PLANETARY RESPONSIBILITIES

Planetary Responsibilities

An Ethics of Timing

Otto Kroesen

Edited by
Frances Huessy

Foreword by
Wayne Cristaudo

WIPF & STOCK · Eugene, Oregon

PLANETARY RESPONSIBILITIES
An Ethics of Timing

Copyright © 2014 Otto Kroesen. All rights reserved. Except for brief quotations in critical publications or reviews, no part of this book may be reproduced in any manner without prior written permission from the publisher. Write: Permissions. Wipf and Stock Publishers, 199 W. 8th Ave., Suite 3, Eugene, OR 97401.

Wipf and Stock
An Imprint of Wipf and Stock Publishers
199 W. 8th Ave., Suite 3
Eugene, OR 97401

www.wipfandstock.com

ISBN 13: 978-1-62564-518-0

Manufactured in the U.S.A. 04/28/2014

Contents

Foreword by Wayne Cristaudo   vii
Preface   xi

1 Four Types of Responsibility   1

2 Four Directions in Ethics   25

3 Rationality, Communication, and Technology   43

4 Multiformity of Man   70

5 The Rhythm of Time: History and Generations   106

6 Fundamental Experiences, Human Qualities, and Cultures   128

7 Western Qualities   153

8 The Christian Way of Dealing with Time   182

Bibliography   209

Foreword

There are few features of the Western world and its influence that are more conspicuous than *spiritual disintegration* and *the fragmentation of knowledge*. We tend to disconnect the different insights into our past, present, and future, and that disconnection is compounded by the fact that our store of knowledge is akin to a vast terrain of silos. This observation is separate from the fact that practitioners of the Human Sciences have never been able to discern—let alone, agree on—core principles around which they might be able to carry on a conversation. Instead, we have roving groups, even within the same disciplines, who "know" what is wrong with other paradigms. They identify a lack of consensus within the Human Sciences and their disciplines, but they cannot convince those enmeshed within them to respond in any enduring or meaningful way. Ethics is as fragmented a discipline as any of the Human Sciences.

Invocations of the *ethical* are ubiquitous today—social theorists and philosophers nearly all trumpet the ethical character of their work, while universities now demand that any research involving a "human subject" must go through an ethics committee. Even the name given to these committees—in the United States, people are familiar with the term *institutional review boards*—can contribute to the conversation-stopping nature of the effort to "protect" the interests of human beings. Of course, that process does not mean that there is any great agreement or compelling argument to be found in such committees or philosophies.

I cannot say that Otto Kroesen's *Planetary Responsibilities: An Ethics of Timing* will finally bring some intellectual coherence into the field of Ethics. It is a discipline with interminable, philosophical ping-pong games taking place among utilitarians, deontologists, and virtue ethicists—not to mention Anglo-American Analytics and Continentals. (There is no way of guaranteeing that this book will be read, let alone received with open minds from such practitioners.)

But I can say that this book represents a major philosophical breakthrough—not only in Ethics but more generally in the Human Sciences and Social Sciences. For it succeeds in doing two major things.

First, it identifies the aspects of responsibility and reality (interior as well as exterior) with which the major ethical paradigms and orientations are preoccupied. Second, it brings Ethics itself into a bigger conversation with the Human and Social Sciences. It achieves this by introducing three different modalities of time into the picture: the different times of (1) daily decisions, (2) biography, and (3) "history as such."

There is one other important aspect to the book that should be mentioned. Its framework is deeply indebted to a little-known German sociologist and historian, Eugen Rosenstock-Huessy. It was Rosenstock-Huessy's ambition in his magnum opus, *Soziologie* (in English, its two volumes are being translated as *The Hegemony of Spaces* and the *Full Count of the Times*), to radically transform the Human or Social Sciences by what he called *a grammatical method*. He argued that what we are and express, long for, and make of our past, present, and future are grammatically encapsulated communications—a function of speech between souls. The register of the human soul is speech and grammar. The names we use are the different responses to each other and to our world and circumstance, in the tasks we make across time and through time. That is to say, the social realities within which we participate express the different forces and human responses whose sediments are stored in our speech.

The collisions of war and revolution are the great cauldrons of new speech and new social formations, new imperatives that express the break with past ways of life that no longer can sustain or nourish us, and equally express frequently violent leaps into new ways of making the future. We follow in the footsteps of founders who take us into unprecedented realities. These realities are possible only because of the inability of tradition to solve catastrophes that confront us.

Otto Kroesen has taken Rosenstock-Huessy's method and applied it to the great ethical dilemmas we face today. Most conspicuously—after taking us through the major different philosophical alternatives within Ethics today, and relating them to the role played by organizations in shaping our existence—he reflects upon the great spiritual traditions that are the enormous forces "trajecting" behind all the peoples of the world. Arching over the book is the great question of how creative concord can be achieved in a world that is open now to vastly different forces that have been shaped by enormous technological, commercial, geopolitical, and administrative forms. These forms pull us all, with our vastly different traditions, priorities, and social memories, into a common world.

Finally, it is symptomatic of Rosenstock-Huessy's and Kroesen's thinking that the book concludes on a religious note. Religious language is the most archaic vessel of names, orientations, and temporal orientation. That language—not to mention its institutional, ethical, and aesthetic legacies—lives with us, still. Among other things, anyone who really wishes to address the circumstance of the contemporary soul and the world cannot let this great traditional current, which has done so much to form the traditions of the West—and now the planet, go unheeded. It is the value of this slim but enormous book that it is mindful of the multiple dimensions we must heed if we wish not only to survive but to flourish with the great tumult of forces that now make us and carry us into a common future.

Wayne Cristaudo
Professor in Politics
Charles Darwin University

Preface

In ethics, the time perspective of moral decisions typically does not receive much attention. What little attention it does receive is blind to the open and unknown future from which, time and again (!), new problems arise and become urgent. Most ethicists assume that our moral makeup is derived merely from the past. But to the extent that we are influenced by moral considerations in our decision-making, we should instead acknowledge that actually it is our belief in the future that urges us to change. Such change also affects our moral makeup. The ethical problems that are left unresolved and are therefore still open, judge us as moral beings, as old-fashioned and antiquated. For that reason in this book I introduce the term "vacant responsibility" into our ethical vocabulary. Open and unresolved problems often represent responsibilities nobody cares about. It is nobody's business. But when we ignore these opportunities, we desert and leave the post vacant where we should stay put. It is the post where a new future knocks at the door. We cannot judge new problems just by the means of old-time norms and values. We must also change our moral values, our moral makeup, and bring them to a higher and more responsive level. Today, this means we should bring our responsibilities to a planetary level. The different values of different cultures will need to open up; they need to live together and create a common future. The word *planetary* doesn't mean the same as the word *global*. Globalization means we live in one economic room. Planetary life represents a journey through time. This is similar in concept to the notion that the planets at one time were constantly on the move and changing direction along undefined paths among the fixed stars of the universe. In a concrete way, this means that individuals and societies will somehow need to inherit each other's values and beliefs, and integrate them into their own makeup. Again this "somehow" does not mean that we end up as gray mice, all of us the same. On the contrary, each of us represents a different repertoire of values, and we will keep doing so. But our different value repertoires are in constant dialogue and are involved in a process of perpetual change, as nomads on the move, in response to each other, changed by what others have to say to us. Peace is not created by a static global citizenry, where we move as cogs in the economic machinery, but by responsive people, able to change direction, to change in response to each other and to the great challenges that face us.

For this reason, I am placing ethics in the context of time. I make use of three different time perspectives: of daily decisions, of our biographies, and of history itself. Using these time perspectives, our moral makeup and values can be traced to well-articulated and long-held historical traditions, both religious and secular. Any differences between the religious and the secular don't matter much for the values themselves. Both secular and religious people want to have these values addressed with respect; nothing else much counts, even if the reasons differ. In addition, values generally have a religious origin, but in the course of time they are articulated in a more secular way. Finally, it is difficult to distinguish where secular culture begins and religion ends. On the one hand, secular goals can be pursued with religious zeal, and on the other, religious values seem to serve secular purposes more than anything else.

For all these reasons, I hope that the secular reader is not shocked by some religious language and that the religious reader does not expect a more supernatural source of ethics beyond the historical time perspective I use. Instead, all readers should look beyond their ethical perspectives and see the repertoire of fundamental orienting experiences that I unfold in this book.

This book starts with the microcosm of daily situations in which moral decisions need to be made. In chapter 1, I propose a distinction among four types of responsibility we typically address nearly every day. But even here, the time perspective can already be felt; that is, new problems often present themselves as responsibilities no one owns. Again, I call these *vacant responsibilities*. The word *vacant* points to the fact that these responsibilities are not merely open, but *left open*, because we walk away from them. They are new problems for which no one feels responsible, largely because these problems do not belong to any established professional practice or institution. Otherwise, they wouldn't be new. In chapter 2, I relate this fourfold analysis of responsibility to more traditional lines of reasoning in ethics. Readers who are not steeped in philosophy might prefer to skip the technicalities of this chapter, although I think it has value in presenting the role of time in the current types of ethics. Chapter 3 tackles an apparent problem that is outside what is commonly understood as ethics—that is, communication and what it entails. However, if it is indeed true that we have to bridge the gap, time and again, between vacant responsibilities and established practices, and that we should learn to change responsibly, by planetary movements—how else can this be done than by . . . talking to each other? So, this chapter sorts out what we do when we communicate.

With chapter 4, we enter the biographical time perspective, going from short-term events to long-term belonging and commitment, and finally to the changing perspectives and imperatives that history forces upon us. Our own biographies are planetary in character, responsive to change, going through crises, yet translating old learning experiences to new paths in time. In chapter 5, I propose to deal with history and time by looking at arcs of time—that is, historical phases or periods that are marked by a clear beginning and end. These arcs of time are not distinct from each other, but can be translated into each other. So each new phase can acquire the essence of a previous phase and save it, reinterpret it, and transpose it into another time. This is another instance of planetary movement and timely change. In chapter 6, I give a short overview of the history of mankind and the main value traditions involved in it. I connect the main values of these traditions to cultural differences, as described in intercultural theory. In chapter 7, I do the same, but with a focus on European or western history. Finally, in chapter 8, I look at four specific traditions that, so to speak, made their mark by going against the normal human pattern: Taoism, Buddhism, Judaism, and Christianity. These four have a distinguished position in the history of humankind in that they have taken as their starting point a creative "no" to the prevailing powers. In spite of their differences, together they open up the capacity for us to face an unknown future, which is really different from the past, even though that past is connected to it. They help us in finding the right rhythm of change and continuity. Now that we have become part of one unified human history, we can discover what we have to say to each other. And in this way, we complement and correct each other by moving in each other's orbit, and feeling each other's gravity.

By no means do I purport to have all this wisdom from within myself. Among many inspiring historians, philosophers, sociologists, and theologians, my primary inspiration comes from the historical language philosophy of Eugen Rosenstock-Huessy. However, I cannot guarantee the reader that I give a "correct" rendering of his thoughts. It is his vision that is the main orientation of this book. But I have reinterpreted it, stylizing and systematizing his viewpoints for the sake of clarity and brevity. Not only are other interpretations possible, but also more nuanced views on details.

My hope is that many readers might benefit from this approach to ethics, especially professionals working in international and intercultural constellations, and in contexts where culture and technology meet. There the need to become more planetary is the most urgent. Our problem is not so much that we need to make the right decisions, but much more that we have to make them together. We also have to make them from different perspectives and according to different situations and paths of time. Moral decisions need to be adapted to different needs. This means that they can differ widely and still be right, but only on one condition: that we move forward in the spirit of speaking to one another, and respond to the imperatives that call upon our names.

1

Four Types of Responsibility

The Idea of Responsibility

Responsibility is a concept that is much misused, and it now seems to be worn out.[1] One should be responsible!

But what does that mean? Don't we often mean "well-mannered" when we use the word *responsible*? "Please act responsibly!" "Act the way a responsible person would."

In the end, it means mostly: Act according to the conventions of responsibility—that is, according to the existing codes of society. Adapt! When responsibility is understood in these terms, we actually take responsibility away from the acting subject.[2] It is not your responsibility anymore. You should comply with what other people expect you to do.

The word *responsibility* is derived from *respondeo*, which means, "to answer."[3] Therefore, shouldn't responsibility mean that you are challenged

---

1. Originally it was not. G. H. van de Bom points out that after World War I, there already was a shift in the ethical vocabulary from *obligation* to *responsibility*. He states, "One has fulfilled his duty and still there remains the gnawing question: Were we, was I, responsible? The responsibility for the future is more limitless and inexhaustible than the responsibility for one's own conduct." Van de Bom, *Oneindige Verantwoordelijkheid* [Infinite Responsibility], 265–66.

2. Bauman, *Postmodern Ethics*, 28 ff., under the heading, "Moral Judgment Expropriated and Reclaimed."

3. This meaning of the term *responsibility* is stressed time and again in the work of the ethics philosopher Emmanuel Levinas. It is the face of the other human being that confronts me and makes my responsibility inevitable.

> The face with which the Other turns to me is not reabsorbed in a representation of the face. To hear his destitution which cries out for justice is not to present an image to oneself, but is to posit oneself as

to give your own irreplaceable answer, and not an answer prescribed by the existing codes of society? Shouldn't responsibility evoke the uniqueness of the person? Certainly, the meaning of responding to a situation in a person's exclusive and unique way is often excluded when the word *responsibility* is used. And it is true that to act responsibly does not always mean acting according to your own conscience. Sometimes it is necessary; sometimes it isn't. We expect bus drivers to drive responsibly. But we do not mean they should therefore drive however they want to, but rather according to the traffic rules. But when we talk about responsible parents, we don't think primarily of rules. Rather, we believe that parents should respond to their child's needs at that particular moment and sometimes (in fact, many times) should forget about rules. It depends on the situation.

To clarify the different meanings of the word *responsibility*, I suggest a distinction among four *kinds,* or *levels,* or *types* of responsibility. The common feature of these four is that one does not act according to one's own whim, but in response to a situation. A situation that requires responsible action is always one in which there is some human presence in front of us, calling for an appropriate "answer," sometimes according to rules, sometimes forgetting about rules.

Functional Responsibility

The term *functional responsibility* relates primarily to the work to be done on the shop floor. It means that individuals act in accordance with the requirements of the job or position they hold in a company. Functional responsibility thus means to carry out an employer's orders according to the regulations, and adhering to a job description and other obligations inherent in one's function. Workers do what they are asked to do. Responsible action, as determined by one's character, as a unique and irreplaceable person is not an issue at this level of responsibility. Functional responsibility makes

---

> responsible, both as more and as less than the being that presents itself in the face. Less, for the face summons me to my obligations and judges me. The being that presents himself in the face comes from a dimension of height, a dimension of transcendence whereby he can present himself as a stranger without opposing me as obstacle or enemy. More, for my position as me consists in being able to respond to this essential destitution of the Other, finding resources for myself. The Other who dominates me in his transcendence is thus the stranger, the widow, and the orphan, to whom I am obligated.

Levinas, *Totality and Infinity,* 1979, p. 215.

people replaceable rather than unique. In today's huge economic system of industry and technology, with its complicated division of labor, people work more effectively when they function as replaceable units. Without this functional division of labor, present-day standardized and large-scale production would be impossible. Functional responsibility can thus be seen as a necessary ingredient of a fully developed industrial society. We need people (and we need, in turn, to be people) who just do what they are told to do. On the shop floor, workers are hired to follow orders, not to talk to one another.

At its most extreme, this kind of attitude brings us to what the psychologist Stanley Milgram called the "agentic state." Milgram performed a famous experiment, which goes as follows: A psychologist poses questions to someone who is seated in another room. That person cannot see the psychologist, but can only hear him. A test subject is seated with the psychologist. Every time the respondent—who, in fact, is playing a role in the experiment—gives a wrong answer, the psychologist orders the test subject to give the respondent an electric shock. Each time the person gives a wrong answer, the voltage of the electric shock is increased. The person in the other room starts screaming and shouting, but again and again the psychologist will ask the test subject to increase the voltage and give the person in the other room the punishment deserved. Some 40 percent of the test subjects were prepared to go as far as 300 volts—enough to cause the death of the unseen respondent. The test subjects proved to be obedient executors of the orders they received from the psychologist. They allowed themselves to be put in what Milgram called the *agentic state*. In the agentic state, the agent is separated both from the intention-conscious sources of the action chain, and from the ultimate effects of the action by a chain of mediators.[4] Any form of functional responsibility as we described above is more or less in the style of this agentic state.

Despite this horrific example, it might be clear that we cannot do without functional responsibility. At times we need to be functioning like a cog in the machine. But there are limits. At a certain point, it should stop. If you do only what you are told to do, your own sense of responsibility is not trained. Thus, functional responsibility is a necessary ingredient, but it cannot be the only type of responsibility.

There has been much debate about the influence of modern industrial society on people's general sense of responsibility. That has to do with the opposition between the private and public spheres and the differences in people's expected behavior in the context of these different environments. In

---

4. Bauman, *Postmodern Ethics*, 125–26. Beauchamp, Tom L. *Philosophical Ethics.* 169–71.

the public sphere, in social intercourse, and in labor organizations, people are expected to give up their responsibility as unique persons. Just do as you are told! In a private context, the reverse is true: Among family and friends we can say pretty much what we want. The consequence of this separation is that in a situation where responsible action would be effective—that is, in the workplace, and within the framework of the social and industrial machinery—the only remaining form of responsibility is functional responsibility. This means that once again people are no longer in charge of their own responsibility; they are agents of someone else's initiative. In the private sphere where people are allowed to say whatever they want, their opinion remains without consequences, since really important issues are not settled in private, but rather by means of public debate and decision making. This unhealthy separation between private and public is a problem often mentioned and studied by sociologists. Modern society, they argue, neither trains people's sense of responsibility nor builds their capacity to act responsibly.[5] This problem makes us aware of the fact that functional responsibility cannot be the only form of responsibility. There must be more.

Collective Responsibility

There is more. Maybe the most natural way for people to respond to a situation is to act not according to requirements of function, but according to the codes of behavior of the group to which they belong. This is what I call *collective responsibility*. Often this expression has a different kind of meaning—that is, several individuals (for instance, a specific department) are collectively responsible for a specific choice. In such a context, collective responsibility means that not just one person at the top, but several individuals together, can be made accountable. The department of a company, for instance, which did not take the safety regulations very seriously, can collectively be made liable. But in such a case, it might be better to speak of *collective liability* instead of *collective responsibility*.

What is meant here by *collective responsibility* is something different. Collective responsibility is characterized by some common leading idea, symbol, or ideology that is shared by the group. Every group has its silent and mostly unwritten codes of behavior, norms, communication patterns, and shoulds and should-nots. In this form of responsibility the collective,

---

5. That is, to mention an example, the contention of Abbe Mowshowitz regarding the social consequences of the implementation of computer technology in *The Conquest of Will*.

the group, dominates one's personal answer to the situation.[6] Even where individual persons act on their own, they still might act according to group codes. In this sense, collective responsibility has nothing to do with the number of people involved. The collective in *collective responsibility* is not the sum of individual persons, but is defined by the symbols and rules that turn individuals into a group. This group can be the family one belongs to. It can be the identification one has with one's nation. It can also be the company one works in, when it has a strong corporate identity and internal cohesion. The group members identify themselves with some larger idea, some common goal or symbol, and the set of practices that goes with it. Individual members do not give an answer of their own, but a group answer. They represent the collective to which they belong. In a positive sense, this can lead to a shared sense of professional responsibility—for instance, when members of a professional group adopt the code of ethics of that group as their own.[7] Professional engineers' associations often adopt a code of ethics to support the collective moral professional behavior of their members. Codes of ethics for behavior in big corporations not only promote moral professional behavior like mission or vision statements, but they also promote a common sense and motivation among all their staff and workers.

---

6. Eugen Rosenstock-Huessy treats the collective as one of the forms of communication:

> A collective is a superlative! The elative or superlative character of a collective use of the words *manhood, virility, beauty, truth* cannot be overlooked lest we misunderstand our ways of life and order. All the Greek gods sprang from this elative quality of collectives or abstractions. Any word can become a fascination on account of the quality for which it stands. Instead of being interested in the many black clouds, instead of wearing black myself, I may be suddenly caught by a kind of awe and admiration for blackness—and when that happens I am bowing to an independent force in life with respect.

Rosenstock-Huessy, *Multiformity of Man*, p. 39.

7. This is the development of engineering ethics that is desired by Michael Davis:

> A profession differs from both businesses and occupational organizations in being designed primarily to serve a certain moral ideal in a certain way. Physicians organized to serve health; lawyers, justice within the law; and so on. . . . .Moral ideals have a claim on us that nonmoral ideals do not. Professions are, by definition, praiseworthy (in the way voluntarily undertaking any laudable responsibilities) because each profession, by definition, undertakes to serve a moral ideal.

Davis, *Thinking Like an Engineer,* 165.

Shell, for instance, was a relatively early adopter of such contemporary codes when it published its General Business Principles in 1976. Often such business principles use beautiful words about honesty, reliability, and responsibility for the general public. But at the same time they remain rather vague. It is not really possible to make the company accountable to them. Nevertheless, both employees and the general public can point to them and the company can use them to promote certain policy choices.

If such a feeling of group solidarity is very strong, the consequence can also be that the rules of the social environment are neglected. We are the best! Outsiders don't understand! Medical specialists sometimes defend one another, or even cover up for one another, if a mistake has been made. The honor of the whole group is at stake. And of course, isn't everybody fully committed to the well-being of the patients?! A company might be so proud of itself that it becomes deaf to external criticism. Even employees who would like to correct the company in such a situation would prefer to remain silent because they do not want to be expelled from the group. The engineer who gave defaming testimony to the U.S. Presidential Commission investigating the *Challenger* disaster in 1986 was dropped by his employer and colleagues because he violated their group identity and pride. He should have remained silent, or at least as silent as possible. He broke with the collective identity and the codes that were part of it. Such pressure might lead to "group think"—that is, uncritical identification with the group, and self-justification of it.

However, to act according to the ethical codes of a company, although it constitutes one form of responsibility, does not make one individually responsible. At its best, it is a form of responsibility by which a whole group or collective attempts to offer a positive contribution to society. At its worst, it is only another way to take responsibility away from the acting subjects and turn them, once again, into agents of the company's will. Collective responsibility, in the end, can turn the person into an agent of group behavior.[8] Therefore, as with any other form of responsibility, collective responsibility becomes negative in its consequences when it is applied as the only form of responsibility.

So we still need another kind of responsibility. Functional responsibility and collective responsibility have their place, but they are not enough. They both can function positively and negatively. The real question is not

---

8. Bauman, *Postmodern Ethics*, 141–42. Bauman criticizes these forms of collective behavior because they can lead to dangerous "eruptions of sociality," conjuring up "vestigal crowds" and "rudimentary tribes." He also warns of the dangers of "socialization" and "sociality," because the group behavior they cultivate can also lead to "disarming and invalidating moral capacities."

so much which form of responsibility is right or wrong, but how long each can last. When to stop and change? We all occasionally need to shift from one type of responsibility to another. That we change, from time to time, is perhaps the most human quality of humans.

Individual and Professional Responsibility

Not everybody is in a position to behave like an individual person. Only able and independent persons can behave like individuals who are capable of taking initiative. A precondition for independence is the capability to choose, given the ability, expertise, awareness, ownership, and freedom to do so. Where this is the case, responsible action can take the form of a conscious act of commitment and choice. The responsibility that requires an independent and free commitment is different from the responsibility that results from group behavior or functional behavior. If people have made a promise and made it voluntarily, then they are obligated to fulfill it. They are bound by their own free commitment and responsibility to act as reliable persons. If people have said something, they should also stand up to it and acknowledge themselves to be the ones who have said what has been said. If you have taken a task upon yourself, then you have to deal with it, professionally, reliably.

In giving a name to this type of responsibility, there is reason to hesitate between "individual" and "professional" responsibility. The features we mentioned, such as *conscious*, *independent*, and *free*, point to the free individual as an agent of this type of responsibility. But we also added *able*. For that reason, we could also label this level of responsibility as *professional*. To be free, we need more than independence and power; we must also possess knowledge and expertise, and such professional qualities as are acquired by training and education. When we think of engineers, it is to a large extent this professional knowledge that makes them independent and free, with respect to the authorities above them.

Professional responsibility differs from functional responsibility in that functional responsibility makes a person act according to the standards and wishes of other people. In professional responsibility, individuals bring their own standards with them. As a professional person, one has the knowledge, abilities, and standards of action of an independent and able person. These standards of behavior might have been acquired during a long period of training and experience. And indeed they have a background in collective education. But if you are a professional, they become part of the individual person you are, and you stand for them and apply them according to your judgment. Many problems between engineers and managers occur because managers would like engineers to behave according to the criterion of functional responsibility, whereas the engineers as professionals refuse to fit into the narrow limits of their function. They have their own independent expertise. One could also state the difference this way: Functional responsibility is a responsibility dependent on the authority of other people, the ones in charge. Professional responsibility is the responsible action of independent people, the sort of responsibility that brings with it individual expertise and (often not recognized) authority. Authority does not depend only on power; knowledge and ability also impart authority. Civil engineers know the necessary thickness of concrete and the amount of steel construction needed to give it strength. They will not allow managers to juggle with the norms.

The same independence is a characteristic of anyone who can enter into a contractual agreement. Contract law supposes and assumes that a contract is drawn up between free and independent parties. This means that only those who are independent enough to really commit themselves to making a contract may enter into a contract. Many labor contracts do not satisfy this requirement because the worker who is hired through the contract does not really have a choice. Collective contracts provide a solution, in part, to this problem. To have a choice means to be in a position to refuse. When engineers are not in a position to refuse a contract, they are reduced to the status of non-professional workers, and they presume their professional responsibility might be easily violated. One of the functions of a professional code of ethics is to strengthen the professional independence of engineers.

As well-trained, intelligent people, engineers often do have much greater independence than the average worker. Managers might regard such independence as inconvenient, but they also need it. It is impossible for a manager to rule only by control. It is impossible to control everything, and ways to avoid control are manifold. Every company or business needs men and women who are committed to its cause. These are individuals who can act on their own account for the sake of the company. They are independent enough to be loyal, as well.[9] This is a paradox. Two seemingly contradictory

---

9. Eugen Rosenstock-Huessy calls the capacity to be independent and at the same time loyal the *capacity for dual relationships*—that is, relationships of partnership.

> In all relations of friendship, of personal liking and antagonism, of jealousy and love, of hate and desire, a third relation prevails, that of dialectic polarity. Friend and foe, you and me, and the little word 'both' betray the existence of dualism. The climax of this dualism is represented by the forms of reproducing the kind.

qualities are combined: freedom and commitment. But it is a paradox indeed, not a real contradiction, because a long-lasting and enduring commitment can only be accepted freely. No company can do without people who have freely embraced its cause. In their individuality, such people represent the spirit or the mission of the company. Such people are men and women who "go for it," not because they are being controlled, but because they have their own commitment and conviction. You cannot really convince people of anything, if they are dependent on you. A person can only fully say "yes" when he or she has, with equal security, the opportunity to say "no." Independence means the possibility to answer "yes" or "no" on one's own individual account. That is also one of the reasons why, in the nineteenth century in so-called "democratic Europe," ownership was a precondition for the right to vote. Ownership was considered a precondition for independence and accountability.

This has an important consequence for the behavior of the company as well. A good cause is needed to attract and keep good workers, instead of structuring a company for maximum profit and just cheating the employees in the name of corporate growth. Many people might be prepared to work for a good salary; but most people also like to work hard for a good cause. This is at least one of the reasons that multinationals are more and more worried about their images, and try to show their commitment to sustainability and the cause of the disadvantaged in society. There is a lot of discussion about whether this concern is more than mere cosmetics. But everybody knows that cosmetics cannot compete with real beauty. That means employees are easier to rally when the company's cause really is a good one.

It is important to distinguish this so-called professional responsibility not only from functional responsibility, but also from collective responsibility. Indeed it is true that many professional norms are group norms. Engineers, for instance, have internalized them during a long education, sometimes unconsciously, sometimes explicitly. A professional judgment, according to this reasoning, applies only such group norms. One could argue then that professional responsibility and collective responsibility are the same. But there is a big difference. A professional cannot act as an automaton. He or she does use the knowledge gathered from a lengthy education, but in many situations a specific contextual judgment is required. In that

---

In partnership, unlike a contract, tasks and duties are not defined in advance:

> In distinction to the growth of the educated and in distinction to the finite behavior of the employee, he who is married or has embraced a cause is trying to regenerate it by his devotion.

Rosenstock-Huessy, *Multiformity of Man*, 45–46, 55.

sense, by applying professional responsibility, one does not participate in existing group norms, but one gives an independent judgment. In this way, not only existing knowledge is applied, but this knowledge is also developed further and renewed in view of the situation at hand.

Yet another feature of professional or individual responsibility is that it is always partial and biased. Every professional might have his or her expertise. But this specialized expertise also has a narrowing effect, because it always emphasizes one or another particular aspect of the problem. As a consequence, a constitutive part of professional responsibility is the capacity to communicate and negotiate with other parties to arrive at a common understanding of the entire problem at hand. Within this process of exchange of information, it is very likely that the one party is not entirely wrong and the other party is not entirely right. This process requires open communication without interference of hierarchical and authoritarian relationships to establish to what extent one or the other party is right or wrong. Without such a process of opposition and dialogue in which the participants dare to say "yes" or "no" to one another and yet are seeking common terms of agreement, the actual truth about the problem might not be established. Such an open dialogue without interference of authority and hierarchy needs authenticity, loyalty, and freedom of speech. In hierarchical working relationships within commercial businesses, this openness is never guaranteed or self-evident, regardless of whether these hierarchies are of western or non-western origin. Open communication always requires a new investment in the human quality of social relationships. It always requires a person who takes the first step, takes the risk.

It is this individual responsibility—of choice and commitment—that is much celebrated and also in many ways disfigured in western culture. It is both celebrated and manipulated. Western people like their freedom. Indeed, we can be proud that this type of individual responsibility is to a large extent the product of western culture, as is explained in chapter 7. Freedom of speech is one of the oldest human rights espoused by western culture. To most people, it now seems self-evident. We in the West dare say "no." We say whatever comes to mind, and thereby are perceived as much less polite than people from southern or eastern cultures. We in the West like to act on our own account and have nothing to do with other people. But this celebrated freedom to act individually and to take our own initiative might be even more manipulated than any group identity. People are easy to seduce: "If you buy such-and-such a product, you will really have a sense of freedom!" In other words, by giving people a sense of freedom, you can make them do whatever you like. Many of the so-called "western-type individuals" do not really stand on their own. Rather, they cling to all sorts of models, idols, and fashions.[10] Every advertisement essentially says to consumers, "If you are really free and if you really do what you want, then you will choose our product." Note the paradox in that message. The paradox of freedom and independence seems to be that in order to grasp them, you must do what everyone else does. This paradox clearly shows how difficult it is to be really independent and committed, really in a position to say "yes" or "no," and to stand by the choice of your conviction.

Professional responsibility also has positive and negative sides. It is sometimes essential, but it too can easily become one-sided. People are easily trapped by the criteria of their own professionalism. They might become deaf and uncommunicative toward the demands and requirements of non-professionals. In addition, people can become too independent. There are many examples of professionals who have built up their own little "kingdoms" within a company, following only their own choices and directives. In such cases, independence becomes independence without loyalty. Freedom becomes a freedom without commitment.

Vacant Responsibility

Sometimes there are events that nobody expected. An unforeseen problem pops up. It is part of nobody's job description. There are no professional codes giving guidance on what to do. They cannot be attributed to the domain of expertise of any professional, at least not according to the usual criteria. That is because they create new problems. They didn't occur previously. Who, for example, is responsible if hackers mess up your computer via the internet? The problem is so new that the law around it has been only recently adapted.

I call this state of affairs—a societal responsibility for which nobody is responsible—*vacant responsibility*. I could also call it *general human and personal responsibility*. It is probably the kind of responsibility that makes us most human, since in difficult situations people show what they are worth. This type of responsibility is one to which you can't say "yes" or "no." Vacant

---

10. This mechanism is beautifully described by René Girard:

> All try in the same way to be different, and when after a while they want to counter the fact that in effect they have become identical, the renunciation of fashion also becomes a fashion in itself. That is why everybody is against fashion; everybody always rejects the existing fashion in order to imitate the inimitable, just like everybody else.

My translation. Girard, *Des Choses Cachées*, 424.

responsibility is involved when, for example, there is a traffic accident and everyone who happens to be at the scene feels the immediate urge to help. That is, everyone at the scene recognizes that a responsibility is not covered and feels called upon to fill that empty obligation. They might not know the persons involved in the accident. It is none of their business. But bystanders can't help but make it their business. There is an immediate response of compassion. That is because in some way or other, we feel that the suffering of totally unknown people does matter. The Jewish-French philosopher Emmanuel Levinas calls this experience *proximity*.[11] What happens to people far away, even those whom you might never actually see, does nevertheless matter to you. These people, despite their distance, become the moral equivalent of neighbors in need. Concern for the suffering of other human beings is perhaps the source of all responsibility and, as far as Levinas is concerned, the source of all humanity and religion, as well. For that reason, Levinas proposes a "humanism of the other human being."[12] Not a humanism to which the individual personality is central, as is usually the case, but a humanism that makes the other person central, transcendent to me.

The Bible contains the story a Samaritan traveler, who sees a man lying by the side of the road, injured and half-dead. A Jewish priest and a Levite have already seen the man, but according to their laws, they cannot celebrate their rites in the temple if they touch the man. It would make them impure. So the responsibility to help the injured man remains a vacant one—not merely empty, but *left open,* calling for action, even if it has been avoided. The vacancy contains the potential to be filled. But this Samaritan, an enemy of the Jews, sees the man and is full of compassion. The story is not exclusively Christian or Jewish. The Samaritan is neither Jew nor Christian. He didn't have a reason to feel responsible, because he was a stranger and he was passing by only coincidentally. Something like an ethics of hospitality lies at the bottom and in the heart of every culture and religion. In parts of Africa, traditional practice requires that some food always be left for the gods. But if a traveler passes by and is hungry, he or she will be offered the food and the people will say that still the gods did get it. In this story, showing hospitality to foreigners and exhibiting moral behavior come down to the same thing as revering the gods.

New situations, challenging situations, emergency situations. These single us out as unique persons. The uniqueness of my answer—which nobody except me can give—makes me the unique person I am; it makes me a person, as such. The more one gives a unique, new answer as a responsible

---

11. Levinas, *Autrement qu'être où au delà de l'essence.* 1974, 77ff.
12. Levinas, *Difficile Liberté,* 1963.

person, the more human one becomes. According to Levinas, it is this primordial responsibility, the concern for the unexpected and unforeseen, for the stranger, the widow and the orphan, that gives us a human face.[13] To have a face is to be able to face another human being, the first one who crosses my path. The answer to the other person is my responsibility, not a functional responsibility, not a collective responsibility, not a professional responsibility requiring an education. It is my own creative answer, the answer I have to give when I am exposed to the other human being who questions my self-sufficient existence. Where I am indispensable, I am unique and irreplaceable. If I don't fill the gap, nobody else will. It is as if there is a vacancy that only I can fill because it was destined for me.

Everybody meets with situations in which they ask themselves, "Should this be my concern?" "Should I care?" It might be that an opportunity is opening up to do things differently and more effectively in an unconventional and unexpected way. Then the question arises as to whether you should take responsibility for doing something different, even if it might bring you disrespect and trouble. Somewhere a challenge might lie in wait for a subject to take responsibility for it. Thomas Edison tried thousands of different kind of wires for the filament in his light bulb. He did not hesitate to stand alone and endure skepticism, because he believed in an extraordinary possibility and made it his responsibility. Or a person might see unanticipated danger instead of opportunity. Will that person dare to speak out and make it his or her business? Every "creative advance into novelty"[14] is in

---

13. Emmanuel Levinas stated this about faces:

> The face resists possession, resists my powers. In its epiphany, in expression, the sensible, still graspable, turns into total resistance to the grasp. This mutation can occur only by the opening of a new dimension. For the resistance to the grasp is not produced as an insurmountable resistance, like the hardness of the rock against which the effort of the hand comes to naught, like the remoteness of a star in the immensity of space. The expression the face introduced into the world does not defy the feebleness of my powers, but my ability for power. The face, still a thing among things, breaks through the form that nevertheless delimits it. This means concretely: the face speaks to me and thereby invites me to a relation incommensurate with a power exercised, be it enjoyment or knowledge. And yet this new dimension opens in the sensible appearance of the face.

Levinas, *Totality and Infinity*, 197–98.

14. The terminology is from Alfred N. Whitehead: "The world is thus faced by the paradox that . . . it craves for novelty and yet is haunted by terror at the loss of the past, with its familiarities and its loved ones. It seeks to escape from time in its character of

a way a new answer to the unheard-of, a new answer to the unknown. Unknown possibilities are as much feared and avoided as are unknown human beings. The future comes to us "clothed" like a stranger asking for hospitality. Every act of creative responsibility has to break with traditional methods and procedures. Mostly such acts are rejected and punished in their own time. It takes time before they can be recognized and appreciated for what they are. The martyrs of one epoch are the heroes of the next. That makes their job a lonely one.

Vacant responsibility is also exercised by "whistleblowers." These are people who feel that the problems and risks their company takes are so huge, that they have to go to the media or the authorities and speak out. They justify their actions by pointing to all kinds of professional codes of ethics. But the law currently offers little protection for whistleblowers. Gradually, however, society is feeling the urge to grant more legal protection to whistleblowers who take responsibility for reporting immoral or illegal practices. This shows that society needs time to make room for new procedures and that responsible action may initially be outlawed. Lawful behavior is not always moral, and moral behavior not always lawful. Responsible action often means entering an unknown future without protection. After some time, institutions might approve these responsible actions, for which there might also eventually be legal protections. The law is always the conservative element in society. That means the moral urge to speak out as a whistleblower might conflict with the law, as the interests of the employer are legally better protected than the interests of the employee.

There is an important reason for distinguishing between professional and vacant responsibilities, although the dividing line between the two might not always be very clear. In some cases, we may be in doubt as to whether to take action because one's professional responsibility is violated or because a vacant responsibility exists. The case of a NASA engineer who tried to prevent the launch of the *Challenger* is an example. He had ascertained that the segments of the two side rockets were not sealed safely and he argued against the launch. He knew that the rubber rings between the segments of the side rockets were not in order. He already had made his point many times to his superiors. He himself had been given the charge to conduct research on the problem, but this was in turn slowed down by management and little money was made available for it. So at the time of crisis, right before the launch, the engineer could give little scientific proof for the dangers he had warned about. Wasn't he motivated foremost by professional judgment?

'perpetually perishing.'" Whitehead, *Process and Reality*. 516.

But he could easily have said, "I have exercised my professional responsibility; I have done what I can."

Nevertheless, at his request on the evening before the launch, several different managers involved in it agreed to a teleconference with the engineer. He tried his utmost to prevent the launch, which was planned for the next day. At that teleconference, management—some of them engineers themselves—disagreed with his analysis, or in other ways concluded that he had insufficient proof of his position and that the pressure to go forward with the launch was too great. Almost unnoticeable in this case, the professional responsibility of the engineer turned into vacant responsibility (see also chapter 3). If this engineer was motivated only by professional judgment and responsibility, he could have concluded himself that he had insufficient evidence. There was little science to establish that the leaks between the segments were dangerous enough to prevent a successful launch. In this case, however, the engineer felt a responsibility beyond that prescribed by his profession. He did more than professional responsibility itself required. He had a "vacant" responsibility, brought into play because the institution for which he worked did not provide procedures and rules to handle the risky situation that had arisen. So he stopped playing by the rules.

It is doubtful whether professional responsibility alone can take a person that far. This engineer too did not go that far, either, before the launch. But afterward, he was honest enough to tell the inside story and disclose the facts before the Presidential Commission.

We might conclude that this kind of responsibility too is right in its own place and time. But it is equally clear that one cannot always be a martyr or a hero. Occasions are rare when we stand alone, no longer covered by tradition, custom, or rule, and we take a lonely stance for that which is nobody's responsibility. Sometimes it is necessary. But the price is high. And it is important to carefully consider the steps we should take in such a case. For instance, should we contact the press immediately? Should we gather more information first? Should we protect ourselves by keeping records of all things that happen and are said, so that we can be prepared in the event the situation leads to a court case? Or should we merely contact a higher authority within or outside the company?

All these steps need due consideration to prevent wild actions which benefit no one.

Table 1. The four kinds of responsibility

	Functional responsibility	Collective responsibility	Professional responsibility	Vacant responsibility
Features	According to job description According to labor division Standardization Replaceable	Codes of the group Communal identity Internal cohesion Collective symbols	Ability and expertise Freedom Independence Contractual	Nobody's responsibility No rules New and unexpected situations
Positive	Effectiveness Clarity	Common motivation and identity Code of ethics in support of moral behavior	Strong commitment Ability to present the company without external controls Ability to communicate	Uniqueness of the person Creativity Compassion
Negative	"Agentic state" Capacity to act responsibly is not trained	"Group think" Everybody outside is wrong	"Little kingdoms" Individualism Manipulated freedom	"High price" Danger of wild actions Danger of more harm than benefit

Increasing Intensity

The four types of responsibility treated thus far show an increasing intensity on the level of personal experience. That does not mean that one type of responsibility has less value than another type, because each type of responsibility is necessary at its own time and place.

Functional responsibility seems the least intense, so to speak. It means to act according only to the prescriptions of the company or to other people's wishes and it implies more or less machinelike behavior. Sometimes this is very important—quite often, as a matter of fact. But the type of responsibility we exercise most often is probably not the most intense.

Compared to functional responsibility, collective responsibility represents an increased level of intensity. At this level, one feels responsible not only for the outside world of matter, functions, and the prescriptive activity of institutions, but also for the group one is part of. This implies more consciousness in that the participants in the group are aware of collective symbols and ideas. To act as the agent of a group therefore seems more responsible than only acting in the context of a function and as part of a system. *More responsible*, again, does not mean that this sort of responsibility is better than functional responsibility. In itself there is no better or worse form of responsibility, because each is necessary in its own place and time. Nevertheless, collective responsibility is of a more intense sort. So we can say that it has an increased level of responsibility beyond functional responsibility. It represents a more intense experience than mere functional behavior.

Professional responsibility, in turn, is more intense than collective responsibility. At the level of professional responsibility, the group no longer decides. Rather, individuals decide according to their ability, independence, and freedom. No longer can an individual hide behind a group or group codes, or behind any form of prescribed moral behavior. It is my decision, for instance, whether I accept the safety standards proposed for a given situation. Surely, I might rely on a professional code of ethics, on my education, and on the procedures for handling such cases. But the decision is on my shoulders, at least partly.

This burden is increased further when we come to the level of responsibility we called *vacant*. Other than functional, collective, or professional responsibility, the concept of *vacant responsibility* is not commonly in use in ethics. I propose the use of this term for cases in which responsibilities are unassigned, have been *left vacant*. They are awaiting action. There is a problem, but there is no agent. These are cases for which there are not yet rules for dealing with a problem one may be confronted with. In such a case action is required, but there is no subject to act.

This sort of responsibility is linked to the imperative as a language form. In imperatives, such as "Walk!" "Learn!" "Take!" and "Do!" actions are required, but no subject is specified. The place of the subject is left open. Imperatives are verbs in search of their subjects. Likewise, vacant responsibility exists at a level that is the most intense of all the responsibilities, and is probably the one least exercised. It would seem that the least intense levels of responsibility are exercised most often, and the most intense forms most seldom. There are only a few rare moments in which we act as unique, responding individuals. But the decisions we take at such singular moments can echo in our lives for many years.

Responsibilities Overlap and Interfere with Each Other

These four types of responsibility do not co-exist peacefully. There are no harmonious relationships among them. Each is in tension, and each often conflicts with the others. There is a constant struggle about the priority to be given to each, in relation to the others. For example, a police officer who experiences the group solidarity of the police force will have difficulty reporting the corrupt practices of colleagues. In this case professional responsibility conflicts with collective responsibility. For police officers reporting corrupt practices is a requirement of their professional behavior. But a sense of belonging to the group, solidarity, and collective codes of behavior, which are also valuable, interfere with this professional responsibility.

In these circumstances, the police officer must choose between two forms of behavior, each of which is valuable unto itself. The question might then be asked, "When does corruption become such a big problem that it is necessary to break up group solidarity?" The question *when?* is one of the most important ethical questions. Another example concerns the creative and future-directed responsibility of an engineer who sees that a new production process might conflict with established procedures. The engineer likes to use new materials, but management doesn't favor it because of the friendly relationships and long chain of contracts they've built up over the years with the people who provide the old materials. The engineer will become frustrated by the lack of cooperation. On the other hand, the established relationships with companies that, up to now, have delivered materials represent a value in themselves. Old habits don't always have to be traded for new ways. Here we see how professional responsibility collides with collective or functional responsibility. Even some "vacant" responsibility might be involved if sensibility for environmental problems already implies more than only a professional attitude. Just performing the function described and prescribed by a job or by the management can be very unprofessional, and even cause a lot of trouble. The manager who directs research might know much less about the production process than the engineer. What should one do? Like life itself, the shop floor is a constant struggle among priorities.

Individual versus Organization

There is a lot of debate in ethical theory and in organization theory about the individual in the organization. It is often said that organizations tend to take responsibility away from the individual, and that the individual as such is reduced to relative powerlessness. For instance, an employee who feels obliged to inform the public about the polluting activities of the company might be supported by a professional code of ethics if that employee takes action against the company. But at the same time, the worker risks making secret company information available to the general public, which in turn conflicts with functional responsibility. Under the worker's functional position within the hierarchy of the company, which is protected by law, making private information public is not allowed. That is, no employee is permitted to disclose secret company information to the general public. In many countries, the worker might even be prosecuted, because contract law generally considers the publication of company secrets as a legitimate reason for dismissal. This is how the law and professional ethical codes can conflict with one another. In fact, this is another example of the tension between two forms of responsibility: functional responsibility and collective responsibility. The law protects the functional division of labor within the hierarchy; professional ethical codes try to protect and stimulate a moral group awareness of professionals.

This opposition between individual and organization is important. But the distinction made among the four responsibilities implies that this is not the only opposition conceivable. Not only does the organization prevent individuals from taking their responsibility. Group codes and company traditions, and the pride and glory people attach to them, also prevent employees from taking appropriate and responsible action. To make matters even more complex, there is also the form of general human responsibility we have called *vacant*.

A lecturer at the University of Technology of Delft supported several development projects in Suriname. This is and was a very professional commitment, because the projects were well organized and of benefit to local people. But he faced a dilemma when Jules Albert Wijdenbosch, a supporter of the country's former military dictator (and now President) Dési Bouterse, came into power. Now this Delft teacher's professional responsibility came into conflict with his vacant responsibility. The projects he developed were excellent. But in this situation of new political leadership under Wijdenbosch, he was troubled by the question of whether his valuable work would benefit the wrong regime. He could easily have stated that this was not his concern because he was acting as a professional engineer. No one forbade him to continue the projects, because there were no rules governing his actions as a professional. There were other parties too, other companies, that took advantage of the new regime and that were not concerned about its dictatorial character. There are many examples of such situations, where societal exploitation, environmental degradation, and human oppression continue, only because there is no agency that takes responsibility upon itself to stop it. The problem is nobody's responsibility. What is present, however, is an opportunity, a vacancy, for a subject to enter and respond to the imperative in the situation. Companies involved in such situations justify their behavior by saying that if they were to stop their activities, others would step in and take their place.

How can one decide which responsibility should have priority? By what justification should the one kind prevail in one situation and another kind in another? That is a difficult problem. First, it is important to have knowledge of the four levels of responsibility. They interfere and overlap, but nonetheless they can be distinguished from one another. As a sort of moral grammar, they help us to map the situation. They offer different moral principles we can cling to, in order to justify one form of behavior over another. Even with a map, however, we have to decide for ourselves what direction to choose. The map offers insight, but it does not yield decisions. The four levels of responsibility are all there, each with its relative weight and importance, but it is impossible to decide in advance which should have priority. The one rule that does apply in this situation is that there is no rule for applying the rules![15]

We can present these four levels of responsible action as four "rules," and take the following points of view into consideration: First, these four need one another, just as they simultaneously contradict and correct one another. Second, no rule can be applied to decide in advance which level of responsible action is relevant in a particular situation. Third, time and opportunity must determine which level at any point in time should have priority, and in which kind of situation. Fourth, the subjective and personal character of any decision to be made is not regrettable but indispensable.

We should therefore not wish to avoid the indispensable element of subjective involvement. Responsible decisions cannot be calculated; they are not the conclusion of a logical chain of arguments. Of course, such a logical chain of arguments is part of the deliberation. But it is the human subject who must decide and respond, and who must stand by the decision that has been made. The element of subjective involvement is necessary, because every situation is a little bit different from past ones. That's why previous experiences and principles are not enough to direct future behavior. The equilibrium among the four levels of responsibility must be found and re-discovered, over and over again. When, for instance, too much stress on functional responsibility leads to damage and suffering, the time is ripe for professional or vacant responsibility to take over. But when has this moment arrived? No one can decide that in advance. Each of us has to decide for him- or herself. That makes life difficult. In ethics, just as in real life, there is no rule for applying the rules. That is what makes us human; not everything

---

15. Berman, *Faith and Order*, 169, fn 95. It is with this expression that Immanuel Kant answers the question of what criteria legal, natural, and civil norms are to be applied to individual cases.

is decided in advance. Decisions provide us with opportunities to make a difference. Human life is always a creative advance into novelty. There is no rule and there can be no rule for novelty. If there were a rule for novelty, such a thing as novelty would cease to exist.

Living in Four Directions

Why did we make a distinction among *four* levels of responsibility? Why four? After all, ethical theory enables us to use any number of distinctions or subdivisions, concepts, and methods. Nothing wrong with that. As long as such theories and concepts help us to understand the situation we are working in, they might be correct and complement one another. Yet this division into four is not accidental. The four levels of responsibility we discerned correspond to the four basic directions of human life (as well as of any other life). That is, past, future, inner and outer.[16] Every life form has an inner center that serves as a starting point for actions into the outer world. Every life form develops from a fixed past to a more or less open future. How are these four levels of responsibility related to these four directions of living processes?

Functional responsibility is directed to the *outward* world of functions, the division of labor and the rest of the machinery of big organizations, the institutions of society, and so on. In functional responsibility, people act as replaceable, and more or less objectified, parts of nature and as a part in the technical process, the system of societal institutions. In resisting the brutal forces of nature, human beings need to make concessions and need to accept that they cannot do otherwise than act as parts of nature themselves to a certain extent. Matter should not matter, but to overcome it, humans do have to act as if they were matter themselves. Force against force.

---

16. Plessner, *Die Stufen*. Helmuth Plessner, in his philosophy of biological and human life, dwells on these four dimensions of the development of time, stressing mostly the inner-outer distinction; Whitehead, *Process and Reality,* p. 516. In what he himself calls his "philosophy of organism," Alfred North Whitehead takes the development of organic forms of life through time as a model for the natural sciences as such, as if nature were also a living thing; Rosenstock-Huessy, *Speech and Reality.* Rosenstock-Huessy is most explicit in using this model, which he calls the "cross of reality," with past and future, inner and outer directions as structuring features of the development of history and of forms of speech; Mark C. Taylor also comes in the neighborhood of this fourfold approach in valuing life as a process of change. He dwells on the theological implications: "If, however, the divine is neither an underlying One, which dissolves differences, nor a transcendent Other, which divides more than unites, but is incarnate in the eternal restlessness of becoming, then life in this world is infinitely valuable." Taylor, *After God,* 377.

Individual or professional responsibility is directed to the *inner* center of initiative and action, speech, thinking, and communication—the human subject. In professional responsibility, we are primarily responsible for what we have in full conscience committed ourselves to. According to the philosophical tradition of the West, all contract law has its foundation in the human subject as a responsible and conscious center of action, human subjects who know what they want and want what they know. The able, independent, rational, and autonomous subject who is free to choose has an important place in western philosophy and is one of the philosophical cornerstones of the western legal system.[17] One can argue that western civilization has a special preference for this one pole of reality, the inner center of a person. We'll come back to that in chapters 6 and 7. As human subjects, we have different images of reality, partial information, and biased knowledge. We need to communicate, speak and listen, to put these viewpoints together and create a common basis of action. That makes the ability to communicate, to speak out and listen, also part of professional responsibility.

Collective responsibility is the result of custom, tradition, and group identity. In that sense it is directed to the *past*. To have a past means to be part of a common history, and such a common history provides people with a common background. Every group has its codes of behavior and traditions

---

17. But there are also reasons to moderate this interpretation, as Berman did in *Faith and Order*, 257–58:

> It should be noted that the Western philosophers have their own history, namely, the history of ideas, and they commonly analyze the meaning of justice by tracing similarities and differences among the various philosophical schools that have analyzed the meaning of justice in the past, starting with Plato and Aristotle. Although they might occasionally discuss concepts of justice found in the writings of Chinese or other non-Western philosophers, they basically write in a tradition which traces its lineage from ancient Greece across the "Middle Ages" to Spinoza, Hobbes, Locke, Hume, Kant, Hegel, and ultimately into the philosophical morass of twentieth-century Europe and America. That is *their* history.
>
> Even from the viewpoint of intellectual history, this genealogy is far too limited. Western theories of justice must be traced not only to ancient Greek philosophy but also to ancient Hebrew moral and religious thought and ancient Roman law. It was the remarkable achievement of the European schoolmen of the late eleventh and twelfth centuries to have combined, for the first time, these three diverse and even mutually antagonistic outlooks—the Hebrew, the Greek, and the Roman—and to have founded on that combination the modern Western disciplines of theology, philosophy, jurisprudence, and political science.

as a result of a history that welded together the members of the group. It is supported by institutions created throughout the group's history.

Vacant responsibility is directed to the *future,* in that it always explores what is as yet unheard and unexplored. Vacant responsibility—recall that it is responsibility for which no one is responsible—is responsibility for what we are not yet accustomed to. It is vacant essentially because it is part of no one's job and is not yet covered by rules. It is a wake-up call for a subject to take action. The issue in question is too new and unexplored. Vacant responsibility always involves problems that are waiting for a person to attend to them. New problems, as yet without solutions at hand, require a creative advance into novelty. To be the first to tackle such a problem is always a thankless task. To really take the issue seriously, we frequently have to throw old habits and customs overboard, and abandon the routines upheld by many colleagues. That is not easily done.

One could ask how the present is dealt with in this approach. From an analytical point of view, one can question the very existence of the present. Every moment of my life, and each word that I speak immediately disappears in the past. And every event that is not yet part of past or present lies hidden in the future. As such, the present is no more than the razor-sharp distinction between past and future. Nevertheless, people do speak without any hesitation about "our time," about "now," or about the time "after the fall of the Wall." That means that people who share the same horizon of meaning live in the same time, in a shared present. The present, as such—that is to say, as physical reality—does not exist. But people do create a common present if they speak and think in the same way.

As such the present coincides with what we called until now the *inner pole of existence*. In speaking about professional responsibility, I already pointed out that every insight is partial and biased. The discussion or confrontation between such insights creates a common present, if people succeed in understanding each other. If, by reciprocally complementing and correcting each other, people create a shared vision, then they live in the same inner space, in the same time, their present.

The everlasting human, moral, ethical, and cultural question is when each of these four directions should take priority: the outer world (the system of objective functions), the inner (the free and committed subject), the past (tradition, group conscience), or the future (the lonely person). This is not only the everlasting question of development and specialization of each culture. It is also the question facing each individual, because every day each of us must answer these four questions:

24 Planetary Responsibilities

1. Which ways of acting and living can today go on as they did in the past?
2. Where should I really dare to take an uncertain course into a new future?
3. Where should I act as a freely choosing subject? To what cause should I commit myself for a longer period?
4. What are the day-to-day functions that I should fulfill?

We need all four directions. When we get pinned down on just one of them, life gets boring and we die. Life means change. We die when we are not allowed to change among the four aggregate states of life. We need surprise. We need customs. We need free, responsible choice. And we also need our functional, daily life rhythm.[18] The perpetual personal and cultural question is how much, when, and in what mix?

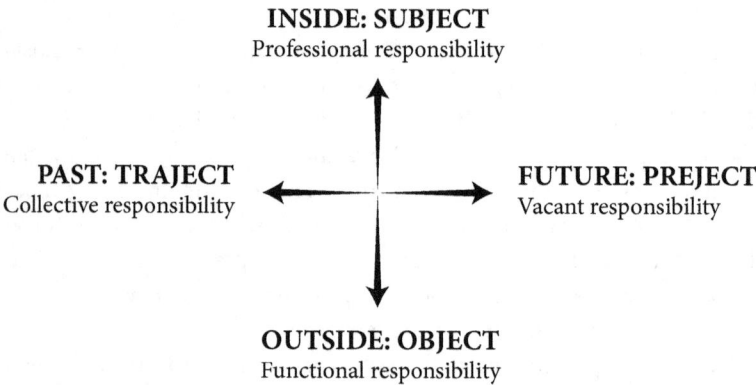

---

18. These four life forms of the human person are more fully developed in Rosenstock-Huessy's *Multiformity of Man*. See chapter 4.

2

Four Directions in Ethics

Introduction

There are many types of ethical theories, and they can be categorized in many different ways. As is always the case, the way they are categorized depends on the judgments and preferences of the one proposing the categories. As a matter of fact, many approaches in ethical theory overlap. The only reason for categorizing them and differentiating among them is that one has something in mind with such a categorization. The one proposing the categories is up to something. A road map for cars looks quite different from a map of bicycle paths or a map for watercraft. In the same way, I have a road map in mind that leads to the categorization I am proposing here. In most cases, divisions are made among consequential ethics, deontological ethics, and virtue ethics. For reasons that I will come back to, I want to add a fourth category, what I call the *ethics of responsibility*. In all ethics, the word *responsibility* plays an important role. Still, there are reasons to label a specific kind of ethics exactly with that word.

No approach in ethics is totally nonsense, just as no method is without its limitations. In *consequential ethics,* the consequences of an act are especially important in judging actions. A good action is an action with good consequences. Of course, there is truth in that.

Deontological ethics however emphasizes obligations and rules, which the subject of the action has to hold on to, no matter whether the consequences are good or bad. Stealing or lying: one simply should not do that, not just because of negative consequences (although those too might be possible), but because you simply shouldn't! There is truth in that, too.

In *virtue ethics* the personal qualities and the character of the person are important. A reliable person will deliver reliable work. A person who has a developed sense of justice is a person from whom one can expect a fair judgment. Once again, there is truth in that.

Because there is truth in all three different approaches, we do not need to make a definite choice among them. We can use them as different viewpoints on one and the same matter. They provide a view on the same matter from different angles. Often they lead to the same results, but they can also contradict each other and lead to different priorities.

I want to name one more approach: *ethics of responsibility*. *Responsibility* is derived from the word *respond*. A new situation asks for a new response. One can never know everything in advance. One always meets unexpected situations. Every now and then, we hear a new appeal. This aspect of newness is emphasized by the approach in the ethics of responsibility. One simply cannot know everything in advance and decide everything in advance. In addition, one can never wipe out the personal and subjective judgment. More than once, ethicists deplored the fact that a "rest of subjectivity" and of personal judgment cannot be erased in moral judgments, no matter how thoroughly the ethical theory is developed.[1] But as long as there is life, life will renew itself and move in unexpected directions. For that reason, not everything should be arranged in advance. The rest of subjectivity, which is a disadvantage according to some, is an asset in as far as I am concerned. Our social reality is not finished yet, and each person has a contribution to make.

It is not my intention to present an extensive treatment of these different ethical theories, but instead to find the right alternation and dynamics among them. Each approach in ethics is inclined to absorb all the attention and to serve as the one and only approach to all problems. However, it is much more important to find the right time and opportunity for each of them. It might sound strange, but indeed these ethical theories are not always right, nor are they always right under all circumstances. Depending on time and opportunity, there will always be one that deserves priority. For

---

1. The American bioethicist Norman Daniels says the following about it:

> Once the foundational claim about moral judgments is removed, however, we have nothing more than a person's moral opinion, however considered. Since such opinions are often the result of self-interest, self-deception, historical and cultural accident, hidden class bias, and so on, just systematizing some of them hardly seems a promising way to provide justification for them or for the principles that order them.

Daniels strives to avoid the historical contingency of our moral reasoning by the use of reason. This, however, cannot fully succeed. A rest remains. Thank God! Daniels, *Justice and Justification,* 83,

that reason, it is important to be able to stop with one approach and switch to another. And it will turn out to be the so-called ethics of responsibility that indicates this rhythm of change and alternation.

Consequential Ethics, Utilitarianism

Utilitarianism is the most well-known type of consequential ethics. If you want to know whether an act is right or wrong, then answer the question of whether people become *happier* from it. In other words, is it somehow *useful* to do this or that? "The largest amount of happiness for the largest number of people," that is the classical expression of the early nineteenth-century British philosopher Jeremy Bentham in this regard. Bentham came to this conclusion because he wanted to get rid of all personal (subjective) preferences in relation to values and virtues. To be effective in the production of happiness—that is the best and most *objective result* one can get.

But who determines what happiness consists of? Well, the people themselves, according to Bentham. One person doesn't need to prescribe how the other person should become happy. Bentham wanted to dissociate himself from all forms of paternalism and interference from the side of the Church or the side of the State.

Bentham lived in an age in which people were very impressed by the achievements of mathematics. After all, it had been discovered how one could use mathematical formulas in describing physical processes. The seventeenth-century Dutch scientist and mathematician, Christiaan Huygens, is the first who succeeded in doing that.[2] He described the movement of the pendulum in a mathematical formula. For us this has become quite normal, but in that time it made a huge impression. People expected a significant amount of influence from that discovery on social life as well. Religious wars and the paternalism and oppression from the side of the Church and State made the idea attractive that society should in fact function as smoothly as nature itself, according to natural laws. On the basis of this expectation, the regularities perceived in nature were called "laws" in an analogy to societal or judiciary laws. In that spirit, Spinoza wrote his *Ethics more geometrico*, a mathematical ethics. If everybody would act according to his reasonable nature, then society would function smoothly. Bentham's idea was that his formula, "the largest amount of happiness for the largest number of people," could function as a sort of mathematical formula in ethics. The only thing one needed to do was to enter the variables, and one could calculate the

---

2. Andriesse, *Titan kan niet slapen* [Titan Cannot Sleep], 90.

result. Such an approach in ethics is also called for that reason a *procedural approach*.³

This approach in ethics is in the background of what is called a *cost-benefit analysis*. If an action causes more happiness or utility than the investment costs, then the result is positive.

Nevertheless, there are some problems with utilitarianism as well as with the principle of happiness as the final criterion for right or wrong. We name some of them:

1. Can all values be reduced to happiness? Why should there be a just society? A utilitarian would answer: Because justice contributes to the largest amount of happiness for everyone. Freedom, beauty, loyalty—all values that exist—are valued only because they lead to happiness. But is this *reduction* justified?

2. Because everybody should account for his own version of "happiness," it becomes an empty concept, a *container concept*, in which you can put whatever content you like. Someone might defend the position: "The airport should grow, because economic activity leads to more usefulness and happiness." Another person has as much right to defend this position: "There should be more forests, because the quietness and rest one can experience in a forest lead to more happiness." Neither position hurts the other, unless the forest should be removed so that the airport has to expand. Then whose "happiness" will win? In other words, behind the term *happiness*, many other values hide themselves: safety, justice, rest, dynamics, beauty, and so forth, all depending on whatever might make somebody somehow satisfied.

3. Unlimited utilitarianism would allow that *minorities fall victim* to the maximization of the happiness of the majority. Often this problem is solved by appealing to the principle of autonomy—namely, that my preference should not be detrimental to the preference of another person (his or her autonomy). But in doing that, one already partially denies the meaning of utilitarianism, in that mere utility is not the only criterion anymore. And how to judge where *my autonomy* stops and the autonomy of the other person begins? His tree might stand in his garden, but its shadow is in mine. Does that violate my autonomy?

---

3. The Canadian philosopher Charles Taylor uses this term and comments: "For utilitarians, rationality is maximizing calculation. *Zweckrationalität* is the crucial form. For the Kantians the definite procedure of practical reason is that of universalization." And this implies in both cases, "that practical wisdom is a matter of seeing an order which in some sense is in nature." Taylor, *Sources of the Self*, 86; Williams, Bernard. *Ethics and the Limits of Philosophy*, 111. This British moral philosopher considers this procedural approach as related to the desire for an "absolute concept" of the world.

4. If somebody wants to realize good consequences or happiness or utility, the problem emerges that one cannot know everything in advance. How to act in a case of a *lack of knowledge*? How then to decide?

All of those objections still do not turn utilitarianism into a nonsensical theory. It remains one of the possible approaches, and it is an open question as to how far it goes. Especially if conceptions of "happiness" of different parties vary a lot in a particular situation, it becomes difficult. Because in that case the happiness of the one stands in the way of the happiness the other. However, once it has been decided what to understand by the word *happiness* or *utility*, the utilitarian approach is very helpful. Once the government has decided to set a special budget for free health care, and another budget for education or safety, for example, then it is decided what should be understood by *utility* in each case. It is important to *establish agreement* about that, first. Utilitarian theory causes confusion if people spar with the word *utility* or *happiness*. But in the meantime, they have put very different values into this container. In that case, the discussion and necessary agreement about background values are unavoidable.

In a certain sense, utilitarianism in the end is back to where it began, because Bentham initially wanted to get rid of these differing value orientations. He considered it impossible that people would find agreement about their subjective preferences. He tried to avoid the problem, but the price he has paid for it is that his objective criterion of "happiness" has become a container concept. This apparently objective concept is colored by everybody in a very subjective way. So his solution becomes unrealistic. We have to conclude that we cannot avoid the question of how subjective and different preferences can be made to agree with each other. That is something that cannot be done "*more geometrico.*"

Deontological Ethics, Universalization

Deontological ethics (*deon* is the Greek word for *obligation*) does not look so much for results, but for *principles*. It might be true that the realization and implementation of such principles can cause problems. For instance, a government can try to prevent monopolies by legislating fair competition. The point of departure or the principle in that case is: fair competition. Despite such legislation, however, some big players might still control the market. In that case, the principle is not wrong or to blame, but the realization of the law's intention is lagging behind. Additional legislation can solve this problem, but sometimes it happens that legislation cannot solve it, either.

In those cases, the consequences might not be good, but the principle, the *intention* behind it, is.

Deontological ethics takes its point of departure from such principles, like justice, honesty, loyalty, and so on. The central question is always how to prove that such principles are valid. One could say: They are part of our human makeup. Or: They are part of the *structure of being human* as a social being. One could also say: They are part of the dignity of being human. Most famous is the foundation of Immanuel Kant's deontological ethics, which can be summarized by the word *universalization*. Just as Bentham tries in utilitarianism to find one formula that can be applied in a quasi-mathematical way to all problems, Kant tries to do that by means of deontological ethics and by means of the concept of universalization. But first, let us explore something about the background of this approach.

Kant too was impressed by the new developments in mathematics. He shares the faith of his time, that man can come to grips with the universe by developing his rational abilities. And he shares in the hope of constructing an ideal and utopian society, the "reign of freedom," merely by reason. But he opposes the empirical ethics of the English, consequential ethics, because it is impossible to know in advance what good consequences are. In such a way, according to Kant, ethics cannot find a solid foundation. He wants to find this solid base and he finds it in the understanding of human beings as reasonable. The highest ability, and as it were, the core of humanity itself, is his *power of reason*. Being human means being (a) reason. It is typical for the eighteenth century to look at it this way. Intuitively, we think differently. Although we too have not completely left it behind us. This belief still shines through in the research on artificial intelligence. If, in science fiction literature or by computer scientists, a computer is imagined in which robots function like human beings, then the point of comparison is still about intelligence—that is, about the power of humans to reason. This is to be imitated or replicated in a computer. It is not about the imitation or replication of passion and emotion. Computers cannot laugh or cry.

In his *Critique of Pure Reason*, Kant has extensively researched the reasonable powers of man and categorized them. Time and space are such categories, because perception always occurs in time and space; and without that, there is no perception. Time and space are therefore forms of our perception, part of our mental makeup. Kant does not attribute them to the reality outside, but they are, as it were, the frame of our brain. Another category in this sense is causality. People cannot avoid searching for causal relationships in their perceptions. Causality however is not bound up with reality. It is a form of perception in our minds. It is a mental category. In his *Critique of Practical Reason*, Kant investigates how reason can also give direction to human action. It is of fundamental importance that reason cannot contradict itself. Reason cannot deny itself, because that would be unreasonable. And therefore impossible for a reason. This state of affairs can be summarized in the logical formula: A = A, and A = not-B. This is a principle that is valid in all circumstances, even in human action. Kant calls it a *categorical imperative. Categorical* in this case means: It is valid in all circumstances. You cannot stop using your reasonable powers. Even our actions therefore should not contradict themselves; and in fact, that is the meaning of the principle of *universalization.*

As far as Kant is concerned, it is the principle of reason that should control all arbitrary impulses of man. Reason does that by means of this procedure of universalization. How does it work? An example: I am the owner of a forest, and I would like to make as much profit as possible within the shortest amount of time. In that case, I cannot do any better than to cut down all the trees of the forest as fast as possible. In the end, I will have my profit. But I will not have a forest anymore. And therefore I have cut off the possibility of making any profit across the longer term. On second thought, I can question whether I am actually making as much possible profit from this approach. Am I not doing something very irrational? I want to make a profit, but the way I do it places a limit on my opportunities for making a profit—a possibly more lucrative profit if the value of either the wood or the currency goes up—in the future. This sounds contradictory. Kant could say: The maxim, "Make as much profit as possible and do that in the shortest amount of time," is internally contradictory and cannot be universalized. Accordingly, Kant concludes that if a person wants to act reasonably, he should act in such a way that the maxim of his action could at the same time be used as a universal law. Or in other words, he should act in such a way that the maxim of his action could be valid for everybody and in all circumstances, without internal contradictions. "Act in such a way that the maxim of your action can become a universal law." That is the first expression of the categorical imperative.

Another example: A lie might bring an advantage in the short term. But if the maxim, "It is all right to lie," would be accepted as a universal law, nobody would trust another human being anymore. If nobody would speak the truth, that would undermine the sense of speaking in the first place. For that reason, this maxim too cannot be universalized. In the case of lying, an additional problem is that a lie is already a contradiction in itself. It is contradictory to reason to lie. The maxim, "It is all right to steal," also cannot be universalized. What would happen if everybody would act like that? Nobody would be safe anymore from other human beings, and that would mean that the one reason (each human being, being a reason!) would deny the existence of another reason. That is something reason cannot do.

This also shows the meaning of the second formulation of the categorical imperative. It sounds like this: Treat every human being not only as a means, but also as *a goal unto himself*. If I let people work for me and I pay them for their labor, then I do treat them as a means to an end. That is, they are instrumental in helping me reach my goal. At the same time, however, I should also treat the employees as a goal unto themselves, respecting their humanity and treating them fairly, for example. "Goal unto himself" means, as far as Kant is concerned: I should treat the other person as a reason, as an embodiment of reason. In every person, humanity should be sacred to me and that humanity consists of the autonomy and freedom of the other person. And this freedom and autonomy in turn consist of his reason. This means that one recognizes the humanity of the other person as a goal in itself by subjecting him only to reasonable laws, which he, on the basis of his own reason, must subscribe to.[4] In our experience, this can lead to rather bizarre forms. For example, Kant might say that the criminal has a "right" to punishment because, if he is reasonable, he should condemn himself.

Now the question is: How far do we get with that approach in ethics, and which problems does it raise?

A first problem concerns the phrasing of maxims. The maxim, "I am allowed to lie," cannot be universalized, as we have seen. But the maxim, "I am allowed to lie if the Gestapo is in search of a person I am hiding," is universalizable. Because it is excellent if everybody acts like that. Not at all contradictory. But in this way, maxims can also be phrased that are universalizable, but doubtful in character. For instance: "Whoever earns more than $100,000 should pay 100% taxes on all he earns beyond that first $100,000." This maxim can be universalized, but is for all kinds of reasons *not so desirable*.

A second problem is more fundamental: You cannot ask yourself all day long whether what you do is universalizable. To brush your teeth, to take the bus, to go shopping—in those cases you do not ask that question. How do you apply the rule in one case and not in another? Kant himself admits: *There is no rule for applying the rule.*[5] What actually happens is that you will

---

4. Kant, *Kritik der Praktischen Vernunft* [Critique of Practical Reason], 210 (A 156).

5. Berman, *Law and Revolution*, Vol. II, 91; see also footnote 106 on page 413. Berman brings that up when he points out that a judge should always sentence equitably. According to him, this does not mean that the law is clear in some cases and not in others, but that a judge should always sentence according to the intention, the spirit, of the law. This does not mean exclusion, but inclusion of one's subjective judgment, of one's own conscience, in the application of the rule. For that reason there is no rule for

first have the *feeling* that something might be wrong, and only after that, the thought occurs that you should start applying, for example, the principle of universalization, if you care about the sustainability of our energy resources. Only if you get worried will you ask: Is our present consumption of fossil fuels universalizable? But if that is the case, an important philosophical question pops up: From what does that feeling arise, that something might be wrong? What makes one question urgent and another trivial?

The *Critique of Practical Reason* is not conclusive in this respect. It is remarkable that Kant poses himself this problem in a subsequent book, the *Critique of the Power of Judgment*.[6] What Kant is saying in that book is that we have an irreducible feeling for *purpose* and *direction*. In other words: That we experience a problem as significant or urgent arises from a faculty of its own that cannot be otherwise explained—a faculty that cannot be reduced to the faculty of reason. Methodically spoken, this is of great importance. It is there in its own right. It is a feeling that remains a feeling, and that cannot be reasonably explained. Instead, it is itself the starting point of reasoning. The feeling is first. The collection of facts and observations can go on and on, but only through all those facts and observations is it possible to have a *concept* of the *whole* by feeling. Somehow, it is as if we smell that something is not all right. And Kant recognizes this as a source of legitimate knowledge in its own right. Only if we are already somehow alarmed may we invoke the help of reason and the principle of universalization. Thinking of our energy resources, for instance, we can collect facts about types of energy, about quantities, and about the places to find them. But these facts as such are not conclusive as to the long-term availability of energy resources. Such a judgment, either the trust that things will go well, or the worry that there is too little for the generations to come, is articulated out of feeling. We will see how that will return in the philosophy of Levinas, albeit in a different form.

---

the application of the rule.

6. Kant does not speak about urgency, but he uses the word *elated*. We have a feeling about what is "elated," of what deserves respect, even though it cannot be deduced immediately from the senses. "Elated is that which, only in order to be thinkable, is shown by a faculty of feeling that surpasses any yardstick of sensual observation." *Kritik der Urteilskraft* [Critique of the Power of Judgment],172 (B 85,86). The whole, which is un-understandable, goes beyond sensual perception (174 [B 88,89]). Kant himself gives the example of the Egyptian pyramids, which one shouldn't perceive from either too close or too far away, in order to understand them as pyramids.

Virtue Ethics: A History of Human Qualities

In comparison to the two other approaches, "virtue ethics" is a rather new phenomenon. And also a remarkable phenomenon. Both utilitarianism and the deontological ethics of Kant strive toward an abstract and timeless formula, with the help of which moral problems can be treated. As we said earlier, they rely on the method of mathematics to do this. Mathematics does not allow for certainties without any proof. Descartes complains about the fact that he was already "spoiled" by his education, before he started to think independently. For that reason he refused to accept any idea about which he could not have a clear and distinct concept. He mistrusted the traditions in which he was raised. And now suddenly, after this Cartesian approach has been dominant for more than two centuries in ethics, too, the twentieth century surprisingly reflects a new interest in tradition and history in the form of virtue ethics.

The Scottish philosopher Alasdair MacIntyre is the most important representative of this line of thought, which introduces a new historical approach in ethics.[7] Virtue ethics does imply a *historical approach*, because virtues or human qualities always are "already there" and they are the product of a historical development. In addition, they also need sustained maintenance. Human qualities like friendliness, sense of justice, and so on, are not innate, but learned. They can be developed further, refined, and also renewed. But they are always part of a history and a culture already, and only within that context do they also reach out separately to individuals.

In antiquity, the qualities of thoughtfulness, courage, and moderation were the three main virtues. Aristotle treats them extensively, and in a certain sense MacIntyre refers back to him. But MacIntyre also attends to the developments after Aristotle, the emergence of the Christian virtues of faith, hope, and love. And he pays attention, for instance, to the qualities of reliability and loyalty in England in the seventeenth and eighteenth centuries.[8] It is not his intention to promote specific virtues, but much more to point to this long-lasting tradition from which we can still learn. This he thinks to be important, because "procedural ethics," like the ethics of Kant and Bentham,

---

7. It is not a coincidence that MacIntyre started his career after the Second World War, as did Levinas. That is related to the fact that science and technology, the development of which starts with Descartes, didn't end in a utopia, but instead in the dystopia of two scientifically and technologically waged world wars. Actually this experience more than anything else puts an end to a merely procedural approach in ethics, no matter how much time it takes even after that to cure the old habit.

8. MacIntyre, *Whose Justice?* This teaching of virtues and human qualities takes place in a historical and sociological context, although sometimes critics seem to forget that.

lacks content. Because both Kant and Bentham introduce a kind of mathematical formula by which all moral problems are to be treated, they propose a specific procedure—that is, the application of their formula. This seems to be precise and scientific, but often the result is that the real questions remain hidden behind a scientific veil of abstract moral reasoning. Those real questions always have to do with the priority struggle between different problems or values or human qualities. And both procedures avoid that question, or at least they do not tackle it. We have already seen that *utility* or *happiness* is a container concept into which everybody can put what he or she wants. And the categorical imperative—or in other words, the *procedure of universalization*—might in itself be a good instrument, but it cannot decide whether a problem is urgent. In other words, Kant's approach does not decide which problems are really important and really matter, nor can it decide which have sufficient priority that they "should be taken to the court of reason." That must have been decided already, before this rational procedure starts. And this decision depends on the value priorities one introduces.

In addition, McIntyre's approach puts not the intellect, but much more the human as such, at the center of attention. The right moral judgment does not depend only on intellect and reasoning. The whole person is speaking in it. MacIntyre gives some important qualifications to his idea of what are "virtues" (I prefer to speak about "human qualities"):

1. They come to be articulated through *practical action*. It does not make sense to call somebody a *righteous person* if that quality is never articulated in his actions. Virtues cannot exist apart from specific practices. Just as a good musician is somebody who can make good music, so too does the quality of a person rest in what he does.

2. They are learned and as such are *part of a biography*. It is impossible suddenly to decide to be sincere, loyal, tough, friendly, and so on, and just be those things from that moment on. These qualities require exercise, training, education, a learning process. It might be true that Descartes complained that he was not happy with his education and the teaching he had been given, but teaching and education are the means by which such human qualities are appropriated and learned in a long process. Without putting it into practice, there is no virtue.

3. These qualities are part of a longer *tradition* and of a *culture*. For that reason, ethics becomes embedded both historically and culturally. For example: From the Middle Ages onward, in western culture it has become typical practice not to keep scientific discoveries secret, but to share them. One should in addition describe them clearly and openly, so that experiments can be repeated by others. In the background is

the motivation to improve the quality of life for people, even as early as the Middle Ages. In the meantime, this approach has become almost a given. Still, it is implicitly learned at universities: to be critical toward your own experiments, to be complete in your information, to be open to outsiders, and to make science available to the public at large.[9]

Because virtues are part of a culture, there is no sharp distinction between *virtues* and *values*. If a culture deems loyalty to be important, we speak of a *value*. If loyalty is characteristic for a specific person, we speak of a *virtue* or *quality*. Different cultures might have different preferences in this respect. In England, loyalty is very much valued. In France a quality like sincerity or honesty is deemed very important.

There is a constant struggle about priorities between such qualities or values. This priority struggle is reinforced by cultural differences within the emerging global society, a problem that is often designated by the term *cultural diversity*. Often women too (not always!), more so than men, attach greater value to other qualities. *Competition, a sense of being connected, compassion, righteousness, safety, individualism, friendship, a critical mind*—all such terms designate values, virtues, or human qualities. At any moment, the right equilibrium needs to be found and the right priority set. That cannot be done by a mathematical formula.

But then how is it done? Is there one supreme value behind all the others that sets and manages the priorities? And which should that be? According to somebody like the twentieth-century American philosopher John Rawls, that value should be fairness: Everybody should, above all, have a fair opportunity. But in this way he brings us more or less back to the Kantian track. Because—according to him, too—fairness implies reasonableness and respect for the individual. And from that moment on, all the problems that we already mentioned in the case of Kant show up again. And then we are back to the beginning.

A different solution would consist of a sociological approach to this problem as practiced in the context of a philosophy of time and timeliness. The social context, practical sense, time, and opportunity in that case decide the priorities of different values and related problems. Within the social context of a family, for instance, care is deemed more important than competition. A group of laborers, working together on the shop floor at a company, doesn't allow for competition among themselves, either. In the world of sports, of course, that is entirely different. And among managers, too. In addition, a particular quality or line of action is desired in any one moment—but later, not any more. Sometimes somebody must raise his

---

9. MacIntyre, *After Virtue*, 187–88.

voice against particularly dangerous developments. But sometimes it is also necessary to remain silent and not push things to the extremes, in order to bear the responsibility for the common good. But where to draw the line? Nobody knows in advance. To speak with Kant once more: There is no rule to apply the rule.

Maybe here the ethics of responsibility, which we have not yet discussed, can help us, because in this line of ethics, opportunity, occasion, and the novelty of each situation play an important role.

Ethics of Responsibility

Is everything in ethics covered by the distinctions among values, obligations, and consequences? Surely, no situation is the same, and each person is always in correlation with his or her own social environment. Every person receives all kinds of appeals, and time and again a *new answer* needs to be given according to circumstances, *place,* and *time.* People are different, and over and over again, each appeal that they make appears in a different way. It is impossible just to repeat the answers from the past.

The philosophy of speech and the ethics of responsibility pay attention to this particular "ethical situation" of having to answer each time in a different way. This is where the philosophy of "dialogue" or "dialogical philosophy" can help.[10] The kernel of being human for this body of philosophy is not Kant's rationality or reason, but speech, *living speech*. To be human is to speak. Or to put it differently, to be human is to be engaged in communication, to give a responsible response. Even thinking comes down to speaking into oneself. To the extent that you are a person, you are at the node of speaking and answering. This approach to ethics moreover has religious connotations, although there are also non-religious interpretations of it.

The French-Jewish philosopher Emmanuel Levinas derives all ethics from this relation of answering to the other human being. The relation to the other human being, in which I am frequently called upon to give a new answer, is for Levinas at the center of philosophical attention. To be *in relation* to another person is the primary experience of being human, and for that reason it is the origin of all ethics. It is not so much an origin in the past, but an origin that everybody experiences in daily life. For instance, in this way: Most of the time we are not aware of the special character of the relation to the

---

10. With representatives like Rosenstock-Huessy (the initiator of this approach), Franz Rosenzweig, Martin Buber, and Ferdinand Ebner; in part, the existentialists Karl Jaspers and Gabriel Marcel; and emphatically also Levinas, who primarily refers his work to that of Rosenzweig.

other human being, and we are quite satisfied with doing our own thing. We are satisfied with our representations of the world, we handle the world, and we work in the world, keeping up what we do. In that way, we are at home with ourselves, just like in our real home. We are what Levinas calls *une force qui va*, a power that follows its course with a naïve sort of complacency, and we enjoy it.[11] Most things that we do are done rather unconsciously, by routine, without alertness, the habitual thing. We are on well-known territory, naïve and satisfied. For Levinas, the technical term for this habitual way of life is the *Self*. And with everything we do, we mostly stay within the confinements of this Self. We even absorb the relationship to other human beings in this Self, because we mostly think we already know the other. But then there are situations in which the other human being emphatically breaks through the wall. This is not specifically in violent situations, but situations or moments in which we feel the vulnerability of the other. This is the open look by which he appears to us as unprotected, and as an unexpected question by which we are confronted. This can refer to a miserable situation, a traffic accident, or imminent danger. But not necessarily. For the one who perceives it, every human being, according to Levinas, is marked by an "essential misery." Anyone I encounter sparks this appeal to an extra alertness and vigilance—that is, responsibility. I can never fully grasp this otherness, and yet it interrupts my self-affirmative course of action, taking away my initiative. And for that reason, I can also write the word *other* with a capital O: *Other*. This appeal, this essential misery, this vulnerability—and at the same time, inviolability—constitutes a moral relationship. This situation appeals to me and I am no longer in control. The initiative is outside me, and as such, it escapes my knowledge and ability. And because I cannot conceive, with my knowledge and ability, the otherness of the other (making a concept of the other), this relationship is in-finite in character. That is, it is beyond the confines of finite knowledge.[12]

Nevertheless, this relationship does have an impact on me. I feel called upon, with my back against the wall, because I cannot escape an answer. I also cannot escape the sincerity that belongs to such an answer. Feeling yourself uneasy is already a way of feeling responsible. Again, this is not because the other is grossly present, but more because of a kind of *weaker presence*, as if I should be alert to my own potential for violence. In the eyes of the other human being, which look upon me without protection, it is already written: "Thou shalt not kill!" This moral appeal is not a conclusion

11. If we enjoy, we are absorbed into the things we enjoy and we do not think of anything else. In that sense enjoyment is unconscious—or perhaps pre-conscious. See Levinas, *Totalité et Infini*, 82 ff.

12. It is important to understand the relationship between conceiving and concept. Thus Levinas, ibid., 161–68.

at the end of a moral argument. It is felt. I feel *exposed* to the call, and now I have to give an answer. I cannot meet the other, empty-handed. My naïve egoism and self-sufficiency are now turned into openness, to exposure to the other, even to longing for the other. Levinas claims that this is a description of our own most original experience. It is not meant to be a norm, as if it should be like this. It is a description of what is happening in every open encounter with the other human being. Every human encounter could be described with the help of the metaphor of somebody who opens his house in order to show hospitality to the other.

Of course there are all kinds of values and rules and norms and obligations and habits. Nothing against that, and they even are necessary. But these norms and values and rules have their origin in this ethical relationship: to prove righteousness to the stranger, the widow, and the orphan; to show hospitality to the other, always in an unexpected way. I cannot fall back on familiar answers, but I have to speak anew, over and over again. If we were already in search of a value behind all other values, or of a rule for the application of the rule, then according to Levinas it is this: the incessant responsibility for the other. Like the other himself, so my responsibility too always appeals to me in other ways.

This situation, in which it is impossible to evade an answer and in which *you* have to come out with it, makes the moral answer that somebody can give personally. You, and no one else, are required to say something or to do something! The *uniqueness of the person* consists exactly of that experience. You are irreplaceable and for that reason unique, not because you are accidentally made up of peculiarities, but because nobody can give the answer that is expected from you. The freedom of a person also resides in this—that is, the possibility not to be determined by origin or environment. But it is a "difficult freedom," because it is a freedom to guarantee for the others, all others. It is impossible to be indifferent.

However, the one who puts all his cards on this approach in ethics can be seduced into the arbitrariness of an "In my opinion . . . " approach. This is definitely not the intention of Levinas. Not every situation is so completely new that there is not an answer already. There are all kinds of social codes and commonly accepted norms and values. Sometimes they need to be followed; sometimes they need to be deviated from. Traffic rules are an example of this. These rules are there so that everybody adheres to them, to avoid collisions. But every now and then, one needs to deviate from the rules, exactly in order to prevent collisions. To act responsibly is comparable to that situation: sometimes it is a matter of following the rules and sometimes just the opposite. There is no fixed rule for the application of ethical rules. In other words, the *rule behind the rules* is: infinite and not defined responsibility.

Background Theory of the Fourfold Responsibility

The reader will have noticed that these four approaches in ethics correspond to the four approaches of the concept of responsibility in the first chapter. Finally, I want to elaborate upon this correlation. I prefer to speak of a kind of affinity between each one of the approaches of the concept of responsibility with one of the approaches in ethics. This is more than an intellectual exercise. It can help us to decide which ethical approach is more relevant in which situation.

Let us start with *functional responsibility*. We have defined functional responsibility as a responsibility in which one exercises one's functional tasks as well as possible, according to the division of labor and the description of a function. We are doing what we are paid to do. We do not need to think much about our daily tasks. The work needs to be done as efficiently as possible. Functional responsibility for that reason is in search of effective action. Whoever emphasizes effective action will automatically cling to *consequential ethics* and *utilitarianism*. Because engineers attach much importance to efficiency, they have a natural inclination toward utilitarian deliberations. Give me insight into the consequences of my actions, give me the numbers and the models; then I will decide if and how the common good is best served. This approach works, once the priorities have been decided upon and have become clear. If the most important decisions concerning life and well-being already have been made, and the people involved agree what is understood by the term *utility*, and as long as the consequences can be calculated in advance, a utilitarian approach is excellent. Both functional responsibility and consequential ethics are focused on the world *outside*.

Collective responsibility means that the answer to a particular situation is determined by the codes of behavior of the group or groups to which one belongs. If, for instance, there is a culture of environmental negligence in a company, then it is difficult for an individual to change that. But the reverse is also true. If, for instance, a company is careful and considerate in relation to labor circumstances and safety, new incoming laborers and managers will adapt easily to that habit. People are inclined to adapt to the values and norms of the group to which they belong, almost without noticing. A common history and a feeling of togetherness are helpful in that respect. For that reason, there is a certain affinity between collective responsibility and *virtue ethics*. Virtues and human qualities are internalized by the common history of the group, common education, and training. One internalizes them and learns them as part of the culture to which one belongs. This belonging to, internalizing, and learning of virtues—thanks to a common history—gives both to virtue ethics, and collective responsibility an orientation *to the past*.

I have described *professional responsibility* as consisting of freedom, independence, ability, the power to coordinate a partial and biased input with other partners, and the ability to have a judgment of your own as an input in the decision-making process. This brings us almost automatically into the neighborhood of *deontological ethics*, which emphasizes obligations toward other parties. Kant, attached as he is to the idea that every human being is "a reason," might argue that a professional judgment coincides with a reasonable judgment. That judgment at the same time treats every human being also as a "goal in himself." A translation of Kant's approach in modern practice is the idea of *informed consent*. This idea is used in the application of risky medical treatments. It means that the people involved are informed as much as possible about the treatment, and on the basis of that information they can give their consent to proceed with it. This method is also used for obtaining social acceptance of technical projects. But then the difficulty immediately arises that separate individuals are no longer involved, but many people concurrently become involved.

Both professional responsibility and deontological ethics are focused on *the inside*, on the *subject*. The fact that I am a subject implies that I have a judgment of my own, that I can be reasonable as well, that I have duties and obligations toward others, and that I can coordinate my views to reach an inter-subjective and shared understanding.

I have defined *vacant responsibility* as the ability to feel responsible for things for which nobody is responsible. In other words, feeling responsible for that which is vulnerable and is waiting for the first person who cares. This not only counts for the weaker person, but also for the "weaker possibility." There should be someone who makes him- or herself responsible for the future. There must be people who explore dangerous and unknown territory. The relationship toward the future, according to Levinas, is comparable to the relationship to the other for whom one needs to make room. For that reason, Levinas' *ethics of responsibility* and the idea of *vacant responsibility* are connected. Always something unexpected is coming up, and always a new and not-calculable answer is necessary. This responsibility appeals to me as a unique and irreplaceable person. Where nothing is arranged, one needs to act on one's own responsibility and one falls back on one's own. This uniqueness often means that one has to stand alone. If virtue ethics or an ethics of human qualities is oriented toward the past and to the group that is participating in a common culture, Levinas' ethics of responsibility is focused on the future—there, where one is at the forefront and needs to go down untrodden paths.

42 Planetary Responsibilities

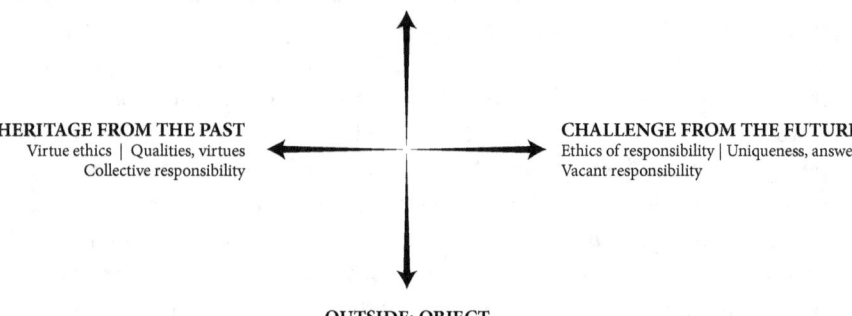

Table 2. The four kinds of ethics

	Consequential ethics	Deontological ethics	Virtue ethics	Ethics of responsibility
Features	Utility, happiness, consequences procedures Cost-benefit analysis Related to the object world	Principles, intention Structure of being human Universalization, Reason and consistency Human as a goal in himself Related to the human subject	Virtues, qualities Expressed in action Part of a biography Historical achievements Related to the past	New situation, new answer In situation, in relation Appeal Uniqueness Related to the future
Limitations	Container concept Reduction Sacrificing minorities Consequences not known	Not desirable, but still universalizable maxims No rule for the application of the rule	Priority struggle between qualities / values Cultural diversity	Danger of arbitrariness and too much subjectivity Danger of lack of orientation
Conditions for application	Agreement about basic values and orientation Decision made about content of "utility"	Feeling of urgency Sense of orientation Agreement about basic values	Dependent upon time and opportunity, social context	"Difficult freedom" Impossibility of indifference: Impossibility of doing nothing

3

Rationality, Communication, and Technology

If we apply moral theory to practical situations, as is the case in ethics of technology, sooner or later it appears that there are limits to what ethical theory can do. Ethical theories can help structure a moral problem. They can help find the right questions to ask. They offer a kind of vocabulary by which moral considerations can be articulated and modeled. But once a decision has to be made, something fuzzy begins to happen. Logic and reason cannot do away with subjective evaluation and, on top of that, they cannot do away with the communication process that leads to action. If these are taken into consideration, suddenly it is impossible to draw a straight line. In this chapter we investigate how this communication process affects the application of moral principles to practical situations. This is done mainly with the help of the language theory of Rosenstock-Huessy and with some examples from the ethics of technology.

A Broad Concept of Rationality

If we study the idea of a reasonable discussion within a group, we frequently discover that rationality is more than only logic. When we exclaim to one another, "Be reasonable!" we mean a lot more than only, "Think logically!" Now, what is more reasonable than thinking logically? The German sociologist Jürgen Habermas claims that whoever comes up with a rational argument makes a threefold claim: (1) The proposition advanced by the speaker is true in actual fact; this is a matter of logic and adequate information; (2) the speaker means what he says—he claims to be honest; he is not lying, and he is not drawing attention to things he does not deem important himself;

he is authentic and open; and (3) he claims the norm implied in his proposition is justified and right. When I, for instance, might say, "This software package is thoroughly tested," I am implying that I have knowledge about the specific testing procedures required. That is, I have the facts and I can give a logical account of this information. Second, I am implying that I am an authentic person, and that I do not lie. Third, I imply that I have some criterion in mind by which I can judge the adequacy of testing procedures. This example shows that logic pertains only to the facts as such. It cannot decide on the authenticity and honesty of the speaker, or about the justification of such and such a norm or value.[1]

If we expand the concept of reason to *reasonableness*,[2] we reach Habermas' concept of *communicative rationality*. Communicative rationality differs from strategic or instrumental action. Instrumental rationality is related to the efficient organization of all kinds of different means to given ends. When I know what I want, and when the goals of my actions are not open to discussion, my communication strategy will be instrumental. The criterion for success is effectiveness, and to that end I will try to mobilize all means. In this way I can try, for instance, to find an optimum between two available actions and I can try in different ways to influence the other stakeholders in the process. As long as I do not give them a say in the determination of my goals, they are objects of my instrumental rationality. As long as I do not take their points of view into consideration as partners in a dialogue, I am manipulating them to adapt to what I want them to do.

So logic is not everything; we also need authenticity. Authenticity is related to *performance*. This means that the person expressing a sentence is not only saying something, but also doing something. He is performing an act by saying something. He is doing something and he wants other people to do something, too. In a sentence like: "The coffee is ready," the people who hear it are informed about a particular condition of the coffee. But the one who utters this sentence would be surprised if somebody were to answer with, "Thank you for the information," and continue his or her work. The sentence is meant to make people stand up and take a break together. One may call that the *performative content* of a sentence.[3] The sentence is an act that tries to perform something, and it is also intended to make the hearer perform something. We all have very sensitive ears in hearing this performative content of any sentence. Implicitly and mostly unconsciously for

1. Jürgen Habermas makes this threefold distinction many times. See, for example, *Between Facts and Norms*, 9, 10, and 18.

2. As Stephen Toulmin does in *Return to Reason*.

3. Rosenstock-Huessy attributes this performative attitude to the language form of the "coniunctivus" and the lyrical, in *Origin of Speech*.

ourselves, we always ask: "Why does this person come with this information at this moment? What does he or she mean by this information? What does he or she want us to do? Is this an order, or a request? Or is it an insult? Or is it flattering?"

The person saying, "This software package is thoroughly tested," makes an implicit claim that not only has he or she enough knowledge to make that claim, but he or she also is provided with a criterion, a value, or a norm by which he or she can make such a judgment. The person who makes the statement, "I am calling this meeting to order," first performs an act by saying that. Before the person said it, the meeting was not yet under way, even though people were in the room, talking to one another. After these words, the meeting has officially begun. But that person also claims to have the authority to do so: Probably he or she is chairing the meeting and there is a recognized rule or norm that it is up to the chairperson to call the meeting to order. Since such norms mostly remain implicit in the sentence, we tend to think that they are not there. But it is just the other way around: Since they are there, they don't need to be mentioned.

There is an ongoing discussion about the question of where such norms and values come from. Are the basic norms universally present in every culture? Or are they part of—so to speak, inscribed in—the makeup of our minds?[4] For our purposes, it is not necessary to go into that debate. It is enough to recognize that even while having an ethical discussion on the origin of moral behavior, we cannot abstract from holding on to such norms: Even during a discussion about norms, we remain polite; we respect the opinion of the other person; we do not resort to violence in order to find a solution to a problem in our discussion, and so on. For that reason, we can bypass these questions and state that in the first instance, they simply are there as part of social life. Their impact on our behavior cannot be suspended; we cannot shake them off. In addition we already have seen that there is an ongoing priority struggle about the question of which norm and value should prevail in which situation, and at which time. Speaking the truth, loyalty to the group, individual career opportunities—these are instances of this ongoing struggle with priorities. All policy makers, all of us who want to participate in the further development of society, have to enter this field of tension of differing and contradicting norms and values. The fact that in principle a norm is universally valid does not help us in particular and specific situations. Factories are not allowed to pollute the social environ-

---

4. David McNaughton, *Moral Vision*, 17 ff. McNaughton, however, knows only of the inward and the outward perspective (cognitive abilities and the reality that corresponds to them). He does not take into consideration that we also live in a field of tension between the learning experiences from the past and the challenges of the future.

ment by the noise they might make. But airports are allowed to do so. As a consequence, it is not enough for a norm or value to be universally valid; it needs to be socially and situationally valid, too.

The Example of the Challenger Disaster of 1986

In this broader concept of rationality that includes information, performance, and the normative dimensions, we find a "tool" for the analysis of decision-making processes. The *Challenger* disaster can serve again as an example.

In 1986, a non-professional astronaut, a female schoolteacher, joined the crew of the space shuttle for the first time. There would be television broadcasts from outer space to promote public support for the space shuttle program of the United States. Millions of people were watching TV, and parents of the schoolteacher's students and the students themselves were present at the launch. As the *Challenger* ascended into the air toward outer space, it exploded, and none of the crew survived. It appeared that the cause of the problem was in the rubber O-rings, which sealed the segments of both the side-rockets of the shuttle. The evening before the launch, a teleconference had taken place between NASA and Thiokol, the company that produced both side-rockets. Some of the engineers had warned that the expected low temperatures (18 degrees Fahrenheit) would cause the rubber O-rings to lose their elasticity and thus there would be a risk of leaks and possibly of the total loss of the space shuttle.[5] That loss is exactly what happened the next day. The engineers tried to have the launch of the space shuttle postponed, but the managers of both NASA and Thiokol did not consider the engineers' case to be strong enough. The subsequent Presidential Commission on the Space Shuttle Challenger Accident conducted an investigation into the process that had led to this disaster, and concluded that on all levels the decision process had been flawed.

Now, here I want to offer a description of those different levels. They entail more than logic and information only. They also entail the levels of *authenticity* and *normativity* that were in play during the decision making.

On all levels, things went wrong. Why did the managers not accept the analysis of the engineers? First, the engineers did not succeed in giving full and coherent information. They had warned before that problems might occur with the O-rings, and they had some information from former launches that could substantiate a correlation between low temperatures during launch and leakages in the side-rockets, but the evidence was not that

---

5. Whitbeck, *Ethics in Engineering Practice and Research*, 133 ff.

convincing. This in turn was a result of the fact that the organization had prevented the engineers from doing more research after they had signaled the problem. The engineers also had a graphic presentation of all launches in which problems had occurred with the O-rings. They did not, however, present a graphical presentation of all launches—including the launches in which there were no problems with the O-rings. Such an approach might have made their case stronger. For that reason, the claim of truth in what they were saying was not sufficiently or logically coercive.

Second, at the end of the teleconference, one of the managers forced the decision by asking his colleagues to put on their management hats. The space shuttle has so many parts that if every tiny problem was taken seriously, no launch might ever take place. At this moment, in fact, open communication was substituted by hierarchical control. The engineers stopped being considered as partners in a dialogue. They were no longer authentically listened to.

Third, there was a problem on the level of normative evaluation. Of course, everybody would agree that safety is paramount; but at that time, the space shuttle program was under high pressure. The costs per launch were enormous, and the organization had not succeeded in speeding up the program to achieve cost efficiencies. In fact, it was the other way around. The shuttle program was slowing down. So in fact there was an unspoken norm or imperative to get along with the launching process. In addition, although there had been leakages more than once and even traces of burning, there had not been failures in other space shuttle launches yet. Therefore, the concern for safety was silently watered down and another norm prevailed. On all three levels—the level of fact, the level of authenticity, and the level of normative evaluation—the decision-making process was not aligned.

Speech and Communication

The example of the *Challenger* serves to make clear how important the communication process is. If the outcome is influenced to such an extent by the quality of the communication process, we should further investigate what happens in the exchange of human speech.

Speech reflects patterns of social relations.[6] Both social relationships and forms of grammar express different types of communication. In this respect, there is a difference in interpretation between Rosenstock-Huessy and Habermas. Rosenstock-Huessy distinguishes four basic modes of

---

6. Rosenstock-Huessy, "Kopernikanische Wendung," 382.

speech and corresponding ways to relate to each other, instead of Habermas' three.

When a group has found its way within social reality, the language it speaks is the "usual" language of established relationships. A lot of small talk goes on, and they repeat views and opinions on which everyone agrees. All kinds of utterances confirm that the group is in harmony and its language in fact serves to create this sense of belonging and harmony. For the most part, half a word is enough. Just like codes of behavior, language repeats itself. On more official occasions, storytelling replaces such short expressions of belonging. When the story of the group is told, the internal relationships are confirmed once again: "The organization has overcome great difficulties!" "The organization has achieved great things!" "The future looks bright!" This is group language.

However, another kind of language is used to confirm hierarchical relationships between superiors and subordinates. Not many words are needed here as well; but instead of a language of harmony and belonging, it is a language of orders, information, and explanation. In the daily command structure, a very clear and unambiguous language is necessary to coordinate the functional behavior of every member of a team. The meaning of the words should be clearly demarcated, just as is the case in an army or in an airplane, where exact orders can be given in only one correct way.

However, much more language is necessary when codes that can direct the behavior of the group have not yet been established. That is the starting point for the real communication problems between people and within organizations. When there is no agreement beforehand, then how can agreement be established? In our modern or postmodern society, it seems that every individual is developing his or her own language, an individual set of terms and communication patterns, a universe of meaning on its own. And if it is not the diversity of individuals, it is the diversity of cultural and subcultural patterns that makes communication terms vague and ambiguous. Even within western culture there are many differences. For instance, an American manager might be delighted to receive feedback from his employees. Now he can manage them better. But in Germany such feedback should be given much more carefully, because a German manager might think the feedback is a means of making him admit his failures.[7] And along with the differences between cultures and individuals, the differences between the types of situations can also increase because of the differentiated professional occupations of modern society. How can common terms, a common language, a common interpretation of reality be established within

---

7. The example is from Trompenaars and Hampden-Turner, *Riding the Waves*.

a situation of growing differences, where we cannot take it for granted that there is common understanding?

Clearly, one needs time; and one needs discussion, opposition, and dialogue to sort things out. More strict hierarchical relationships cannot solve the problem. There seems to be an easy way out: Let us have more of the language of clear hierarchical relationships, and we can do away with all discussion and all confusion. And for a while it works. But after a while, it appears that beneath the surface, everybody was doing something different. The boss cannot be everywhere, and as soon as she has left—and even while she is there—her subordinates might not do their own thing, but certainly do things their own way. Nothing can prevent that from happening, as long as there are real and significant reasons for it, to the extent that there are really different options, competing lines of action, and contradictory viewpoints. They cannot be brushed away only by hierarchy. They need to be solved by discussion and by dialogue, and that takes time.

The *most loyal opposition* is the official term by which the opposition is named in the British Parliament. The United Kingdom has the oldest parliamentary system, and it makes decisions final. In its early days, the English Parliament consisted of the lower nobility called the *House of Commons*, which opposed the King and the high nobility.[8] English society of the seventeenth and eighteenth centuries was ruled by a balance of—or an equilibrium between—these two forces, neither of which could overrule the other. The power of the King and the opposition from the House of Commons were the two poles of its political system. This was new within western history, the idea, that "the enemy" is not depicted as unworthy or as a monster, but as a partner in the process. Such a dialogue cannot be conducted without tensions; it is a combination of working together, and yet being opposed to one another. The idea that contradicting forces can work together without abandoning their differences is a mental and cultural achievement of the social and political history of Europe (even if we have to admit that Europe sinned many times against the principles by which it was created). The idea has always been that top-down relationships should be balanced by corrections and criticisms from below (see chapter 7).

Sometimes people think that the communication gap is overcome when they have the same understanding of the situation, the same conceptual and symbolic horizon. They use the same words for the same things. But alas, this is not enough. There is no communication without some level of benevolence. First, the correspondence needs to be established between

---

8. Rosenstock-Huessy, *Out of Revolution*, 257 ff.

different people before the information can flow.⁹ So to speak, the communication line needs to be opened before the messages can come through.

An example: An American firm wanted to sell a particular product to a company in Brazil. The computer system they wanted to sell was of a superior technical quality and their presentation by PowerPoint was beautiful, clear, and effective. Their only problem was that they arrived in Brazil in the morning and they had to leave at the end of the afternoon. But they calculated that even within this short time, it should also be possible to have lunch together with the representatives of the Brazilian company. Things worked out differently because they had to wait for more than an hour, waiting for the Brazilian representatives to show up. They had to rush through their presentation to catch their plane at the end of the day.

Meanwhile, a Swedish company offered a competing technology clearly of inferior quality. But they took the time and stayed in Brazil for more than a week. They made friends and established relationships of loyalty and trust with the representatives of the Brazilian company. The Brazilian company decided to buy the inferior product from the Swedish company because their representatives felt these people were friendly and reliable, in case problems would occur.[10]

It should not be forgotten that communication is not there for its own sake. It should end in a common line of action. This is difficult. "Don't we all agree on the fact that . . . ?" How often does a chairman try to prevent any real opposition by such a trick? It is just one more attempt to brush away real differences. In order to overcome such differences and to achieve some form of effective action, agreement is necessary (as already pointed out) on three levels: First, on the level of information, the facts on the table; then on the level of the different ways of expressing those facts; and finally on the normative evaluation of them. It is not difficult to see how these three levels of communication influence one another. Many so-called facts already are on the table as interpreted facts—and in addition are interpreted from a particular evaluative moral viewpoint. One can take the vigorous discussions on the global greenhouse effect as an example. There is not even a normative agreement regarding what might count as a fact: Even the facts need to be legitimized and authorized before they can be recognized and "count" as a fact. In many cases, if they do not suit the "model," they do not "count."

---

9. Levinas has pointed out that rationality cannot do without sincerity, which prevents people from merely playing a role in a drama that absorbs them. The *droiture de la relation* prevents people from being taken in, despite their fear and trembling. In that sense, rationality cannot exist without a relationship to ethics. *Totalité et Infini*, 177.

10. The example is from Trompenaars and Hampden-Turner, *Riding the Waves*.

Of course, the participants in a dialogue do not need to agree on everything in order to commit themselves to some or other line of action. Differences will remain, and they are even fruitful. When a particular course of action is supported from different viewpoints and evaluations, one might expect that this course of action even has better credentials. When a man wants to buy a car because it is cost-effective, and his wife wants to buy the same car because it is safe, and the son wants to buy it because it is fast, and the daughter because of it looks nice, then the family might have found exactly the right car. Different viewpoints might contradict one another; but they can also correct one another, or influence one another in a creative way so that the result might be better than what every individual at first would have come up with. In other words, the starting point of a dialogue lies in the recognition of the fact that the different participants begin from different starting points. They have a partial view on reality, not only in the sense of partial information, but also a partial and biased understanding of it within their personal frames of reference. They might also have a partial and biased normative valuation of it. A real discussion about taking common action can therefore be compared to a design process. The mutual learning process within a dialogue is not only a process of mutual adaptation, but also (and even more) a process of change.

This is an important point, here: Dialogue and communicative interaction imply *change*. Facts, interpretations, and their normative evaluations undergo a change when other people are really listened to. The views, interpretations, and evaluations of the other person, when I have really listened, will become mine to a certain extent.

To return to our example, if the son's first priority for the car is its speed, then after some discussion he might admit that his mother is not entirely wrong that the car should also be safe and have good brakes, for instance. Nobody has the one, definite, and absolute view on reality; but everybody might have a point. Maybe the truth does not exist in an absolute sense, but it still does in a relative sense, just as we say in the expression, "There is truth in that." Maybe the truth consists of the right sequence of partial truths that follow one another, correct one another, and adjust one another when they enter the discussion in the right place and at the right time.

Imperatives, Facts, and "Beliefs"

If an exchange of views—and if change itself—are necessary, how do we get people to cooperate? That is the problem of any hierarchical organization that accepts the fact that the hierarchical command structure is not enough to keep the organization on track. How can individual workers be convinced that they do not work for only the money, but also for the good cause the company represents? Don't we need some higher cause or goal in order to open people up toward each other and get them to cooperate?[11] Of course, any big corporation might push away that question by saying that they are not in the business of philanthropy, and therefore have no mission-driven, internal need for workers to embrace an altruistic corporate theme. Oil companies, for instance, produce and distribute oil so that investors receive a reasonable return on their investments. But on the other hand: What is the sense of producing oil if people are not served by it? Here lies a test for every organization: If the organization is not doing an indispensable and valuable job, it can expect to be valued and praised neither by the general public nor by its own employees.[12] In that case, it seems that the company is not answering to a real need, a real imperative. New imperatives, needs, and values will instead mobilize the energy and power of society.[13]

Sometimes the creation of cooperative relationships and the creation of a common representation of the truth are in tension with each other. Relationships of correspondence and mutual responsibility are created by paying attention to every individual *in particular*. People try to adapt to each other by looking each other in the eye. But developing a sense of the good cause and legitimate role of the company within society requires paying attention to the broad picture and to an *encompassing* vision of the future. That is something else. There is a risk that the truth falls victim to our nice and friendly human relationships. The reverse can also occur. There is also a risk that I do not like somebody and so I do not listen to what that person has to say. We cannot sort out what the real imperatives are if we like each other too much and avoid saying what the other person does not like.

It is also not easy to establish whether we only use different words for the same thing or, on the contrary, even articulate a different view while using the same words. How do we phrase what really matters? It is necessary to distinguish the real imperatives from the illusory ones. What should one think, for example, about large-scale transportation by airplanes? Millions

---

11. Leon Martel analyzes the quality of workers' employment in this sense in his *High Performers*.

12. A major proponent of servant leadership, Robert Greenleaf, has said that "[t]he test of greatness in a dream is that is has the energy to lift people out of their moribund ways to a level of being and relating from which the future can be faced with more hope than most of us can summon today." Cited by Joseph Jaworski, in "Destiny and the Leader, 258–71 and 263.

13. Rosenstock-Huessy. *Origin of Speech*, 110 ff.

of people are carried by airplane, and airline companies plan for more passengers per flight in the future, ordering planes with more than 800 seats. Is this wrong, because of the noise and the pollution and the waste of energy? Or is it justified and even necessary in order to establish peaceful relationships between people on a global scale by furthering mutual understanding? How should we understand and create a vision for the use of airplanes in human transportation? Which option should we choose?

We can also frame the dilemma as a matter of urgency. What is more urgent: the question of sustainability, or the opportunity for ordinary people to make contacts worldwide? Such a technological dilemma also existed at the beginning of the car industry. Before the Second World War, Daimler-Benz in Germany had chosen to build a car for the happy few—expensive and of high quality. Henry Ford, on the contrary, introduced a mass-produced car, increased the wages of his employees, and thereby created the mass consumer society. In retrospect, which was a better course of action? Would it have been possible to prevent Nazism if Germany had chosen to develop in the direction of a mass consumer society in the early 1920s, too?

By asking such questions, we introduce the normative and historical dimension, the dimension of imperatives and necessities that legitimize and authorize such-and-such a policy. Since the question, "How do we want to live?" is a normative question, it is clear that the development of technology is affected by it, and in turn it also affects this normative question. When such normative questions on urgent needs and historical imperatives[14] find agreement within society, they can provoke a lot of organizational energy and creativity. It sounds peculiar, but the industrial capacity and the capacity to invent and to organize was never used more effectively than during the time of the Second World War in Great Britain and in America. Here was the just cause to which everybody could dedicate himself or herself. On a smaller scale, we can mention a Dutch example: In the early days of the Philips factory, which became big by producing light bulbs, there was a competition going on between the two brothers directing the company. One tried to sell as many light bulbs as he could; the other tried to produce as much as he could. If he produced more than his brother could sell, he challenged his brother to sell more. And the other way around. Although these two brothers directed the company in quite an authoritarian way, the energy of their joyful competition flowed throughout the whole company.

---

14. The normative dimension, which remains abstract in the work of Habermas, is historicized in the work of Rosenstock-Huessy. It is discovered, developed, and renewed by historical experiences.

They were highly respected, and by their effort they convinced the employees of the good cause they were working for.[15]

In this way, in fact, another language beyond the mere language of communication is introduced. And also another kind of relationship. It is the language of norms, values, and imperatives that claims the energy of their adherents. The persons who introduce and articulate such a language are opening ways into the future. These are creative persons who often stand alone. Or it can also be small companies experimenting with new technologies or new forms of organization. They are the creative leaders. This language is not so much a language of many words, but often a language of short names, the exact meaning of which is not yet clear. Such short names are a matter of preference and political sense; they are more a matter of belief and sensitivity than of analysis.

Normative and evocative language does not mobilize our intellectual capacity nearly as much as does our sense of the future, or our sense of urgency, our sense of timeliness, our priorities, and our concrete imperatives. This language of short names and imperatives introduces new ways of handling problems, the outcome of which was not clear beforehand. When such imperatives or values are articulated, we understand them only halfway. We need time to develop an understanding of what we say. *A sustainable future*—it is a challenging, short expression, a kernel of a name for a whole set of problems. But who exactly knows what it is? *Flexible labor relations*—somehow everybody can feel that something is going on, here: Ongoing learning, new borders (or no borders at all?) between private and public life, and so on. But what will come of it? *Globalization*—indeed, more and more companies are working on a global scale, but what really will it mean? Will it result in one, big monoculture? Will it result in a division of labor among different cultures? Nobody knows. Such short names are future-oriented imperatives that can be explained and implemented only in the course of time, when we try to find our way with them. If we follow them, we will discover what we mean. There is no experiment that can solve such problems, except for the experiment of social and political life itself. Or in other words, they receive content only as concepts, once they have been taken seriously as names for a problem yet to be solved.

Nevertheless, imperatives and necessities do affect the quality of communication between people. We already emphasized that it takes time and energy to establish a dialogue between opposing forces. On this level, the level of communication and commitment, it is necessary to pay attention to every particular contribution of individuals or from individual departments,

---

15. Wennekes, *De Aartsvaders*, 283 ff.

and so on. Their contribution should be honored, lest the company fall apart and become a company full of political struggles among competing "tribes." But people and departments within organizations also need to be convinced before they invest this level of energy in each other. In order to overcome their differences, and in order to overcome their stubborn individualism, people need more than authentic communication and mutual love. They also need to recognize a common value or imperative, or norm or assignment that they all have to subscribe to as a matter of historical urgency.

People do overcome their differences only when it is really necessary. Times of crisis, if only financial crisis, often provoke the energy by which the members of an organization are not only prepared to work harder, but also—and this is the secret of large-scale production and big organizations!—are more willing to cooperate and to coordinate their efforts. It is true that many times short and shallow slogans are used within companies to provoke such energy and commitment. Managers often try to combine the qualities of a preacher and of a general. What the hierarchical structure cannot achieve, they try to achieve by the slogans of the day, using whatever slogan they can find. The most popular these days seems to be, "We are the best!" Of course, such artificial slogans do not work. They do not really convince people. Everybody knows he is belied by such language. But that does not make the normative language of imperatives superfluous. These mistaken slogans only represent the wrong solution for the real problem. Besides communicative commitment, an important imperative or appeal is necessary to bind people together. To say it in more popular words: The organization is not only in need of passion, but also of a mission.

Four Types of Language

So far, we have distinguished four types of language.

- *Informative* language. The language of information. Information should be clear. Meanings of concepts should be clearly demarcated. The word changes into a concept when its meaning is clearly defined, and from now on is used in that definite sense. From that moment on, words lose their ambiguity, just as they also lose their flexibility. They can mean only one thing. Such language is used for things in the world outside: facts, data, know-how. Such language is also instrumental in a chain of top-down relationships, a command structure within a hierarchy, in order to give clear orders and assignments—and to be sure that people as well as machines and so on are functioning well. It is the language of logic and coherence and clarity.

- *Formative* or narrative language. The language of belonging to the group. These are the day-to-day words and stories and expressions that seem not to have much meaning, except to confirm that members belong to the group. Half a word is often enough. The meaning of the words is not clearly demarcated, but this "defect" of language is compensated for by a kind of silent mutual understanding. Silent in the sense that mutual understanding does not need many words. Language is repetitive. It is the language of a meaningful, shared history that is kept alive within the group produced by that history.

- *Communicative* or *performative* language. This is the language of dialogue in which people are seeking one another, and seeking mutual understanding, common agreement, and effective action to which everybody will commit himself or herself. The language within a dialogue does not have the same definitional clarity as instrumental language. There are many misunderstandings, and the clarity of conceptual and instrumental language is still searched for. Within a discussion we often hear, "What do you mean?" Partial and biased views are put together to change, correct, and complement one another. Because the meaning of the words shifts from one context to the other in an associative way, such language is logical and coherent only in a limited sense. A discussion is not yet a discursive chain of arguments.

- *Normative* language. This is the language of imperatives, urgency, moral considerations, and necessity. We invoke a future by short expressions, a future that is not yet realized. Since it is not there, it is not yet known. It is merely on the agenda. It calls forth discussion and action. Problems are signaled and named so that they might be put on the agenda, but it is not yet clear how such problems should be treated. True, they have received a name, but such names work like imperatives: They provoke discussion, and only in the end, when the solution is found, can clear concepts be delineated.

These four types of language can be presented graphically.

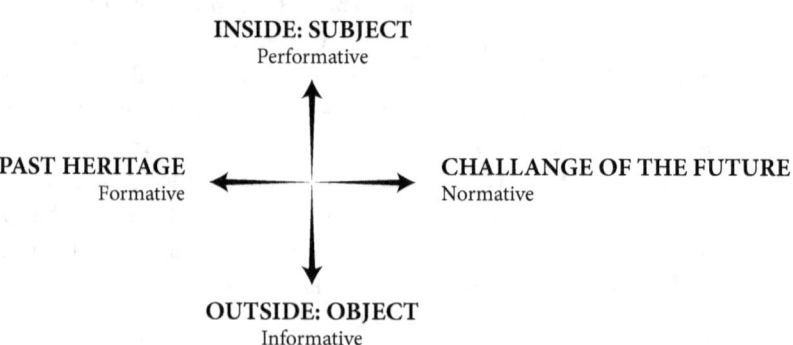

Table 3. The four kinds of language

Informative	Formative / narrative	Performative / communicative	Normative
Indicative Clear concepts Definitions Instrumental language Pointing to the world outside According to the division of labor	Participate Stories Half a word is enough Language of belonging Group narrative History and tradition Repetitive Norms and values (traditional)	Subjunctive Words Propositions that are proposals Associative language Discussion Dialogue Finding agreement Trial and error Coping with differences	Imperative Names and vocatives Overwhelming New situation Unstructured problems Unexplored Norms and values (surplus of meaning)

Values and Imperatives

We have put the terms *values* and *norms* at the future side of names and imperatives, and that is not entirely correct. Values and norms actually are generalizations of concrete names and imperatives that we have experienced. All experience is concrete.[16] We could have put them also—and maybe even more appropriately—on the side of the past. Values and norms, like justice, equality, benevolence, virtue, and so on, are always the values and norms as we know them already. We have a history with such norms and values in which they have found their development and expression. A norm like *justice* can be considered a container of past experiences with that term, through its expression and development.[17] The concept *justice* has many layers or ramifications of meaning. Do we mean *distributive justice*, in which equality is very important? Or do we mean *retributive justice*, in which the meaning of punishment is implied? Do we mean *justice* in the sense of a utopian situation in the future, in which there will be no more suffering? Or does *justice* merely mean that every individual should have a fair opportunity? Or do we mean *justice* in the sense of "due process of law"? And how can justice be better exercised? Do we need independent judges to

---

16. The concrete experience plays an ontological role. There is no initial (ontological) value like safety or loyalty, which then becomes concrete under certain circumstances (empirically). The order is the opposite. See Levinas, *Totalité et Infini*, 148.

17. Alasdair MacIntyre shows how different philosophical and cultural traditions, and social orders, express divergent notions of what *justice* might mean.

pass sentence? Or do we need a jury as representatives of the general public? Does not the difference among all these options affect the content of justice itself? Is the group the bearer of the right judgment, or is it the individual?

All these meanings of the word *justice* contain and summarize our past experiences and applications of the word. And whenever we are confronted with new problems and circumstances, the first thing we do is cling to the moral concepts we know. And thereby we cling to our past moral experiences and solutions.[18] In fact, what we then do is try to judge whether the new situation also falls under these well-known values and ideas. It is worth noting that *fall* is the literal meaning of the word *case*. It comes from the Latin word *Casus*.

To take an example: When we decided long ago to create laws that would protect intellectual property, and then saw the emergence of digitized information—which makes it easy to copy intellectual products, even without loss of quality—we now try to understand the new moral situation in terms of former ones. That is, we now try to decide whether a copy of a computer program "falls" under the same rule. At the same time, however, norms and values that we know from the past are also, for their part, pointing toward the future. They have an unexplored reservoir of meaning, a surplus. To a certain extent, concepts like *benevolence, duty,* and *love* are not yet fully "known." They are open for future experiences. And from the perspective of future experiences, they can be like sponges and receive a new and more encompassing meaning. Martin Luther King, Jr., for example, gave a new meaning to the word *equality*, in spite of the fact that this concept was already highly respected in the United States. But until the 1960s, equality did not count for African-Americans. At the same time, exactly because the idea of equality was highly respected in the United States, the civil rights movement could claim that concept, and ask for legal rights "in the name of justice." In a sense, this well-known concept contained a surprising meaning that has now become explicit. For that reason, such moral concepts can be put at the pole of the past (we do have some experience with them), and also at the pole of the future (they still contain several surprises for us). Thus, we could call terms like *justice* and *equality* "concepts," in as far as they define and summarize past experiences and developments. On the other hand, and at other times, we should call such terms *names*, as we hear in an expression like, "In the name of justice, I proclaim . . . "

Concepts have a well-known content; names point to a future yet to be explored.[19] Words are in their multiplicity of meanings the

---

18. Past and future are not totally separated. The past is never finished.
19. Rosenstock-Huessy, *Impure Thinker,* 42:

bridge between names and concepts. If we add the pole of the past, of mutual understanding and storytelling, the following sequence is the result: Names—words—stories—concepts.

A Field of Contradictory Constraints

We have four options for social behavior, and they are covered by four types of language. The language of dialogue and discussion, in which the meaning of the words is still shifting from context to context, is quite different from the clear language of concepts and instrumental language, in which the meaning of the words is clearly demarcated. And the short, powerful expressions in which a new future makes itself felt and is named are quite different from the sometimes-whispered and sometimes-storytelling language in which belonging to the group and the heritage of the past are imparted to us.

These four poles of reality—words, concepts, names, and stories—put us in a field of contradictory constraints. Names, and to a certain extent norms and values as well, represent the future in the form of urgent questions and imperatives. But the new questions entering our agenda, however urgent they might be, are not yet in the minds and the hearts of society at large. Or in other words, they are in opposition to the heritage of the past. A society, a group, or a company is used to a particular line of action, a particular set of practices, and a particular vocabulary of shared views on reality—and how to handle it. It is difficult to change any of these. Even if people are open to change, this is only a partial solution, because high ideals and norms not only meet resistance from inherited practices, but also meet with resistance from the realities in the world outside. It is the effective language of hierarchical relationships that primarily has to deal with the forces of the outside world: The struggle against nature, the competition for a market share, and so on, are conducted most efficiently through a centrally controlled and directed division of labor in which everybody automatically knows what to do. And managers with a clear eye on the market forces, aware of the dangers and risks of competition, will quite soon feel uneasy if they are confronted with time-consuming discussions to reach agreement among different parties.

> The right words, i.e. "names," guarantees responsiveness. Responsiveness is the lying open for being empowered. We have long spoken of an open mind. But the mind is open for conceptual understanding of the things outside. The other openness of any human being is to an appeal made to him in the power of his name.

In times of crisis, it is tempting to opt for a shortcut, to skip dialogue and rely on the hierarchical chain of command. In practice, however, the question must always be: How do we achieve the right equilibrium among these four forces, each of which is indispensable? The question is not whether we need the chain of command or whether dialogue would be better, but how much hierarchy, how much dialogue? How much change, and how much continuity? And in what sequence? When is the proper time for dialogue? When should hierarchy do the work? When is change necessary? And when is it worthwhile to preserve valuable experiences from the past?

For example, if a farmer will act from a position of altruism and introduce environmentally friendly production methods, he or she still needs to avoid the danger that the products will become too expensive in a competitive market. Institutions, groups, or individual persons can survive only if they know how to cope with all four fronts: past history, future challenge, inner dialogue, outside competition.

Institutions, ideas, human persons, and moral notions—all of them need to be related to these four fronts in order to be real. If they stand on their own, they lack reality and effectiveness. And they will not survive. A person can have a beautiful idea. But when he or she is alone and cannot fall back on the established insights of some community, the idea is too new and he or she will not be able to realize it. Likewise, if support for the idea can be found, but it is impossible to realize it in the world outside, the idea will also lack reality. During the twentieth century, scientists spent more than thirty years researching a bacterium believed to cause cancer. This was not just an idea of some individual; it found broad support and funding from governments and universities. But the entire research effort never yielded any positive results, simply because cancer is not caused by bacteria.

A new idea will not find enough support if it remains only the idea of one individual. The idea itself will improve if many people contribute to it by offering their incomplete and biased views on the problem at hand. Let us say that it should be possible to acquire and store energy from hydrogen fusion. It takes time and a lot of effort from very different disciplines and scholars to turn the idea into reality. In such a discussion, scientists discuss their perspectives, exchange their biases, offer up differing opinions, and conduct research in different directions (often using different hypotheses). But in the end, probably all of these partial contributions will have meaning for the realization of the initial idea. This insight has a definite bearing on the main question of this chapter: how moral values and norms on one side, and participation within a group—driven by communication—on the other side, affect each other.

Moral norms and values need to dovetail with communicative interaction. Moral norms and values do not have an abstract existence apart from the reality of the other poles we mentioned. They need to go through the entire circle of communication. A real, moral imperative can be turned into reality only by going through the whole communicative process. That means:

- These norms and values need to be felt and articulated, named.
- There should be a discussion about different and partial ways to implement them.
- A new imperative should somehow connect to older experiences of the group or organization.
- It should be possible for such an imperative to be implemented in concrete, practical, and technical ways.

When and where these four elements come together, or one after one another—that is, when and where the four poles of reality meet—begins the gradual change of an initial idea or imperative into a matter of fact.

Citigroup Center in New York

As an example of the four poles of reality coming together in a particular situation, we consider the architectural case of the Citigroup Center building in New York City, a technically innovative design, but confronted with serious and dangerous construction flaws.[20]

After the completion of the Citigroup Center building (also known as *601 Lexington Avenue*), the structural engineer, William J. LeMessurier, discovered that the building was vulnerable to hurricanes. In his design, he had given the building a quite new and special structure. In one corner of the building, he had to integrate an existing church into the structure and therefore the stilts bearing the building's load were not on the corner but in the middle of the outer walls. Large diagonal girders were used throughout the building to transfer the weight to the stilts. According to his design, the elements of the construction were to be welded together; welding makes the construction stronger than if bolts are used. When LeMessurier later found out that the construction team had used the cost-cutting measure of applying bolts instead of welding the support beams, he was concerned. But because he had been using the building as an interesting subject for a lecture on quartering winds—that is, winds that occur diagonally and thus

---

20. Whitbeck, *Ethics in Engineering Practice and Research*, 146 ff.

hit two sides of the building simultaneously—he decided to calculate further what would happen under particular wind conditions. He discovered that stresses on particular structural elements would increase by 40 percent, and stress on certain joints would increase by 160 percent. During a heavy storm, the whole building might start vibrating and would be vulnerable to total collapse. This discovery caused him to become alarmed.

Technically the solution to the problem was not difficult. Structural Band-aids over the bolted joints would make the building strong enough. But LeMessurier could not avoid disclosing that the building was vulnerable, and he needed to take responsibility for that disclosure. He contacted Citigroup's chairman, lawyers, and engineers and explained the situation to them. The costs of fixing the problem were estimated to amount to $1 million. The chairman recognized the importance of the tower as the company's new corporate emblem, and therefore readily agreed to the repair proposal. They involved city officials and made an evacuation plan for the building and the surrounding neighborhood, in case things went wrong. They issued a press release, indicating that the building was being slightly improved so that it could withstand stronger winds. The repairs were completed at night when the tenants in the building—which was now occupied—weren't there, thus causing no inconvenience to them. Citigroup filed an insurance liability claim against LeMessurier's company (which had supplied the construction team) to cover all of the added costs, and LeMessurier's insurance company offered $2 million for the claim. Citigroup eventually agreed to settle the claim and close the matter. LeMessurier's good reputation was rescued because his secretary was able to convince the insurance company that LeMessurier had acted in a commendable away. He had acted immediately, appropriately, and effectively.

How do the four types of speech come luckily together in this case?

1. Although the building was estimated to be safe, the change from welds to bolts, in combination with the computations performed to test the building for quartering winds, alarmed the architect who had designed the building. The building appeared not to fit the normative level of safety required. At risk for total loss of the building (and its surrounding neighborhood), a new imperative made itself felt.
2. LeMessurier could not solve the problem alone. He was searching for support in an open and honest way, and asked for different contributions from other parties. In this case, dialogue and communication came together to create a common present.
3. It was quite easy to find agreement and come to speaking terms with other parties. They agreed to a common strategy for repairing the

building without notifying the press or alarming the neighborhood, while at the same time securing the interests of the tenants.

4. All of this was done relatively easily, because the technical solution was not too difficult to implement. It was simple and efficient.

In this case, the four directions of reality came together very luckily. It is noteworthy that the repairs to 601 Lexington Avenue were deemed to be sufficient for the building to withstand a 700-year storm.[21] The structure withstood Hurricane Sandy in November 2012, in which sustained winds of 50 to 55 miles per hour pounded the city for a day, with gusts up to 80 miles per hour.

We can conclude: Only in situations in which there is an imperative, where people respond to it authentically and honestly, where a common course of action is designed, and when the outside world of physical reality offers possibilities for implementing the required actions—only then can changes be realized.

Tension between Gradual and Radical Solutions

Only when these four elements come together or follow up each other can a new idea be turned into a reality. For that reason, it is unavoidable that individual moral judgments become effective only in a slow and time-consuming process of communication and realization. But the same process allows their full meaning to be concretely discovered and advanced. There is too much emphasis in ethics on the judgment of individuals—as if ethics is finished after the individual has given its judgments or opinion. It might be true that it is typically individuals—not a group—who discover and articulate an imperative for the first time. But that articulation is only the beginning of a process of communication and realization in which many parties are involved. Without doubt, the consequence is that the first inspiration is watered down so that it can reach the next audience. But it also means that the original imperative is made concrete. It means that the world offers technical options that at least to some degree effectively (and perhaps quantitatively) meet the imperative. The hard, necessary, and empathic imperative for *sustainable development* can thus—if it is recognized as such in the first place!—be realized only in part by environmental regulations that are slowly introduced, one after the other. But that does not mean that there is no result at all. The original imperative maintains its power and attraction, relative to whatever small result might be reached in the moment.

21. Roberts, *Wind Wizard*, 32–128.

The consequence of all this is a lasting tension between gradual steps forward and radical, necessary solutions. On the one side, there is the necessity to hold on to fundamental changes; on the other hand, one can be grateful for every millimeter of progress. If that is the case, however, it might not be the primary task of ethics to give a judgment, case by case, with the help of moral considerations and theories. It might be more important to coach and supervise the process and keep it alive. In this moral tension, in which one side has to give in and the other remains unsatisfied because of the failure to meet the imperative, we still see the process of progress. We keep attention alive between unfulfilled promises and daily reality. Instead of timeless philosophical judgments, we see developing a social and communicative process of change. In such a way, we might be able to turn an abstract philosophy of individual judgments by reflective theory into a sociological process of communicative action and gradual change.

Oil and Gas Reserves of Shell

We can see this relationship between communication and ethics in the story of the disclosures about Shell's reserves of oil and gas in January 2004, when the registered oil and gas reserves were suddenly downgraded by some 20 percent. What happened? What did people do? What can we learn from it?

In the middle of 2001, Walter Van de Vijver had succeeded Philip Watts as chief executive of Shell's unit, "Exploration and Production." From the start of his being in charge, Van de Vijver consistently expressed the position that reserves booked during the time of his predecessor were "aggressive" or "premature."[22] On February 11, 2002, he brought to the attention of the central managing directors that 2.3 billion barrels were overbooked, according to the U.S. Securities and Exchange Commission (SEC) rules.

Now, the SEC rules stemmed from 1978. The Shell Guidelines about booking oil and gas reserves are different from the SEC rules, and Shell only slowly incorporated the more strict rules of the SEC. The report of Davis Polk & Wardwell, the U.S. law firm hired to investigate the case, speaks of "inadequate understanding of the application and meaning of the SEC proved reserves disclosure rules."[23] Differences in interpretation relate to the impossibility of exactly measuring the reserves, "arbitrary determinations," estimates of production during the time of license, and so on. The Shell Guidelines on future production estimates are more exact, but the SEC rules

---

22. *Report of Davis Polk & Wardwell*, Executive Summary, 4.
23. Ibid., 6.

have the power of legal authority, as least to the extent that Shell wants to operate in the United States.

The reserves booked during the term of Philip Watts were not even compliant with the Shell Guidelines. Van de Vijver repeatedly complained he was hampered in being able to meet Shell's business targets because of this. Van de Vijver—as well as Watts, who in the meantime had become his direct superior—however, wanted to "manage" the problem over time by declaring certain projects were mature, extending licenses, and succeeding in finding new reserves through exploration. In spite of the fact that this strategy failed, Watts was pressuring Van de Vijver to keep the reserve rates still at 100 percent across the next year. In his e-mails, Van de Vijver on one hand—that is, to Watts—complains about "becoming sick and tired about lying about the extent of our reserves issues,"[24] and on the other hand—to his subordinates—delivers an encouraging message about reaching planning goals, warning them about an "enormous blow to the group's credibility with the market"[25] if they could not deliver the same results as the previous year. Van de Vijver wrote: "I would prefer to restate our 1/1/03 reserves and de-book all remaining legacies to allow for a clean start." On December 2, 2003, a memorandum warned that the company was exposed to liability according to the SEC rules; Van de Vijver warned: "This is absolute dynamite, not at all what I expected and needs to be destroyed."[26] He later commented that he did not expect an analysis of the problem but a solution for it. In the end, it was not a moral stance, but fear for legal liability, that led senior management to the disclosures of January 9, 2004.

The Davis Polk report goes into the question of why colleagues and subordinates did not make attempts to bring the matter into the open. The Group Reserves Auditor speculated that if he would have taken more initiative in this respect, his position might have been at risk: "It would have been a clear break with all my predecessors and it could probably have cost me my job in those days, but I should have."[27]

In addition to this "Shell culture" of not confronting each other, the report mentions several weak spots in managerial lines, and in checks and balances, mainly with respect to lawful procedure and legal liability. One of the recommendations of the report is to remove reserves from scorecards and reduce job rotation, because "several control failures could be attributed

24. Ibid., 8.
25. Ibid. 9, and Part 3, 41.
26. Ibid, 10.
27. Ibid., 13.

to the short tenure of certain individuals in key functions."[28] About the Shell culture, the report states:

> In order to create a culture of compliance, it is essential that Shell's senior management emphasize to all employees that integrity and compliance concerns must be raised with the internal audit or legal functions and must be investigated thoroughly and openly, regardless of who is involved. This policy should be communicated forcefully and frequently.[29]

From this, I put forward some observations and interpretations about the question: Which types of language are used in this case and what are the consequences?

1. *The outside front*: Both Philip Watts and Walter van de Vijver were focused on the market forces, success, efficiency, and short-term results. The same orientation is expressed in the importance of individual "scorecards." It is also expressed in the anxiety about the credibility on the market, which threatened Shell if the oil and gas reserves were not to be kept at the same high level. We have seen already that short-term efficiency and hierarchical control go together. For that reason, it is no surprise that both Watts and Van de Vijver use the language of the hierarchical control chain. But, as appeared before, this proves to be inadequate and one-sided, and in the long term, even ineffective if other forms of speech do not come to the rescue.

2. *The front of the past*: Apparently within Shell, there was a particular company culture, a set of codes, dos and don'ts—such as not speaking against those in authority, and keeping your head down if problems occur. Do not interfere with other people's problems. Such group codes were stronger than the power of the individual to stand alone and go against the flow. When Van de Vijver brought the problem to the attention of the directors, they left it to him and to Watts to find a solution, and they did not get involved. Why not? This question is the more pressing since at least 200 managers within Shell were informed about the problems relating to the oil and gas reserves.

3. *The front of the future*: Van de Vijver, fed up with lying, does have an acute eye on the moral side of the problem. He would prefer to start afresh. But at the same time, he is so absorbed by the established codes of keeping silent and is so preoccupied with the immediate threats from the market that he pushes the responsibility for the long-term

28. Ibid., Appendix, 8.
29. Ibid.

credibility of Shell into the background. It was not moral responsibility or care for credibility, but the threat of liability claims, that caused the disclosures of January 2004.

4. *The inner front*: At all levels, there was not enough space for open dialogue, for criticism, or for taking differences seriously. If there had been, it would have been possible to turn those differences into common understanding. It would also have been possible to gain sufficient support to bridge the gulf between—on the one side, established practices and group codes—and on the other, moral norms and credibility. An open dialogue was not possible, and as a result a "shared present" could not be created.

5. *Moral bifurcation*: It is not always possible to translate moral imperatives immediately into effective action. The result is a tension between reality and the desired outcome. Realizing moral issues for that reason mostly appears to be too thin, if compared to what actually would be necessary. But such a moral bifurcation does not have to lead to a full dichotomy in which moral concerns remain a private business, as in the case of Van de Vijver. Open dialogue could have bridged the gap by maintaining an ongoing flow of change from the imperative toward the actual practice.

The Normative Dimension and Moral Bifurcation

Now the question arises: What do you do if the four poles of reality do not come together that easily? Sometimes there might be a norm that people would like to have kept, but the norm cannot be met physically and technically. Airplanes, for instance—even the more quiet ones—do make noise and will probably make noise in the future. Nevertheless, if it could be possible to keep the norm more strictly and produce quiet airplanes, this course of action would definitely be preferred. The situation becomes more difficult if a norm is there and is necessary, but cannot be kept because there is no consensus to keep it. In other words, not enough support. In Dutch building and construction companies, there was for a long time no consensus on preventing fraud and corruption. There were silent agreements on prices and tenders, for example. That means that the norm of fair competition did not mean much. If the norm of fair competition is not enforced by law, then what can one do as an individual? Until just a few years ago, nobody could discuss the subject, let alone start partial and diverse initiatives to bridge the gap between established practices and necessary changes. They did not stand a chance within this sector of the economy. Instead, it was taboo. New practices gradually came into being only after someone blew the whistle (the phase of the imperative), after a lot of upheaval and discussion (the phase of communication and dialogue), and after a national commission conducted a parliamentary research (the phase of establishing new codes of conduct). These new practices are installed now (the phase of technical and legal implementation).

In other cases however, there might be better opportunities to bridge the gap between established practices and necessary changes, if policy lines become less rigid and more open for internal discussion and dialogue. Individuals frequently complain about the lack of opportunities to change something within their organizations. Too often, they are right. Nevertheless, one can stretch the opportunities for change further, if one has the capacity and the ability to conduct policy discussions openly and honestly. Too often individuals claim that there is no possibility for change, even though they have never tried it. There is always room for dialogue, discussion, and for gaining support for a new approach, all of which will do more justice to new imperatives. But that room is not used to its full potential. Too many times, people think the discussion stops when they have made their opinions known. This is actually only the starting point. And too often they also forget that such a process takes time, and that superiors and colleagues will not be convinced overnight. What they most often forget is the fact that I myself too might be wrong and will need to change my views. Even my opponent might have a point.

Dialogue and discussion are a difficult process. The process invites concurrent interference from imperatives and values, partial and biased views, correct and incorrect information, and logical chains of reasoning (or not that logical, after all). The participants in such discussions do not need to come up with the one final solution. They need only enough agreement to take the one efficient action that meets the problem in primarily a provisional way, and maybe only partially. As a consequence, the new need—the imperative or norm—will mostly be met only for the time being. In this way, no definite and final solutions are created in design processes, but only optimal ones. They need further correction, or they need to be supplemented and developed further. For that reason, the participants within a discussion are put in a constant field of tension between the two questions: What is necessary? and: What is possible? The term *possible* can be used also in the context of consensus, something that receives some sort of majority support. This field of tension needs to be accepted as part of the process in which provisional solutions follow each other up, in order to meet each other's limitations. This is what I have called an *unavoidable moral bifurcation*. Sometimes, however, if urgent problems are not taken seriously, a situation might arise in which one cannot do otherwise than go against the group and finally become a nasty whistleblower. If nobody has the courage to do that, in the end it will be the disaster itself that blows the whistle. But then it is too late.

4

Multiformity of Man

In chapters 1 and 2, I have suggested that subjective involvement is not detrimental to ethical judgment, but on the contrary, helpful and meaningful. Ethics is not a matter of objective science. A person's subjective stance has a say in the truth of things. That is because—as chapter 3, about communication, explained—our judgment is not and should not be formed only by the past. It is as much formed by where we are headed and by the interaction among different persons and roles, responding differently to the imperatives representing the future. Our future is constituted by today's serious imperatives that we recognize. The promise of names and words each represents the future we are heading to. Of course, this means not only that our subjectivity is involved in the creation of a future from moment to moment, but also that our complete biographies have a say in our moral judgments. In Dostoyevsky's *Brothers Karamazov*, both Dmitri and Ivan are equally guilty, and in the end, Dmitri escapes punishment; the other brother, Ivan, freely takes punishment upon him. And according to the author, this contrary evolving of their biographies fits each of their characters. In the same vein, different biographies might provide to our common future different contributions, even contradictory contributions. And still these contradictory contributions might both be indispensable, just as Dmitri and Ivan are still part of one and the same family. This chapter explores how a human being's biography can be shaped by his or her involvement in life, labor, partnership, and history.

Management and Man

Top-down

Visual representations of organizations are typically shaped like a pyramid. Thanks to this image, the term *top managers* is now customary. Below top management, there is of course middle management, and finally there are the regular employees or the workers at the bottom. It is the task of the top to organize the company from within, and to devise a competitive market strategy to meet the market forces outside the company. So in this representation, both the inner front and the outer front are taken care of by top management. The question can be asked: Is that it?

In mainstream management literature, it is. Henry Mintzberg, who summarizes a lot of management theory in his classic work, *Structures in Five*,[1] gives us two more basic structures beyond top and middle management, and the regular staff. These are—first, the administrative unit with the task of unifying the organization's internal processes; and second, the auxiliary units. These units do not have a well-recognized place within the overall structure, but they do have a function. An example of this might be a Research and Development Department, or the cleaning personnel, or whatever function there might be that serves the organization in general. It is quite strange to find the Research and Development Department, the engineers, represented in this image as an auxiliary unit—coming, as it were, from outside, and not belonging to the core structure of the organization. But this is a consequence of how organizations are treated according to the general image of a management pyramid.

Time and Space

By using this scheme, how organizations are structured according to space is emphasized more than their development through time. The spatial representation of organizations is also a static representation. Further, it has an important side-effect, in that the top automatically becomes the subject of the organization, and the workers at the bottom come to be treated as "objects." They are the passive element relative to the activity from the top. They need to be organized, stimulated, and activated—in sum, "managed."

Do organizations really exist as spatial structures, with thinking managers and acting subjects at the top, and working employees at the bottom, treated as objects of the policies and strategies from the top? The odd thing

---

1. Mintzberg, *Structures in Fives*.

is, that in spite of the spatial and static representation of industrial organizations, nothing changes more or faster than industrial organizations. Industrial organizations depend on technological progress on one side, and on market demand on the other. Both are subject to rapid change. If such fast changes were not there, management would be an easy job. But as a consequence both of the progress of science and technology and of customer demand, management becomes a competitive race at top speed. The existing method of production is prescribed not by management, but by the interaction between technological development and the needs of society. In other words, the engineers (to whom Mintzberg cannot give a place within his pyramid structure) and the interaction between engineering and society have a decisive role to play. In this process, change is so predominant that even the engineers themselves might be left behind by the development of technology—for example, if they have to abandon a whole line of reasoning, or if their training proves to be incongruous with new technological discoveries. Neither engineers nor managers have control over this process; both try to respond to it as well as they can. That means that even the managers are not "on top," with an overview over the process as a whole. They themselves are "enveloped" by a process of change, and they try to respond to it and coordinate the diverse priorities that change urges upon them.

Change

It is the pace of change that causes the managerial problem. This becomes even clearer if we look at the contrary element of change and innovation: the repetitive tasks and daily rhythm of the labor force. In former times and in small workshops, the same person might have been the creative innovator one day a week, a repetitive worker four days a week, and a manager of his own activities one day a week. The three forces were in one hand. Now they are split apart into three. In fact, four, because the labor force from which the other three forces are split off, remains. Labor implies a repetitive and accurate implementation and realization of an already-designed product within the production process. In fact, besides the two fronts of inside and outside, we now discover two other fronts: past and future. If engineers are standing at the front of the future, in search of new designs and production processes, the labor force is standing at the front of the past, by daily repetition of productive work, according to prescribed rules and manuals. Through this, we understand better the meaning of *management*. It is the task of management to reconcile the speedy rhythm of innovation with the repetitive and automated production by a rationalized labor force.

The managers have to make these two factors—innovation and repetition—cooperate, and reconcile them like past and future. It is up to them to create a "common present," which means a common perception of reality, mutual understanding, and a shared horizon between these two forces. In that sense, managers are not on top of the organization, but they constitute the inner front of the organization. If a common present is not there, no cooperation is possible. People do not live automatically within a common horizon, sharing their perceptions of reality. Time and again, a common horizon needs to be created and installed. And it is a job that does not lend itself to "done, and done." Because change is going too fast for that. It can be done only for the time being, and for as long as it lasts. After a while, the process needs to start all over again. And it is the task of the manager to handle that process in such a way that also the fourth front is taken into consideration: The outer front of society and market forces. It is not enough that the inner forces of a company have an agreement of how to operate. Their options, conceptions, and perceptions should also be viable and realizable in the world outside constituted by society.

A Biological Paradigm

Therefore, at the root of the industrial system, there are not only the opposing interests of labor and management, as though there were a dual relation with only two parties involved. In reality there also is a forward front, where engineers are constantly innovating in technology and methods of production; and there is the backward front, where machines and rationalized hands repeat the routines resulting from the inventions and production methods of the past. Management, itself placed at the inner front, has to mediate between these two poles, while at the same time reckoning with a fourth one, the outward front of sales and marketing, which takes care of the day-to-day survival in a competitive market. The orientation on four fronts—past, future, inner, and outer—is a feature of every living creature (see chapter 1).

In order to survive, a creature needs an inner will, conception, and perception of how to tackle the forces outside; and it needs a development through time in which old achievements and new challenges find equilibrium. Every living group or organization has to delegate specialists to these four fronts—the new, the old, the external, and the inner life of a group. For that reason, management does not handle workers as objects in space. Instead, it handles always-changing relationships of engineers, workers, machines, and market forces.

Dependence and Uncertainty

This view of management has two consequences. First, the industrial system has priority over the individual factory or company. Individual companies are at the mercy of the industrial system at large, dependent as they are on the next phase in its development. An individual company cannot go its own way, independent of the rest. No actor on its own can manipulate market forces, needs, and imperatives in the way that it wants to. Second, workers within this system are living in a state of suspense. Nothing is ever settled, once and for all. Nobody can trust that a company has permanent work for him or her. One day a person might be sure of his or her job; the next day, everything is different. Just like the industrial system and the factories and companies themselves, the individual person is for that reason becoming more aware of his existence through time, more aware of change, and of the necessity to look at short periods of time from a longer perspective. What does that mean?

The Mechanization of Time

Minutes

Much literature has been written about the changing time perspective of the industrial age. The American philosopher of technology Lewis Mumford, and later the economist David Landes, have written about the progressive and increasing significance of the clock, beginning with the Middle Ages. At first, only hours were measured; later minutes and even seconds were counted. Increasingly, labor has been subjected to discipline in the context of time. In the well-established custom of paying for labor by the hour, the Industrial Age probably has gone to the extreme in this respect. Even doctors and professors calculate their labor and payment in hours per week or per month. How far away we are from the time in which it was an embarrassment to be paid by the day!

When Odysseus visited Achilles in the underworld, Achilles deplored his death to such an extent that he would even be satisfied to return as a day laborer—if only he could come back to life again. It seems that nothing was more humiliating than to be paid by the day. Today, the value of top managers and other professionals is spoken about in terms of their pay by the hour, and doctors by the number of patients seen or procedures completed.

Overhead

How could it come this far? To each reason for this reversal of values, the industrial age added the ideology of factory accounting. The ideology of factory accounting tries to calculate the productive wage by counting the pieces of work produced during one hour. All the other expenses are counted as overhead by means of extra charges of 100, 200, or whatever percent. In this counting procedure, the productive labor is considered basic for the whole business, and the efforts of engineers and administrative staff are considered a superstructure, even by the employers themselves. Under this process, it is hidden and forgotten that—let's say, for the first 200 pieces—careful attention is necessary, and that for the other 800, fast routines are all that are needed. The whole procedure is abstract, because actually the work of the engineers, managers, and administrators is no less "basic" for the whole production process than is the so-called "basic" productive labor. This process serves only as a tool for calculating prices and wages. But if taken seriously, it shortens the time perspective of the workers. It makes it more difficult to connect the lost moments of time.

Lifetimes

This lack of connection becomes even more visible if we realize that even the day laborer of former times lived a natural life on the rhythm of the seasons. The working day lasted as long as the sun would shine: a long day in summertime, sometimes no more than six hours a day in winter. Even half a day was counted as a day, because subdivisions of the day seemed meaningless. Generally, people were paid by the month or by the year. State officials and civil servants were paid in this way. The year also was the normal time for honorary services to the community, like being a town mayor or a member of a jury or committee. For that reason, payment by the year was not related to the amount of work done within a year, but to a period within a person's lifetime. Lifetime employment meant that the appointment was not related to an objective scheme of production, but to the lifetime of a person. This can be illustrated by the German civil servants, who were famous for their thrift. They were not overpaid, but the perspective of lifetime employment gave them oversight over time and the energy to save money for longer periods of time—for instance, for their son's education, for their silver wedding anniversary, etc. They were in a position to survey and dispose of their whole lifetimes.

Production Time

Here we are at the root cause of the change: The payment system in pre-industrial time was oriented to a person's lifetime. The time perspective of modern industry has a totally different orientation. In the time of the machine, of science and technology, what counts is production time. That means that in the end, the calendar of industrial time is oriented toward the external physical processes in nature. It is often said that the farmer of times gone by lived a natural life, and from that point of view, one can argue that the farmer too was related to the calendar of astronomical time. But to this man, nature means something different. Nature regulated the rhythm of sowing and harvesting, of summer and winter, cold and heat. The farmer rested when the soil rested. That makes farming and harvesting entirely different from producing. The fertility of the soil is not subjected to scientific control. Harvesting and planting were the rhythm of local group life. The farmer lived with the year of the earth, not in the year of Copernicus.

The Calendar of Physics

In the time of industry and technology, what dominates is not the time of seasons and life rhythms, but natural production time, the time of physical processes. The time spans are taken from the solar calendar, from neutralized time in which the life-rhythm of human beings no longer has a voice. Night and day make no difference for this calendar. Machines can work around the clock. The system of shifts is a natural expression of this calendar. In the twenty-first century, the shifts are going on planet-wide. The worker in San Francisco passes his work on to a colleague in Calcutta at the end of the working day. These shifts are more human than the shifts of former times in that the worker does not have to work at night. But the principle is the same. Nature knows no rest. People need rest. The time of physical processes is a time without feasts, without resting periods, and it never stops. It is without intensification and without relaxation. The working hours are indifferent toward one another. When a bridge is built, it can be built in, say, 700,000 hours by 700,000 workers; and then every worker would need to work one hour. Or it can be built in 700 days by 1,000 workers. But the change in quantity of workers does not mean a change in quality. In both cases, the life of human beings and their rhythm needs to adapt to the indifferent process of time of physical nature.

Inhuman Calculation

In the context of the abstract calendar of scientific and technological production, human labor is treated as a part of nature. True, man is a part of nature, too. But whenever human beings are treated according to the laws of physics, their full humanity is not taken into consideration. The treatment of human beings by the laws of nature strips them from what is specifically human to them. The desire to calculate human work forces in advance takes away their future. In as far the future can be known in advance, it loses its specific quality of being an (unknown) future. To have a future means to stand before unknown and undiscovered territory. It is specifically human to live through time, or even more to organize time in different periods. It is specifically human to be partly unknown, to have an unexplored future. Calculation in advance takes away the natural rhythm of life of human beings and their sense of the future. For this reason, any concern for the more distant future in terms of sickness, accident, or old age needs to be removed from the shoulders of the employees, so that they are concerned only with daily life. Under the dictatorship of the daily rhythm, the humanity of human beings crumbles away. The true proletarization of the worker has not so much to do with payment, but more with workers' perspective on time.

Living from moment to moment, in the daily activities of production and caring for material needs, the person is not trained to respond to larger and farther-reaching imperatives. As part of the workforce, a person only has to meet the requirements of production calculations: targets. By contrast, in former times even a shoemaker took the responsibility for his little shop. And in addition, he had to care for the next generation and to teach the craft to younger people—which could take quite a lot of his working time. Of course, this man was plagued by other evils such as poverty and disease—for him and for his family. These are evils that our technological era has solved quite well.

But it did not solve these problems without a price. The price paid for the mechanization of time by modern industry is the shrinking of the time perspective of its employees. The workforce lives only in the present, not even knowing that it is repeating the past.

Future

A real future means a change in quality, surprise, and promise, a challenge. The future does not come toward us in a continuous straight line. A life without surprises is boring. The fully lived present cannot do without such an openness toward the future. The question must arise: How can the mechanization of time be counterbalanced by a way of life in which the full time perspective of past, present, and future—with its changes and surprises, in its commitments, and in its breaks and ruptures—is restored and explored?

Arcs of Time

Time is mechanized, and this achievement of the industrial era is now regulating a global economy around the clock. It regulates the clock in production plans, in a systematic division of labor, and in ordering and re-ordering market forces over and over again, according to the newly discovered preferences of the consumers. This method of relating to time has become almost totalitarian. It is out of balance. Humans are not a part of nature. Humans are not a "resource" to be compared with "natural resources," as is presumed in the term *human resources management*. The humanity of human beings rests in their relationship to time. Animals might live from moment to moment. It is specifically human to connect these fragments of time and of momentary life to one another in eras, in arcs of time. It is specifically human to disconnect and connect past and future in manifold ways. The great question of our time is how to restore this relationship to time within a fully developed industrial era in which the computer has caused an increase in calculation and communication capabilities beyond imagination.

The Living Reality of a Team

Individuals?

In modern industry, even in the information era, the myth still prevails that companies hire individual workers. With the help of bonuses and premiums and individual career opportunities, these workers can be motivated to become high performers. This strategy, however, does not work in situations in which work means primarily *labor*. The word *work*, more than the word *labor*, can point to something lasting. Whether it is a piece of art, or a bridge, or a computer program, if we use the term *work*, something enduring has been achieved, something an individual can attach his or her name to. The word *labor* denotes tasks that are repetitive in character, that pile up in huge quantities one after the other, and by which nothing lasting is achieved.

Examples are cleaning work, responding to many e-mails related to trivial things, watching the production process (without any internal relation to the results), finishing the report of a meeting. Such tasks are anonymous in character, which means they do not make a difference as to who is performing them. One person can do it as well as another. Many times in doing such work, the people involved are not working on their own, in fact. And even if they do, they know that at the desks beside them, other people are performing the same tedious tasks in the same routine way. And in addition, they feel their dependence on their co-workers to get the job done. These experiences connect them to each other. For that reason, in this kind of work—more adequately named *labor*—the urge to adapt to the rhythm of the group is much stronger than individual stimuli from above. This proves that people do not work only for the money. But it proves even more so that large-scale high-tech production is not a matter of individual performance. The machinery of modern industry, even the "machinery" of an administrative unit, can go on day and night without weekends or holidays. The individual worker cannot match the performance of this high-tech machinery. And for this reason, the technology itself of modern industry presses the experience upon the workers that individual performance cannot do the job. They need co-workers, working together, to equal the energy and endurance of the technology.

If a job has the character of "labor," it is always done by a plurality of people. This plurality acts and feels together, and they labor under the pressure of repetitive and tedious, never-ending tasks. During the break, they have their coffee or go for a walk. They might have their habits and jokes, teasing each other either in a positive or a negative sense, and talk about football and the news. These all help to make their labor bearable again. Although their work mostly has been planned in advance, such a group of co-workers does not function mechanically like the technology they might work with. Instead, the group functions as a living reality. Being together on the job gives a feeling of belonging and solidarity. A team therefore should never be treated merely as a labor force that can adjust to the requirements of the production plan. It has a rhythm and a life of its own, a shared attitude related to the work it has to do. In all that, the interest of the group comes ahead of the interest of the individual.

Three Is One

It might be true that working in shifts has been pushed to the background in modern industry, but that does not alter the fact that working in shifts still provides the real paradigm for the way in which technology is mastered by humans. Working in shifts symbolizes the perpetuity of physical processes. The machine can go on for 24 hours, but at least three persons are required to work 8 hours each, to match this performance of technology. These three people signify that people have to line up together in order to overcome the dangers of nature in a laborious struggle. This is an unavoidable aspect of human life relative to the forces of nature. "Three equals one" is the formula that captures this eternal law of human existence.[2] In this way, it is also the adequate expression of the life form of a team, people working together as a labor force, "rubbing elbows" with physical processes. Today it might be primarily the machinery that masters nature, and people seem to be necessary only to direct and watch over this process. That does not alter the eternal law of human existence itself, because throughout history, the struggle with nature—called *labor*—has proceeded in such a way that people had to line up in order to match the overwhelming and perpetual forces of nature. Regardless of individual illness, weakness, or death, the struggle against nature had to continue.

The "three" in this formula therefore means that the labor is not done by an individual, but that it is social in character, since one has to rely on at least one predecessor and one successor. In the struggle against the forces of nature, an individual worker has to be replaceable. The work has to go on, even in case one person needs to give up.

In the days of hunting, the individual did not mean much in the fight against the mammoth, and that principle has not changed. Today, the individual does not mean much in a chemical processing plant, or in the production of an airplane. The laborious struggle against nature—or today, with the watching-over of modern technology (called *labor*)—can therefore still be expressed in the formula: Three equals one. Three atomic individuals form together one living molecule. They have to stand shoulder to shoulder.

Keeping up with the Average

The "three" in this formula should not be taken too literally. The labor group amounts to five or fifteen participants working together, but at least it is more than two. The optimum of such a group might differ, depending on circumstances. These participants are not the result of adding individuals one by one, up to the total of fifteen. The sum is more than the individual parts. A working group is a living creature. Working groups often show great solidarity. The participants feel that it is up to them to finish the job together, and that their individual efforts do not make a big difference. For

---

2. This formula is explained more extensively in the *Multiformity of Man*, the booklet of Rosenstock-Huessy that I follow and from which I summarize the line of argument in this chapter.

that reason, incentive plans and premium systems do not work because they are aimed at the worker as an individual, and they try to stimulate competition. It is "not done" to excel in individual performance when you know that for the final result, you are dependent on the other participants of the group. Keeping up the morale of the group means adjusting to the average output of the group. It is not wise for a manager to promote competition within such a group. Competition, ambition, and honor can be developed only between such groups.

Team Spirit

The meaning and the importance of such working groups has not yet been sufficiently investigated. If the inner dynamics of a working group were to be taken more seriously, it could be used more consciously, too. Group solidarity and relying on one's co-workers produces a pre-reflective kind of mutual recognition within a group. Jokes and humor keep the good spirit going, and maintain a good atmosphere. Managers should have the wisdom not to interfere in the work rhythm of such a group, unless absolutely necessary. Such a group of co-workers typically feels the same about issues they confront in their work. Such feelings are different from opinions.

Opinions can be formed after reflection, but the feeling of a group results from their common labor. In the 1990s, new, more rational time schedules of the Dutch Railway Company did not take into account what made the workers take pleasure in working together and keeping the system going. The managers underestimated the trouble the workers took to run the trains right and on time; they also underestimated the honor that these workers put into this effort. They re-organized the work in such a way that the employees no longer had an overview of what was going on; in this way, these employees felt that part of their professional responsibility had been taken away. That responsibility was put into the hands of rational managers.

The situation worsened after these "rational" interventions were in place. The Dutch Railway Company still has a hard time bringing back the good working atmosphere of former times. The all-too-rational managers not only underestimated, but also never even saw, how these workers had formed a group with a life and a spirit of its own, with feelings of its own, even if these features of human life might look irrational from the point of view of an outsider (which each rational manager had effectively become). Lucky is the company in which groups of co-workers really form a molecule together, connected by the pressure of the labor they share.

How can such groups be constituted? How can an environment be created, how can conditions be put in place so that such groups can come to life? How can a real team be built?

For How Long?

The optimal size of the group is not the only thing that deserves further study. The optimum life cycle of such a group does, too. How long can the participants of a working group go along without being bored or irritated by one another on the job? What would happen if participants in a group were to engage consciously in such a group for five or seven years, and if after that period they would join another group? Would that not mean that all the possibilities and qualities of the participants would come together more cohesively than if such groups were to be formed at random? What would happen if the membership of the group might be changed at random, too, or if the entire group were to be dissolved all of a sudden, at the convenience of management? The positive qualities of the individuals would find better expression if the negative qualities, controversies, and irritations were to be taken into consideration only for a limited period of time. The work group does not require a lifetime commitment. But it does require commitment for a certain time. Because it will come to an end at some point, it can unfold its potentialities better than it would if it seemed to be able to go on in perpetuity. Because it will come to an end, it can become more of a living reality. The price of life is death.

If a group knows that for a particular time it works together, and if it knows that this time will be limited, then it knows that within this time span it will have to make the best of it. This is their time. If all the possibilities and qualities of such a group have come to fruition, then in the end such a group will cease to live. The participants will be bored by one another; it has been enough. But if a lifetime commitment were to be required, the group might even not come to life. This would require too great a commitment. When too much is asked, less is given.

Temporary Belonging

The factory itself is not built for eternity. Since churches and states survive across hundreds or thousands of years, people tend to think that factories should do the same. But factories and companies do not aim at long-lasting efforts. They take care of transitory work, of the material conditions of life. And they are influenced by the demands of always-changing technologies.

That companies sometimes survive a long time is due to the many changes they allow during their existence. Technologies change and communication media change, with the result that companies and enterprises spread out across the globe. Participation in mechanized production processes within a globalized economy has uprooted people all over the world. Participation in the living molecule of the working group can balance this process of rapid change and mechanization of time, and at the same time adapt to them. The recognized membership of a working group survives change, and at the same time can integrate changes within its own rhythm of change. This microorganism can balance the fast-changing rhythm of factory life, because it has a life of its own. The working group within a factory, temporary though it might be, nevertheless might give its participants a sense of belonging and security, just the way artisans in former times had their own professional corporations.

Space, Time, and the Life-Rhythm of the Group

In the era of technology, humans and nature have become integrated. The physical processes of nature, under control of technology, tend to absorb human reality into their mechanized rhythms. Human beings tend to be treated as a part of nature, too, in the economic plans and strategies of competing companies. This can be counterbalanced by human reality when this reality, from its perspective, makes an impact on the physical and technological processes of nature in the process of production. This would not only bring humans under the regime of nature, but in turn also bring nature under the regimens of humans. The mechanization of production processes and the impact of science and technology in general tend to bring human beings under the regimens of nature by treating them in the production plan as just another natural force. Thus, the time-connecting human being is brought under the regimen of nature, of space. On the other hand, by creating cooperating teams for a limited time, to handle the forces of nature, the time-building human once more takes the initiative by bringing nature, technology, and machinery under the regimen of time. Human beings within the industrial system are not to be treated as a "resource," like other natural resources. Instead, living work groups, molecules of production, can restore the dignity of workers as human beings. This occurs not because humans act mechanically, but because they handle natural resources according to their rhythm. We live in a time of intense reverence for the development of technology. This excitement about the achievements of technology is almost idolatry. In turn, this idolatry has brought us great scientific and technological advances. But when this means that people are treated as production forces to be turned on and off at will, a reaction becomes necessary. The recognition of the working group as a living molecule of production can restore human beings to their rightful place among the other elements of nature.

That does not mean that the formula *three equals one* is the end of all wisdom in human relationships. It serves the treatment of reality outside, the labor in which the resources of wild nature are brought under human control. But this is not the only social task that human beings have to perform. Companies have temporary and transitory forms. Physical processes also have a temporary nature. In this, they do not match the longer-lasting scope of a human lifetime. Human beings live in time perspectives other than only the short time period of production. Human beings eventually have to survive each team they are part of. How can they manage to do that?

Identity: To Add Consciousness to Life

Collective Consciousness

The mechanization of time within modern industry has devastating consequences when it is applied to human beings. It is true that physical nature too is part of being human. But it is a distortion of their humanity if people are treated only in this way.

The first measure to counterbalance this one-sided treatment of human beings as "matter" in "space" consisted of emphasizing the meaning of the work group. A plurality of workers sharing their life rhythm and joining one another in the laborious struggle against the forces of nature is already more than a mechanized part of nature, or of technology. But in this way too, justice is done a human being only in part. Human beings are more than labor forces. That is already true within the context of a factory or a company, where the only thing that matters is what things and people are and can do. The system of production treats human beings as "one of many," a treatment that is expressed in the formula *three equals one*. Even in this formula, *three equals one*, the labor forces are already recognized in their basic humanity—that is, as members of a group that conquers nature by the solidarity of their struggle with it. But it is obvious that people will not be satisfied if they are counted only as one of many. They would still feel treated as a number and lack a sense of identity, of conscious self-assertion. The first thing they will do if they are treated in that way is to cling to some encompassing symbol of self-awareness by which they can assert themselves to counter the anonymous treatment as part of a labor force. In effect, that is what happened during the nineteenth century. When the employers "bought" a labor force on the market, as if it were one raw material among others, the laborers, treated in this way, clung to the collective identity of "Labor!" With this expression, they protested their functionalization and expressed their group pride and self-assertion. This is almost an instinctive reaction every time when people—say, students; say, patients, or even professors—are treated by society as merely this number of people which they happen to be a part of.

For example, when doctors are criticized for the high cost of their services, or for not carrying out their work accurately, they will stand up and emphasize the honor of their profession, and perhaps cite the oath of Hippocrates. And they will assert themselves by some sort of a collective identity like *medicine*, or *medical care*, or whatever term can function as a symbol to express the dignity of their profession. In this way, they cling to a collective symbol of who they are. You would not see a single person standing up for himself and saying, "I am not like the others; I am a better medical doctor." Nobody would want to be singled out as the exception. Instinctively, everybody would defend the collective dignity and identity of the group to which he or she belongs to, and is proud of.

All Equals One

Labor is a collective concept. So is *youth*. Such words are abstractions, just as are *the nation*, or *feudalism*, or *man*. The nation, for instance, consists of many departments of civil services, municipalities, government, or parliament, and so on. Only by abstraction can they be summed up as *nation*. The nation is more than the sum of all these different entities, just as the forest is more than the sum of the trees. In such abstract concepts, the (invisible, non-empirical) whole behind the parts is articulated. For this reason, they are more than quantitative or statistical concepts. They express the quality of the parts. To name the different departments, services, and institutions of government by the collective idea *state* makes these departments visible in a particular quality—in this case, their duration through time, authority, and orderliness. Such collective concepts are more or less aggrandized and elevated, like flags high above the crowd. In a sense, the collective concept is a superlative. It makes the thing or person referred to dignified and important. One might count 1, 2, or 3 men, but when somebody talks about *manhood*, or *virility*, one might add *admiration* and *fascination* to the mere objective designation of *men*.

By the admiration and fascination of these collective symbols, people adopt a religious relationship toward these elevated expressions. Words that cannot be mentioned or named without due respect are, in a sense, already religious terms. They express a relationship of reverence. Such concepts are more than concepts. They provide orientation and direction. They require no metaphysical system, and in that sense they do not require belief in a religion or God. Nevertheless, it is difficult, if not impossible, to exist without some form of religious attitude. Names expressed with respect and honor have a "binding force," which is the precise meaning of the word *religion*. Any symbol of identity or belonging that people adhere to, functions as a religious force. The Greeks too had such a relationship to their gods. In the name *Aphrodite*, sexuality was honored; in *Ares*, manhood and struggle; and in *Athena*, wisdom. In the same way, professions and subcultures within society identify themselves with their respective collective symbols. They give the members of this subculture an identity: "We are . . . " Since the *we* in this equation involves an indefinite number of people, we could symbolize this equation with the formula: *All equals one*.

The Binding Force of Symbols

Communism made intense use of this need for collective symbols. In this way, the Communist Party tried to force an encompassing solidarity upon the masses, bypassing the plurality of the work group expressed in the formula *three equals one*. By doing this, the Communists asked too much from the workers and made them live in an abstract world of anonymous historical processes. It is asking too much if people are required to be in solidarity with the entire labor force and to interpret one's personal life only as a drop in this ocean of "solidarity."

A person cannot feel solidarity with all humanity, because *all humanity* represents only an abstract thought; you cannot see or experience "all humanity." But you can feel solidarity with your co-workers. When the minimum solidarity of the work group is recognized, as the formula *three equals one* does, an opportunity is created for a process of growth of solidarity. It is difficult to be in solidarity with an anonymous whole, merely via abstract reasoning. From the experience of solidarity in a work group, however, the circle of solidarity can be gradually widened. Communism did not give what it promised, but merely provided the mechanized masses with a common symbol of identity. Here we find a strange paradox. Although communism aimed at changing the material conditions of life, in fact it served a spiritual need, the need for identity. It gave a group of people the opportunity for self-assertion, self-idealization, and a corresponding claim for recognition. It provided a common background and a future to long for.

This tendency is recognizable in all collectives. Collectives draw inspiration as much from a romantic past as from a utopian future. By doing this, they offer an escape from the too-narrow prison of our daily existence. And that is exactly what we need them to do. We cannot do without, even if that would mean that we cannot do without some form of illusion. Some readers might be inclined to be critical and to say that it is too easy to ascribe importance to identifications with a symbol, or to a tradition or a group of people to which one merely and coincidentally happens to belong. But the order of life is the reverse of the order of thought. Or in other words: First, human beings (including you yourself, dear critical reader) identify with such collective symbols and take them for granted and integrate them into their lives. Only after that has occurred can criticism enter and cast doubt on the validity of such-and-such a symbol or group identity. And even then, it is possible to criticize and cast doubt on one particular symbol of identity only from the point of view of another symbol of identity. That symbol and that identity might be deemed more important, but it still constitutes an alternative group identity, even if this symbol of identity is "reason," or "rationality," in the name of which an intellectual might like to criticize collective symbols.

Education and Identity

A common education within society also fulfills exactly this function—namely, to collect experience, to give boys and girls the experience of a common life and a common background. It gives them a common language they can refer to for the rest of their lives. It passes on the treasures of experience of the human race. Later on in life, men and women will become more and more individualized. As a consequence, it will become more difficult to find common ground. This is why we need a common refuge in education, where we have been speaking the same language and experiencing solidarity and friendship—from the first phases of our lives, onward. This collective background makes us part of the great stream of tradition of human life.

Within the time span of education, individual responsibility is not yet fully developed. This burden is taken away from the individual and postponed. Other people are responsible. In this way, we install in ourselves a happy state of growth, of dreams, and hope. Actually, this is exactly the way in which the workers, who identified themselves with the collective symbol of "labor" were not yet fully living in the present. They in fact did not claim the present; they claimed only that the future was their domain. Neither Socialism nor Communism changed the working conditions of the individual workers. They did not restore the individual worker to his or her full personality. The individual worker within Communism was as de-personalized as a worker in a capitalist society, probably even more. He or she still did not count for more than a working force within the functional machinery of a company. But what Communism did give to the workers was a collective aspiration, an identity.

This collective identity can be seen as the first phase in counterbalancing the functionalization of workers within modern industry. In that sense, Socialism and Communism had a function in educating the masses. Collective concepts like *man*, *youth*, and *woman*, do not belong to objective reality. They provide us with a dream, and create an opportunity for development and growth to the extent that they give people something to long for. They intensify a particular quality of existence by which a "we"-group merely may assert itself.

Collective Service

However, this can become a dangerous and violent process. A group clinging to such a collective identity might be inclined to criminalize and victimize the world outside. Professions with a strong group consciousness and a strong feeling of doing the right thing might easily end up feeling misunderstood by society in general, and close their frontiers. They might do their own thing in spite of, or even against, the rest of society. But there is also a natural outlet for such collective instincts and conscious group identities. This outlet is collective service.

Just as in an army, where the collective awareness of the group is directed to fight the enemy, the collective identity and group pride that young people in modern society are seeking can and should be directed to the service of society. Especially in situations of crisis and need. In this way, a sense of belonging and collective aspirations of pride and honor can be satisfied by the deep human instinct for collective service.

Fragmentary Consciousness

The danger inherent in groups with a strong identity and pride might be exclusiveness and violence. But the danger of layers of society without such a strong identity might consist of a lack of self-esteem, a lack of belonging, and a fragmentary, uprooted existence. Many people in our society do not specifically cling to one symbol or collective identity, but instead jump from one to the other. This is similar to their being in a shopping center, where they might try on different clothes. The stream of information and the rhythm of change, and a diversity of claims directed at them makes it difficult to exercise some form of lasting membership in relation to a tradition, a group, or a movement. The effect of this is a strong skepticism, which takes a detached attitude toward all commitment and tradition. People feel they come from nowhere, and their existence has no destination. There is no priority among values, symbols, or groups. The problem of western societies seems to be not so much that its members are too deeply rooted in a particular form of membership, but that they are influenced by so many fragmentary opinions and conceptions of reality that they cannot take root and adhere to some truth or conviction at all. But this lack of identity could just as easily turn into its opposite. The strongest fundamentalists and most violent neo-tribal groups often consist of former, uprooted relativists who can no longer endure the uncertainty of being nobody and of never belonging to anything.

From Consciousness to Self-consciousness

Consciousness, as it is expressed by collective symbols, still is pre-reflective. One does not become part of a collective merely by reflection. On the contrary, reflection can begin only after becoming part of a collective identity provided by history, by the surrounding society, and by symbols and realities that already existed before we entered history. A person first needs to receive a common education to become part of its culture, and to internalize its existing codes. A person also needs to identify with these streams of historical life before he or she can say: Now, actually, what am I doing? What is my personal contribution? What is my part of truth within this symphony?

Only by asking these questions can consciousness change into self-consciousness. Now a person is thrown back on his or her own, and from this moment on, he or she starts seeking real partnership.

Commitment and Partnership

Making a difference

A human being can be a member of a collective only for a limited period. A person can participate for a long time in a group and, as it were, be absorbed by it. In that state of aggregation, the person does not differentiate between his or her individuality and the participation in the group. In opinions, gestures, and acts, such a person confirms the common life of the group. Such a person would never say, "But I . . . " because in that act, the participation in the collective identity of the group would stop. From there, real individuality has its starting point and from that point on, participation can be exchanged for partnership.

Individuality Is Not Atomistic

In a sense, a person who says "I" is saying "no." Why would somebody want to say anything at all, when he or she agrees to all of what is said, already? A person who says, "I think . . . " has the intention of saying something different from what is said before.

"You can think what you want, but I think that . . . " The *I* in this sentence is—more or less—opposing the other participants in a discussion. At the same time, however, the person expressing this sentence is involved in a dialogue. This means that he or she is in search of support of his or her vision, or confirmation of it, and even correction of it. The person expressing antagonism and opposition is also in search of a partner who might contribute to his view on reality—or change it, or confirm it. This is quite contradictory. As long as a person identifies with the collective symbols of a group or tradition, that person is not yet acting as an individual. But as soon as a person says, as an individual, "I," he or she is both responding to other people and opposing other people. As such, that person is not on his or her own, either. Would there really exist an abstract, individual person making choices all on his own, independent from other human beings?

On the contrary, it might be true that human beings discover themselves only as independent persons when they express their own judgments in response to the judgments they have heard before. If this is true, individuals, like atoms in space, are in fact non-existent. The image of a nod in a network would fit the situation better. To be a person means to be connected, to be related. And also saying, "But I . . . " or "No, but . . . " means to relate to what is said before and to continue the "great conversation" of mankind. People who express their own opinions do not want to stand on their own. But they express their views in the hope that other persons can receive these views within the framework of their own "belief systems," and weave them into the fabric of their own.

On the other hand, an individual might receive suggestions from others and connect them to his own partial views, in order to complete the picture. In this process of mutual exchange, the differences are not necessarily overcome, because in that case duality would end up in collectivism. But in a sense, the differences are also reconfirmed as different, but necessary, views and contributions, so that they can reach one and the same purpose, or so that they can meet one and the same problem.

Duality: Different Contributions

In many languages, the dual has a peculiar grammatical form, as in Latin or in Greek. The dual form expresses a personal identity, related to another person who occupies another role, even though it might be different, but it corresponds to the first one. An example of such a dual relationship is that between a mother and father who each has a special role within a family, but they are related to and in correspondence with each other. They call upon one another, correcting and complementing each other. The more the mother is a mother, the more the father can become a father. They can exchange roles, of course, and often this is necessary if one of the partners is not there. But they contribute to one and the same result within their differences in approach. This occurs even in spite of their different approaches, or more to the point, thanks to their differences and their internal diversity. A dual relationship exists where diversity is found within unity. Two different persons are working together to the same end.

In a dual relationship, *two equals one*. These two people do not have a common identity as in collectivism, because they are really and irreversibly different. Their contributions, opinions, and qualities are different. But their differences are related to each other in such a way that they support each other and are integrated into one another. Integration in this sense does not mean unity, but the awareness and sensibility for the right timing—that is, to know when one's own contribution should stop and when to let the partner take over. Real partners are integrated into one another in that way. And only when the partners are integrated into one another in such a way can we speak of more than a sexual relationship. Instead, something durable and sustainable has come into existence. We can speak of marriage.

Partnership

At first sight, it might seem as if marriage has nothing to do with human relationships within an organization. It seems that in an organization, only individuals are working together in some form of pluralism or collectivity, people who identify with the same traditions, the same symbols, the same awareness, and group codes as the other members of a group. But in the meantime, no company or organization can survive if it is not carried forward by people who have fallen in love with it. If there is no commitment with the organization, individuals will refuse to take that one extra step that is always necessary to achieve something important.

In the case of a molecular relationship of pluralism, the workers adapt themselves to the rhythm of the group as a whole. But the committed individual is concerned with the benefit of the cause, with the organization as a whole, or with the partner he feels responsible for. It is not enough if workers or employees are functioning as parts within a big machine. As parts within the apparatus, the employees are no more than replaceable units, and consequently they will not feel any responsibility for the welfare and success of the organization as a whole. That is none of their business. They are just employees. As employees they are "employed" in the service of the goals of other people. The labor time is no longer their own time. To be hired as an employee means not so much to trade one's labor for money, but instead to trade one's time. When individual persons feel it is their business whether their organization reaches its goals and ideals, produces its results, and renders its services—then, from that moment on, they become committed. They have become more than only employees. They no longer feel their time taken away from them, but the time they work for the company has become their personal time as well. It has become part of their lives. The work they do for the company has become part of their personal fulfillment. They have become partners: a durable relationship of loyalty has developed. They left the law of pluralism and the law of collectivism behind them and entered the law of dualism: *Two equals one.*

This idea of partnership explains the huge disappointment of many employees when suddenly their work is considered redundant by the organization, or if they get fired in times of crisis. This does not mean only a financial loss or a loss of status. It brings disappointment. People feel hurt and become skeptical, just as is the case when a love affair has failed. It means a break in their commitment and a loss of partnership. They feel dumped.

Fire

For contemporary objectifying science, it is difficult to say something significant about dual relationships and longer-lasting commitments. It is difficult to measure commitment. It is impossible to measure it within the context of one working day. The social scientist who would like employees to fill in a questionnaire that will help map the character of relationships within a factory or a company will probably get the wrong answers or no answer at all.

He or she can register only the small tasks that pile up every day. And even if the social scientist would ask employees the question whether they feel committed and loyal to the company, the answers are likely to come from within the limits of political correctness. Questionnaires do not reckon with factors of shame and hesitation that always have to be overcome before people can honestly express their deeper feelings and convictions. These emotions ordinarily cannot be measured or shown in the results of social research.

Scientists themselves are no different. For instance, if you were to attend a conference of social researchers, you might expect to hear a lot of small talk, competition, jealousy, and ambition. The fire inside these social researchers, committed to the progress of social science, might not even come to play. And in a questionnaire about the conference, this fire would show up only if it were politically correct to express such a commitment.

These days it is politically correct for social researchers to show only a detached attitude toward the objects of research. They cannot express their real commitment. Such a commitment can only be expressed in course of time, if hesitation and shame can be overcome at the right moment, and only because trust, loyalty, and commitment slowly drove to that result.

Time Spans

We can better understand the character of dual relationships if we consider the time spans involved in the different kinds of relationships treated so far. In the work group, which has multiple members and where the law of *three equals one* prevails, short time spans are dominant. In everyday life, many small actions pile up, waiting to be fulfilled by such a work group. The group as a whole will most probably need to refresh its membership between three and seven years after it begins. The collective, where the law of *infinity equals one* prevails, might last hundreds of years and overarch the individual life spans of many people and generations. Partnership in turn involves yet another time span. Partners who have fallen in love with each other and other types of dual relationships involve or express a conscious commitment. For this reason partnership organizes the conscious and responsible phase of the human biography. It might last twenty, thirty, or more years, if the commitment is not broken for some compelling reason.

Mediation between Truth and Love: Reproduction

Every time a person says, "For my part, I would think . . . " or "As far as I am concerned . . ." he expresses his part of the truth, which means he expresses the part of reality that he has experienced so intensely that he feels responsible for it, and with which he has more or less "fallen in love." Marriage is love connected not just to the reproduction of the kind. Every time a person feels responsible for some part of reality, for an ongoing process, for whatever it might be, he feels committed to its survival, or to its reproduction, its continuation through time. A person committed to his company will struggle for its continuation through time, and to its reproduction on a larger scale. In this endeavor, he or she will be committed to searching for more partners who are prepared to invest in this process of reproduction. A real discussion, not an ephemeral play with words, is always a search for partnership, for shared responsibility.

In a discussion, the participants marry their partial and biased insights to one another. By expressing their views, they change each other, integrating the part of reality of their partner into their own view of the matter at stake. Without a communicative commitment to find a common truth to act on, they might carry on a discussion forever, without conclusion. Rationality without commitment will always find a different angle, will give a twist to the argument, will reconstruct the facts from a different viewpoint. Reason and a consistent line of argumentation are, without doubt, a necessary part of finding truth. But if it is left to reasoning alone, no truth will be agreed upon, ever. A "reasonable" discussion without commitment to the other party will never come to a conclusion. And so it happens over and over again, when people are involved in a discussion without loyalty, commitment, and trust. They tend to talk (or even better, negotiate) longer and longer about smaller and smaller issues. When our reasoning is not connected to love, it will lose itself in endless constructions and reconstructions of reality.

For instance, if North Korea and South Korea enter into a dialogue about a common future, they will easily find the events in history that prove they belong together. But when there is no commitment to a common united future, history will only provide "evidence" of disagreements, never to be reasoned away. And the two sides will start talking about the size of the chairs or the flags on the table. Only when intellectual insight or reason is coupled with love, loyalty, and commitment—in common language, this is typically called *openness* to the other party—a viable definition of *reality* can be found. That definition is at least viable enough for common action, for the time being. Without this understanding, no common ground will be found.

This common conviction might not be the end of all wisdom, since it can change. This will, for instance, happen when another partner enters the discussion, expressing his part of reality. But even if such a truth is open to further development, when it is established within the context of a mutual relationship and partnership, it will work for the time being and only as long as it lasts. Is it a miracle then, that dual relationships in biology, as well as in society, are fertile in the sense of both reproducing and renewing the kind?

Unity within Multiformity: The Soul

The Necessity of Unity

Following the description of the different modes of human existence presented thus far, we might want to ask the question: How can human beings find unity within the necessary alternation of these modes of being and ways of life?

Labor is indispensable. This is the law of pluralism, of *three equals one*. It is necessary to grow by participating in long-lasting collectives, traditions, ideals, and symbols of a particular group. This is the law of collectivism. To have a fully developed life also means to be able to love and be committed to a higher cause—this is the law of dualism.

But how can unity be found? The question becomes even more urgent when we take the three possible time spans into consideration. The short time spans—day, month, or year—are a matter of labor time, counted in terms of hours or days. Historical time spans of collective symbols usually overarch the lifetime of the individual. Dualism, partnership, and commitment organize the conscious part of human existence. So the possibilities of designing different time spans seem to be exhausted.

Reason

Let us first establish where the unity of human beings is *not* to be found. It is still the myth of our time that the unity of human beings is to be found in the thinking individual. His or her reason or thought is presumed to be at the core of the human person. The "I think" seems to accompany every experience in human life, so that by thought, an individual gathers his or her life experience into one narrative story. At first sight, this solution might seem self-evident, but it overlooks how many times the narrative story of a human life is re-ordered and receives a totally different meaning. This comes after a deep rupture and in the light of unexpected, new experiences.

In other words, beneath the surface of our ordinary stream of consciousness, life seems to have its own rhythm, bringing new things or modes of being, which we experience. These come to mind only after the fact.

If that is true, the conscious part of our life is not decisive. It draws the conclusion and gives articulation only to a new direction of life that our—let us call it *soul*—has embarked on. Whether we call it *soul* or use a different name does not make much difference, but the fact is that in many situations, some part of us already has made the decision. Our intellectual life can do nothing else but express the decision that one part of us, often called *emotion* or *passion*, made.

Ruptures

Many of us have grown up with the assumption that reason has the capacity to lead. This is a myth, and nothing more than that.

The philosopher Descartes used to complain about his youth; before the time he could use his reason as a grown-up person, he was impressed by so many confusing ideas that in retrospect he would have liked to have been endowed with reason from the days of his childhood, onward. For him, his humanity began when he started to think and reason. The sleeping, emotional, passionate side of his existence was left out, and his reason was emphasized and revered. But our experiences tell us the contrary: We become no more conscious of ourselves than after a stupid action for which we blame ourselves. Our "emotional" side makes us conscious and awakens us from our naive and thoughtless ways of doing things.

"How could you do this, John?" we say to ourselves on such a moment, after making a mistake. And how many times are we not really thinking at all! At the high point of our experience, our consciousness even loses its capacity to capture what is going on. An overwhelming love affair, the sudden appearance of a disease, or the death of a loved one all constitute experiences that often leave us stupefied, without a thought, without any articulation or understanding. It might sound paradoxical that at these breaking points in our lives, we become conscious of our biographical unity. At such moments, we are shocked and we feel lost. And indeed, we are broken apart. We cannot continue along the lines of action that worked so far, and we do not know how to go forward into an unknown and certainly different future. Part of us happens to be thrown into the future, while another part of us from which we might not want to dissociate ourselves, is left behind in the past. At such intervals, when part of us dies and another part is seeking a new future, we discover ourselves as living souls that can be hurt. At such a breaking point, we need somehow to translate the essence of the life we conducted so far into a new future. The real value, intention, love and life, inspiration and responsibility, which were at the core of my former life now need to find a totally different form and a new course—and inspiration. The ability to change—the plasticity and shapelessness it implies, the experience of being nowhere and still having to be incarnated in another life form—is the experience that we might call by the word *soul*.

Reason as an Elative Symbol

The thinking individual is a mere shadow, compared to the soul as the inner biographical unity—caught between past and future, and subject to change. I am immersed in life, not because I think. When I think, I distance my experiences from myself, objectifying them by a detached view. To think and reason means to take a detached stance in relation to the surrounding world, as well as to our living experiences. Thinking involves stepping outside the stream of life, abstracting from it as if we were not ourselves, but someone else looking at us. Both *reason* and *thinking* call upon us to take that attitude, just as *labor* or *youth* call upon us to relate to our experiences in a special mood. Therefore *reason* and *mind* are intensifying and aggrandizing collectives, just like any other symbols that give human beings a sense of belonging and meaning. They are—we used the term earlier— "elative" in character. These can be symbols like nationality, professionalism, and status. By the symbol of *reason*, modern intellectuals belong to the clan of *thinkers*. So it can be concluded that the faculty of reasoning is not a self-evident starting point; but it starts with an act of identification.

Soul: Connecting the Times

If the biographical unity of our existence is not constituted by the faculty of reasoning and thinking, then how is it constituted? Human beings have different appearances, and they need frequently to change the forms of existence during their lifetimes. During a particular period, they develop their human potential mainly in one direction. After some time, such a period naturally comes to an end. It is natural for the youth to live under the authority of other people, and to live as part of a collective (for example, a group of peers), but it is also natural that such a period comes to an end. At a certain age, a person will experience his half-ness and incompleteness. This person will enter the search for partnership and stop living in the collective mode from that time on. He or she will enter upon a time of conscious choice and commitment, taking responsibility for his own life and for the future. He or she will seek a partner to whom that future can be entrusted.

All commitments too are subject to change. A commitment to a particular job in a particular company might suddenly come to an end if the person has outgrown this commitment, or if suddenly the social and organizational setup of a particular company is turned upside down, either from inner necessity or by the impact of the market forces. All of a sudden, a person might lose his job or feel bored by the fruitless repetition of an outdated function. Confronted with such a breakdown of commitment, the people will feel hurt. They might experience their situation as a time of crisis. Crisis means judgment. They are forced to judge anew and to readjust their commitments. In order to restore the unity of their prior biographical identity, they need to find the inspiration and orientation of their whole life, all over again. They need to find the vision, their orientation, the love they live by. At least something that outlasts their former commitments. Such a belief or inspiration or vision can introduce them again into a new commitment, a new phase of their existence, a new life form. But that means that in situations of crisis, people need to discover a new, or an already existing larger imperative. This imperative might have been only partly realized in a former commitment, but it now can be realized and renewed within the context of a new commitment, new partnership, or a new love. The soul is not a fixed entity, but a process. It is the plasticity of human life and love, the power to overcome a partial death and to enter upon a new life. The soul in that sense is indeed the time-traveling part of human beings. It listens to a new imperative from the future, and so it creates a new order of human life or society. It is the power to change from one social form or life form to the other.

The Soul: A Time-out

In that sense, the soul does not point to yet another time span. Instead, it signifies the ruptures, the crises—and at the same time, the deeper continuity—among time spans, the times of life, and periods. For hundreds of years, the people who emigrated to the United States of America lived two lives. Their lifetime was broken into a time before they left, and a totally different life and social form after they entered America. On one hand, migrating meant a rupture and a confrontation with a new imperative and in that sense a time-out. On the other hand, however, there was a continuity of inspiration, a continuity of the living soul of love and longing, connecting both phases of their lives by translating old inspirations in a new context.

Modulation

The biographical unity of a person's life can be compared to a musical composition. A musical composition might start out with one theme and be developed to a certain length, being interrupted by another theme that could be a counterpoint to the former one. There will be a phase of turmoil and also a phase of nearby silence. The melodic line or theme of one part can be taken up and re-cast, and developed in an unexpected way. The music will go further from modulation to modulation, continuously taking up a former theme in a new key, and yet it still is one piece of music: The inner life of the music is constituted by one breath, and one soul is expressed in it.

From time to time, we need to recompose our lives and to grow through a time of change and crisis. But in retrospect, crisis and change might lead to just another variation on the inner center of longing and inspiration. This is our soul, which resounds and echoes in the one person we are. The word *person* is related to *persono,* the voice sounding through the mask, in the theaters of antiquity: In our person we echo, we take over, and renew the old inspirations and commitments that made us human. And we express them and renew them in order to pass them on to the next generation.

Micro and Macro Man

This process of revival and renewal makes the human soul the pivotal point in history and in periods of time. So here we find a connection between the particular microcosm of the individual and the development of humankind. Human beings do not establish the truth merely as individuals. Establishing the truth is a social process, in which "the truth" is readjusted and reconfirmed by different participants in the conversation. The truth is the set of agreed-upon things such as convictions, procedures, and meaning-giving symbols. Of course, it is not arbitrary whether some proposition is accepted as "the truth." The different partners in a dialogue have their values, orientations, accepted facts, and procedures, and they bring them together to complete and readjust the total picture. That means that "the truth" at least needs to be accepted within the framework of the already-established different viewpoints that the partners within the dialogue have inherited from the past. They might have to give up part of their convictions to reach agreement. But they will not give up their convictions just for no particular reason and let their interpretation of life be turned upside down, just like that. In addition to the need for agreement on the inner horizon, the truth that is agreed upon for the time being will be exposed to outside reality.

This means it should at least work to a noticeable degree. People might, for example, agree or not agree on the temperature measurement method of Fahrenheit or Celsius, and that is arbitrary. (Well, no, it is not arbitrary, but it is a matter of the inner horizon.) But they cannot decide that water will boil at 90 degrees Celsius instead of 100. That simply does not work.

Historical Traditions as a Composition, and the Individual as the Musician

The individual is not the source of the self, nor of the cultural and spiritual baggage that comes with an individual. Individual convictions, meaning-giving values, orientations, accepted facts, and procedures are derived from social relationships as they develop through history. This is a history with many layers, full of contradictions and conflicts, and of trends and opposing trends. It looks as if the debate going on throughout history is reproduced in the minds and hearts of individuals, trying to make sense of the universe they live in. Different views and interpretational schemes come toward me from history, from my social context, and again different voices are reproduced and echoed in my inner deliberations. That does not make the individual meaningless. Trends and values inherited from the past receive a new modulation and are applied in a new context, by which their meaning is enriched. In this way they are passed on to the next generation. Every individual can be, and is to a certain degree, a source of creativity. But it is not creativity in an empty space. It is like a painter painting a landscape, and not just reproducing what can be seen. The painter re-creates what the senses receive. Social institutions, social habits, human qualities, and historical achievements are the treasures from the past. Every individual draws from them and takes part in them. Language is particularly the treasure of experience in which the achievements of former generations are articulated in a network of meaning of words and names. It is quite common to look only at a personal biography to understand a person's world view and orientation. If the circle is widened, family relations can enter, allowing formative experiences received from parents, brothers, and sisters, and the way the individual responds to them. If the circle is widened even further via family relationships, teachers, meaningful persons, stories, and literature, the whole experience of mankind and the evaluations of these experiences are handed over to the present generation. This insight is, to a large extent, contrary to common convictions. These we have inherited from the French Revolution and thereafter, when the private person and reason were considered to be the source of convictions and meanings.

The French Revolution—in fact, that precursor of the French Revolution, Descartes—wanted to get rid of the formative experiences from the past. These would merely consist of confusing opinions, unreasonable convictions, and distortions of the truth. Instead, the truth should be settled by clear reasoning and logic and a natural experience of the world. But this is also the approach of the French Revolution, and in it has become part of the common inheritance of humanity. If parents ask their children, or if teachers ask their students: "What do you think, yourselves?" then actually they reproduce the way of handling human experience in day-to-day language. This was introduced by Descartes. Implicitly, the individual is considered to be the source of meaning. If we leave this view aside—or better, integrate it again in a much broader vision of reality—then we can adjust or complete this vision by the metaphor of human beings as nodes in a network of relationships. In these relationships they not only exist in the present but come from the past and stretch out into the future. In that approach, the individual is a kind of a microcosmos in which the great experiences of humanity are reflected and refracted. Reflected, because the individual harbors a wide variety of past experiences expressed in the words and names he or she uses. Refracted, because the individual adds a new twist or modulation to these experiences in light of new imperatives and challenges.

Historical Achievements, Moral Qualities

In a sense, the human individual is too small to be completely human. It would be impossible for an individual to develop to full potential without the help of contemporaries and without the heritage of former generations. This means not only that the individual receives the achievements of the past, but also that what an individual has developed as a new quality of being needs to be passed on to the future. Human society and history become a kind of common stock and a kind of aggrandizement of individual contributions. Often these achievements have their origin in a revolutionary outburst of creativity. Only after some time are they taken over by society. They then become part of the continuous stream of history. In our common memory, all the human potentialities are essentially stored up, and we continuously revive and renew them in order to meet future challenges. Particular human qualities have happened to be special achievements of only some branches of history and society. For instance, the human capacity to smile and be detached, and in a state of full inner harmony has never been developed as fully as in the China of Confucius. The capacity to revolutionize society frequently, while always keeping the perspective of the future open and never resting in the status quo, was first fully developed in Europe.

Planetary Responsibilities

Protected by Institutions

Such human qualities are the product of individual or generational investments in the "common stock" of humanity. But they are also incorporated and incarnated in social institutions. We install institutions, regulations, and authorities to guarantee the reproduction and maintenance of the human qualities developed in one or another society. Without a parliament, for instance, and without freedom of press—and the laws protecting them—an open political debate would not last long. Further, an open critical attitude belonging to this practice would easily be suppressed, or lost and forgotten. In this institutional form, human achievements become part of our collective consciousness and are imparted to us by education and socialization.

Summarizing: Five Time Frames

In this chapter, I have distinguished five time perspectives that together constitute the makeup of the human biography. They differ in length—and for that reason, in quality, too—starting with matter and ending up by connecting human beings to history and its revolutionary evolving from past to future. Each human being in his or her subjective and personal biography gives a twist to inherited qualities and contributes to the re-creation of history. These qualities are handed down to the next generation, translated and renewed through all the crises of our human existence.

Table 4. The five time frames of life

Matter	Life	Consciousness	Love	Faith
Physical time: natural time Machine time: seconds, hours Neutralized, mechanical time, causality	Labor time, The molecule of the labor group, 3 = 1 4—7 years (?), a biological rhythm of its own, to counter nature	Collectivism, belonging to the group through symbolic representations like *youth*, *labor*, etc. ∞ = 1, Collectives can last hundreds of years, naïve participation in them cannot outlast 15 years	Partnership, reproduction, Re-creation, 2 = 1 15 to 30 years of conscious choice and commitment, a lifetime, marriage	Uniqueness, change through crisis, translation from one era to the other, Soul 1 = 1 Responding to a new imperative, a moment, a flash

In table 4, I used the words that Rosenstock-Huessy derived from Paracelsus in naming these five different time frames: matter, life, consciousness, love, and faith.[3] *The Multiformity of Man*, which provided the guide for my line of argument in this chapter, in my interpretation has a silent connection to the interpretation Rosenstock-Huessy gives to the work of Paracelsus. If we look at it that way, it also becomes apparent that the different time perspectives support each other and come to the rescue of each other. If people live too much in one perspective—for instance, if they are occupied only by material things—sooner or later they need compensation by one of the other perspectives. In one of his lectures, Rosenstock-Huessy commented on the way of life of Americans, saying that they lived only in column 1 and column 5, shown here in table 4, implying that their usual materialism now and then was counterbalanced by (what they perceive as) their mission for humanity. We can also present the different time frames and perspectives according to the cross of reality. This gives the following picture:

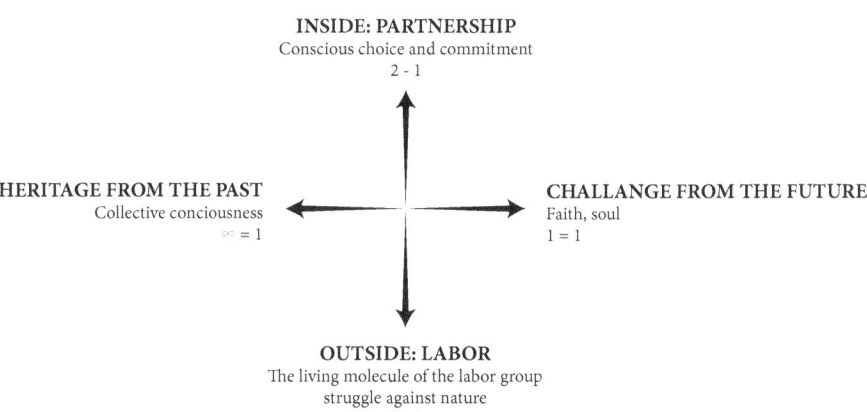

If we take into account that in each next step the human being becomes an increasingly greater part of the full human history, we can also use the following picture:

5. ENTERING HISTORY THROUGH FAITH: through ruptures and crisis, both biography and history are re-created

4. PARTNERSHIP: concious commitment of love, 15-30 years, a lifetime, manage

3. CONSCIOUSNESS: participating in symbols and leading ideas of the spirit of the time, 4-10 years, renewal every 15 years

2. THE RHYTHM OF THE LABOR GROUP: cooperation against nature, 3-7 years

1. PHYSICAL, MECHANICAL TIME: causality

3. Rosenstock-Huessy, "Heilkraft und Wahrheit," 1952, 114–37.

In the course of our biographies, we increasingly learn to live in a longer perspective of time. We learn how to connect the times, both biographically and historically. Little children do not know of any time; they live in the moment. Working merely for survival, even if it is part of the labor group, does not give a much broader time perspective than living by the day. Depending on the context and type of work, such labor groups might last three to seven years. If longer perspectives of time do not come to the rescue, they probably will not survive that long. If some group identity and belonging does not help, nothing is more boring than mechanical labor. But how long can such a group last, a group that gathers around a common flag or symbol that promises a future of hope?

Future of hope? Yes, we have to keep in mind that groups gathering around a collective idea and a common identity derive hope for the future from that, even though this means that they are realizing a symbol that came to them only from the past. If, for instance, a group of young people participates in a team that produces a faster car than any other team, this will give them a feeling of promising self-assertion and innovation, even though they built the car according to existing knowledge and traditions. New ways are seldom invented as a group. Sooner or later, the members of such a group will discover that they are merely repeating what they already learned to do. The members of a student association will also impart a sense of belonging and probably also a sense of innovation to each other, because each generation has its own inventions, discoveries, and fashions. Nevertheless, after some four or five years, the members will discover that it was more of the same, and their participation in the student association will feel repetitive. It is not as new as they thought. They have seen it all. They will start doubting the value of their membership and feel as if they are once again alone. That, in turn, is a good starting point for real partnership. In a lasting relation of partnership, each has a contribution to make. The creative tension between inherently different partners will keep a relationship alive more and for a longer time than is allowed by belonging to the same idea and group. The student association might last more than hundreds of years, but the participation of the different students does not last more than seven to ten years.

A partner—or a cause, even—to be married to, mobilizes stronger energies than collective identities can. But even such a commitment can become lifeless and obsolete. A person can also be committed to the wrong cause! Wrong partnership! Then a new love, a new imperative, is necessary. And often through crises, the commitment to causes and marriages either is renewed or broken down. In both cases, old inspirations need to be translated into new contexts by an act of faithful translation by which a human soul, moving through loneliness, is revived and rescued. To save your soul might not be so much a matter of transporting your soul to some afterlife, but to be able to translate an old love and inspiration into a new situation without becoming unfaithful to it.

5

The Rhythm of Time
History and Generations

Introduction

In the previous chapters, I have put forward what Rosenstock-Huessy called the *cross of reality*. We always live in four directions—two spaces and two times: inside and outside, past and future. We have already drawn some arrows and made a spatial representation of these four. That illustration provides some understanding, but it also has negative consequences, perhaps exactly because it makes it too understandable. It seems to be a model alongside other models. And our time is rather indifferent to models. Why not try another model tomorrow and throw away this one? It is just a construction, after all.

However, Rosenstock-Huessy's teaching of time can help us trace reality behind the model: the reality of time, as we experience it. Spatial concepts are always more or less construed. The stream of experience, which passes through us in time, can be articulated in language. And such articulation can be more or less to the point, more or less thorough. But nevertheless, what we experience in time is not construed or made up. What a person feels is what a person feels. Language might articulate it, albeit in different ways. Of course, everybody has his or her own version of the experiences through common time, but that does not make them arbitrary. One cannot deny what one feels. Such feelings and experiences might complement each other and correct each other. They are biased and partial aspects of the truth, but as experiences, they are undeniable. With history, it is the same as with our experience as living people. If two people share their experiences about a third person, they will express their own respective versions of that experience. But mostly the person about whom they talk remains recognizable as one and the same. They discover different aspects of this person.

In this way, I will put forward here Rosenstock-Huessy's teaching of time. By doing that, I will also provide the background method of his approach to culture and history. And that in turn can serve as a preliminary exercise for the next two chapters. In them, I will give a sort of pedigree of the achievements of the great streams of culture in the history of humanity (chapter 6) and of the western, especially European, history (chapter 7). The background of chapter 5 here might teach the reader that human qualities and historical achievements are not static. They are constantly on the move, susceptible to further developments, creative junctures, and mixtures. They are also open to new learning experiences at the crossroads of different cultures. If globalization means more than westernization of the whole world, then it should be something like that: the heritage of different cultures being made available for each other and re-created in view of a common future of peace and justice.

Time and Space Are Not Homogeneous

In philosophy—and for that reason, also in historiography—the dominant opinion is that space and time are homogeneous. Without this assumption, the natural sciences would not have been possible. At any point in space and time, the same natural laws should be valid. Only thanks to this axiom could Newton conceptualize the apple falling from a tree, and the moon revolving around the Earth, with both covered by one and the same natural law. Nevertheless, concrete human experience has a different approach to time and space. It is difficult to enter a cathedral without feeling something of the atmosphere of respect and devotion that such a room evokes. A person who visits a former concentration camp cannot avoid being affected by what once happened there. A person who returns after many years to the place where he or she was first kissed cannot remain indifferent to such a place.

Just as a particular room might give a more intense impression than another one, different times also have a different intensity. That counts for the individual as well as for society as a whole. A person can be completely blinded by his or her new love, or by all the possibilities of a new technical invention. After a period of euphoria and amazement and enthusiasm, slowly but surely a more even time experience enters. We alternate between impassioned peaks of time and normal daily experiences. Historians do not usually take into account the differences between such peaks and the more common experiences of human beings. The result is a kind of historiography in which temperament and temperature of the historical actors seem to be more or less even, or are treated as if they were. And for that reason, often the true dynamics behind history are not understood.

For instance, one could argue that it was a measureless presumption of Napoleon to try to bring Russia to its knees. Or one could speak of it as if it were a strategic mistake, that in his cool calculation and estimation of the political and military power play, some sort of failure occurred. However, whoever takes into account the spirit of the French Revolution can become sensitive to the inevitability of the event. All of France lived under the influence of such a revolutionary upheaval—so much so, in fact, that they were beyond themselves. This messianic élan drives a passion that makes a rational balancing of costs and returns impossible. Exactly because of this passion, Napoleon and his troops had already won many battles. On several occasions, he had turned the impossible into a reality. Why not once more? And even in its failure, the campaign for Russia was still a statement by France to the rest of the world. After the Battle of Waterloo, the language of the French Revolution slowly but surely was taken over by the other nations as well: in Europe, a liberal culture was established within the frame of reference of national states with one language, one more or less natural territory, and one capital. This was the model of the French nation-state. Even Germany and Italy took over the model and became national states, which they were not before.

Peaks in History

History looks different as soon as we become aware of the differences in the intensity of experiences. For this same reason, we are also struck by different events in history. In both the chapter on communication and the chapter on responsibility, I have pointed to the different aggregate states in which language and responsibility can put people. This chapter adds to those insights and applies them to historical developments. This chapter attends to the course of this fourfold rhythm in the historical process through the generations.

The small account of history I present here is derived from the perspective of language. It looks at the question of how large groups of people, across long periods of time and over large areas, manage to speak more or less the same language. This is not an accidental or arbitrary starting point. The question of all questions, the main question of history, is exactly this question, because its answers explain how people make peace, establish ordered societies, and create relationships built on justice. Peace can be concluded only *expressis verbis*. Language itself therefore probably does not originate in hunting or in daily intercourse, where people used signs to indicate things to each other. Instead, it originated in the question of war and peace. Only if people bend under the weight of commonly recognized names and imperatives can they put aside their rivalry and egoism and realize something together. The very word *order*, as used in the expression *social order*, refers to *order* in the sense of command. That means there must be something like a commonly experienced imperative, urged upon them by need and necessity—that is, by time. People do not create communities only as a matter of coziness. They pull themselves together and push their differences aside so that they can ward off calamity or repair the damage from a calamity. The primary historical questions for that reason are: How do we get to the point that people do not fight each other out of fear and hatred, but bend under the same social order in the light of a common need? How do we get to the point that they do not let themselves be chased away as random individuals, each on his own, but turn toward each other and toward the commonly experienced need, take the responsibility for each other, and face their problems together? Wherever that happens, a new foundation for future culture has been laid. At such moments, a new language is spoken. And wherever such a thing has happened, we can speak of an historical event. All other events in history are more or less only of passing interest.

Often in the margin of history, creative minorities have laid such a new foundation for the future. As a consequence, historiography typically does not pay much attention to such events. Only when such a creative minority succeeds and comes to power, it becomes visible. And that happens only when the first revolutionary élan has ebbed away. But then historiography, not aware of the peace-creating power of language, frequently points to completely different causes for whatever success there has been in concluding peace.

For example, historians usually ascribe the period of human welfare of the Italian Renaissance to the enlightened spirit of trade and city life at that time. As the rationale goes, the Renaissance was a movement that wrested itself away from the tutelage of church authorities and identified with the Greek and Roman culture of antiquity. That ascription, however, confuses cause and consequence. The enlightened spirit of trade and traffic is not the cause behind the period of better human welfare, but the *consequence* of it. Only if people are better off, it is usually supposed, can tolerance and enlightenment be enjoyed. The toil and trouble necessary to get to this point, however, has a totally different motivation. More often than not, historians overlook the origin of the Italian cities as grounded in the struggle between pope and emperor. When the pope and the papal party within church and society resisted the attempts by emperors and kings to instrumentalize the church and its offices, at last it was agreed that the emperor would no longer enter the territory of northern Italy, south of the Alps, with his army. As a result of that agreement, ordinary knights, people in bondage, and serfs saw their opportunity for emancipation. From the end of the eleventh century and the beginning of the twelfth century onward, they founded many cities as sworn communities. This beginning in northern Italy was soon copied throughout the rest of Europe. They fought with and without weapons for their city rights against the nobility and the emperor (and as often with support of the emperor and kings against the local nobility, as well). And on that basis, they acquired and developed their civil liberties. They profited from the language introduced by the papal revolution in the Middle Ages—the language of universal justice to which the two rival parties (pope and emperor) let themselves be bound to settle their disputes. That neither party was above the law and that there was, or at least should be, the rule of law and by law, is a unique and exceptional combination in history. That such a thing could happen was a true revolution—with all of the corresponding sacrifice, enthusiasm, and passion.[1]

Four Aggregate States

Rosenstock-Huessy speaks frequently about the four aggregate states of language. Just as air, water, earth, and fire constitute different aggregate states of matter, the grammatical forms of the subjunctive, the indicative, the past perfect (or pluperfect) tense, and the imperative represent different states of the human soul.[2] And just as is the case with the natural elements—earth, air, water, and fire—people in the one mood are barely recognizable to people in another. An old man can forget the enthusiasm of his youth altogether and completely become "earth." A young man can be full of enthusiasm and on "fire" to such an extent that he totally lacks any understanding of the life experience of the elder. Whoever feels himself spoken to in the imperative like a "you!" and is totally overwhelmed by the electrification from that,

---

1. Rosenstock-Huessy, *Out of Revolution;* Berman, *Law and Revolution,* Vol. I; Braudel, *Civilization and Capitalism.*

2. The pluperfect tense expresses action that is already past, from a perspective that it is over and done with (a perfect aspect, signaled by the participle). An example is: "She *had arrived* at 3 o'clock, when I was not at home."

does not know of any self-reflection. He or she will "completely go for it" and does not calculate the price that anyone has to pay for it. People who live like that are so convinced of themselves, and their imperative "rages" in them to such an extent, that other people even get scared. They will not let themselves be stopped in any way. That counts for people like Pope Gregory VII, who started the struggle of investiture in 1075, just as it counts for Luther, for Cromwell, for Robespierre, and for Lenin—all of whom acted as if they were possessed. Often they had to convince even their closest companions. Their temper totally suits the fire of a revolutionary period. The *geuzen* (a nickname meaning "beggars") who took Den Briel (in the Netherlands), the people who stormed the Bastille—for calm, historical reporters looking back on them, they were out of their minds.

Whoever dares to take a courageous step forward in the tension between crisis and opportunity often stands alone. He or she makes it, thanks only to the driving power of such an imperative that calls forth the sacrifice. Although one can artificially and by rhetoric try to evoke such a tension, if crisis and necessity are not present, the creditworthiness of such rhetoric quickly fades away. The lies of Hitler and Mussolini did not come from the depths of living souls. Yes, they did articulate the crisis experienced by the people, but their respective solutions to those crises were merely reproductions of the outworn language of an old past. They used revolutionary language to prevent revolution from coming. They were in this sense counter-revolutionary.

Only if we book the first successes in the fierce spirit of the beginning do we open up room for opposing voices. The imperative is now clearly and without dispute on the agenda, and from now on, people from different points of view can be allowed to contribute to the solution of the problem. This requires a different temper or mood from the one that is present in the people who "completely go for it." One can, for instance, think of the theologians and jurists immediately after the papal revolution, whose job it was to underpin the claims of the pope against the emperor, with the help of theological and legal arguments. People who devote themselves to such reflection need time and rest in order to do that. Their mood is less ardent than that of the people of the first hour. They need space and air. In open competition, different options can coexist at this stage. Quite soon the imperial party could fully participate in the debate, in order to reach an equilibrium between the power claims of the pope and the emperor. If this debate were aimed at some form of agreement, the opposing parties need in some way to be mutually penetrable. They make propositions, ask for approval, and somehow must let the truth of the other party also weigh against themselves. They cannot afford only to speak; they also need to listen. They need to be able somehow to create a "common present" with the other party.

If a revolutionary movement enters this phase, other types of human beings also enter the floor. There is more willingness for compromise so that the new and the old can coexist, to a degree. This gives "air." And in this way, a slow growth of the new principle of life becomes possible, while the old can once again prove its lasting meaning, but in the new context.

Thinking of the different phases in the creation of the Netherlands during the Eighty Years' War (the Dutch War of Independence), we can point to the *smeekschrift der edelen* (petition of the nobles), William of Orange, Den Briel, Alkmaar, Haarlem, and Leiden as standing on the frontline of the future, representing the fire at the beginning. The period of Oldenbarnevelt and Maurits, the competition between the Synod of Dordrecht, and the more liberal States-General until the Peace of Münster in 1648, a period still full of unrest, can be considered the second period. During this time, different solutions were tried, with the idea that eventually the new and the old could exist beside one another. The period of 1648 until 1672, the "year of disaster," was a period the new principle of life was presumed to be beyond all discussion and could have an impact, thanks to the common conviction behind it. It was a period of presumption because, as participants in the accepted truth, the new community did not take under consideration any viewpoints outside the in-group. This is the period of the "past perfect tense" in which, thanks to a common history, a group of people learned to say *we*, with all the positive and negative consequences accompanying such a phenomenon. It was a period of power, thanks to that common conviction; but it was also a period of one-sidedness, as well. Eventually, that meant that the new revolutionary group would collide with other groups in the world outside, groups that would have a different picture of the world. And as a matter of fact, even the new revolutionary group could not be in total control.

For Holland, the eighteenth century is a period of relative humiliation and stagnation. Only after the French Revolution, from 1815 on, when the seven provinces become one national state, a new equilibrium can be found between the *we* of the Dutch and the other nations. They know who they are, one to another, and are able to look upon themselves also from the outside, as seen by someone else. From that moment on, the period of the indicative slowly sets in: It becomes possible to objectify oneself as much as possible, and to give an impartial account of the whole history. One can start to gather facts. And being Dutch has become just one common experience among others. It no longer gives one a high feeling of *we*, but it becomes a matter of fact, documented in a passport.

Modern historiography to a large extent operates in the indicative. In detailed research the facts are gathered, hypotheses are put forward, and the research never leads to more than partial evidence and the assurance of the necessity of further research. The historian who researches the French Revolution in such an "indicative" state of mind after the actual course of events might find it completely obtuse why the storming of the Bastille should have been such an important turning point. There were no more than seven prisoners in the Bastille anyhow, and it was only one of many confrontations between the old regime and the revolutionary forces. The revolutionary meaning of the storming of the Bastille does not consist of the fact as such, but of the revolutionary mood this event evoked, and by which it was evoked. The Bastille was the prison for political dissidents. The people, in other words, robbed the king symbolically of his power to sanction. Whoever does not *sense* the symbolic meaning of this event, and has no internal connection to the different aggregate state in which the participants lived through it, cannot be helped out by research on the facts, statistics, and archived documents. And such a person can arbitrarily construe a different starting point for the French Revolution.

Spengler and Rosenstock

To get a better understanding of Rosenstock-Huessy's view on history, let us compare the historical method of his contemporary, the German philosopher of history, Oswald Spengler. In Rosenstock-Huessy's conception, a new history starts with a new event, a command, an order, articulated in time like an imperative interrupting the natural course of history and pointing to new ways that can become a reality only if people listen to the message. In Spengler's conception of history, this element of listening to an imperative is missing, although he too has the courage to bring order into large historical periods. But in his conception, history is without revelation—that is, it has no starting point in an eruptive imperative. It is a natural process of growth and decline. As such, it is not related to human speech, born out of necessity and need.

In many ways, the approach of Rosenstock-Huessy and the one of Spengler are related. Both of them look not only at the historical facts, but also at the starting point of the life experience that is expressed in those facts. Spengler's *Der Untergang des Abendlandes* [Decline of the West] first appeared in 1917, in the middle of World War I.[3] Rosenstock-Huessy wrote to his wife, Margrit: "He is thinking my thoughts."[4] According to Rosenstock-Huessy, Spengler shows deep insight in history and he is also to a high degree influenced by Goethe, again like Rosenstock-Huessy. But

3. Spengler, *Untergang des Abendlandes*.
4. Dated March 31, 1919, unpublished.

he does not have a sense of language and destination. For that reason, one can say that he talks about history minus revelation, minus the imperative. Spengler traces the life feeling, which he hears in the great symbols of the different cultures, back to natural life. The life experience of the farmer in the landscape is at the origin of every high culture, according to Spengler.

Let us take the example of Egypt, farmers living on a small strip of land along the Nile. The Egyptians, surrounded by the colossal mountainsides at the shores of the Nile, founded the pyramid empire. This culture can be symbolized by the line, because the statues and the temples force the visitors to move forward in one direction, from south to north. Colossal buildings on both sides of the roads and of the Nile create the impression of a continuous movement. The Greeks, on the contrary, have built their temples on the top of a hill, surrounded by the city as if it were the center of the world. For many reasons, the point is the suitable symbol for the Greeks, who did not seek for the big perspective in which their city-state was connected with the rest of the world, but lived in the here and now. In time as well, the Greeks did not search for continuity. They did not prepare for the future and did not anticipate it. They fell prey to the rivalry between the city-states and could easily rush into war from one day to the next. The symbol for this life in the here and now is the naked statue, standing freely in space.

Spengler too comes up with a fourfold rhythm, the rhythm of nature: spring, summer, autumn, and winter. In a specific landscape, a particular life feeling binds people together as adherents of one common symbol. If this dawning life form carries on and becomes the dominant culture, city life emerges and the original life feeling starts flourishing in expressions of art and culture, as well as in social life and science. Autumn sets in at the moment this culture turns into a civilization—that is, by the increasing urbanization and all the artificial life that living in cities brings with it. Then people lose their roots in the landscape and their contact with the original feeling of life. *Civilization* is the name for the period in which people no longer believe wholeheartedly in their ideals. Instead, they start thinking about and reflecting on them, and try to retrace—by reflection and deliberation—what for past generations was a self-evident conviction. Eventually this period of civilization, autumn, turns into the period of cultural petrification: winter time. With an inner skepticism, the old cultural baggage is dragged further into the future. People no longer know why they are who they are, and do not share their original inspiration, anymore. This also is the time in which great leaders use their charisma to put their stamp on politics and on the masses, which already are wavering in their convictions. It is the period of Caesarism, as Spengler calls it, according to whom the Roman Empire in its imperial phase is an example of such a petrified culture.

It is typified by charismatic dictators who manipulate the waves, trends, and opinions of the masses. But Spengler sees the same thing happening in the Europe in which he lived.

Rosenstock-Huessy notes that Spengler's work became a success in Germany, exactly because Spengler looked upon the decline of a culture as if it were just a natural phenomenon.[5] If that were the case, the loss of the war and the humiliating Peace of Versailles would be nothing more than an inevitable process for which nobody was to be blamed. Polemically, Rosenstock-Huessy calls his essay on Spengler, "*Die Selbstmord Europas,*" the suicide of Europe. Europe did not perish because of petrification, but instead committed suicide because it consciously tried to deny and destroy the values on which it was based.

And Spengler contributed to that by his quasi-biological understanding of the growth and decline of cultures. In Spengler's view, the different cultures that developed in the course of history do not have any real contact with each other. They cannot understand each other and they are not accessible to each other. On the surface, it might seem as if they inherit a lot from each other, but the life feeling of each culture stands on its own. The Egyptians tried to establish an empire of eternal duration; the Greeks, by contrast, lived in a point of time without real consciousness of past and future. Despite superficial similarities, these human types are total strangers to each other and cannot understand each other. As far as Spengler is concerned, this is also the case with the innerconstitution of European history and culture. Spengler uses the term *Faustian* to describe the European feeling of life. He means that it is full of unrest with the here and now, and is in a constant state of needing and longing to look further both in space and time. He ascribes this life feeling to the forests of Northern Europe, and to the daring voyages of the Vikings and Normans.[6] The Gothic churches, the oil painting, and the European philosophy of numbers are all "symbols" of one and the same feeling of life. In the churches, the walls stretch upward to such an extent that ceiling and walls cannot be discerned from each other. The oil painting expresses depth. The European philosophy of numbers moves between the infinitely small and the infinitely big. These symbols express the urge to see every independent phenomenon in a greater frame of reference, in a wider perspective. The invention of perspective itself is just such a symbol, because it looks from the future and from far away, back to the moment.[7] It always seeks after the connection with the

---

5. Rosenstock-Huessy, "Der Selbstmord Europas," 45–84.
6. Spengler, *Untergang des Abendlandes*, 253, 255.
7. Ibid., 336.

totality of things. This culture too knows its spring, its summer, its autumn, and winter. And in the end the culture perishes.

Spengler looks upon his own work as being part of the final phase of this culture, because in his work, he puts this culture itself into perspective from its beginning to its end. The period of Caesarism and mass culture lies before him, in the future. At the outset, Spengler hailed the Nazis and their "heathen" way of thinking (rooted in blood and soil). This became something the Nazis could use to produce their ideology. Only slowly did Spengler distance himself from their appropriation of his way of thinking.

Twofold or Threefold

With his fourfold classification—spring, summer, autumn, and winter—Spengler comes close to the aggregate states that Rosenstock-Huessy spoke of. So too was it the case with his conviction that the symbols of a culture express the life feeling under the surface of it. What Spengler lacks, however, is the primacy of language, and within that, first and foremost the imperative, the discovery of a new marching order in the middle of life at a time of crisis. From the unconscious, almost vegetable-like life in the landscape, so to speak, a new feeling of life automatically emerges. As this life feeling becomes more conscious and explicit, people lose the inner contact with this existential layer. As time goes by, every conviction becomes petrified, because it is subjected to too much consciousness and reflection. Unconscious conviction occurs in the beginning; over-reflection and skepticism mark the end of a culture. That is also the reason that one culture does not have anything to say to another one. To bring about communication between cultures, it would be necessary for the petrification of a particular culture to be experienced as a crisis—a crisis that requires a solution. It would be necessary for people to allow in their lifetimes the rupture between a past that should be done away with and the new future on which they embark. Such breaking points, these periods of crisis, are also the connection and translation points between the different periods of time. They allow a translation of the person's heritage before the crisis, and of the person's heritage after the crisis.

The experience of crisis and the sensibility for a new imperative are both necessary for the emerging development to come about. It can take a long time before a society runs into a deadlock, and even more time before this is experienced as a crisis. If no new opportunity looms on the horizon of creating a new level of peace and a new order of society, the status quo is experienced as an inevitable destiny or fate. And on the other hand, if a new idea, a new imperative comes "too early," if people do not experience and recognize the existing situation somehow as a crisis, this new language has little chance of finding acceptance. Everybody wishes to go along established lines as long as possible.

Rosenstock-Huessy replaces Spengler's twofold rhythm with a threefold rhythm, the pre-formal, the formal, and informal language.[8] Pre-formal language is open to the influences of all kinds of cultural traditions, but it did not find its own unique marching orders and destiny, yet. Some signs might already implicitly announce where the future emphasis will lie. Language becomes formal if the "high word" emerges, and if in a time of crisis people try to ward off the threat by putting a new imperative and a new marching order on the agenda. Language in such cases becomes formal, in the sense of solemn, impassioned, and ardent. These are moments that require the right words, because people's lives depend on them.

During the French Revolution, *patriotism* was a "high word." The party of the patriots wanted to overcome the division of the land in counties, duchies, shires, cities, and regional parliaments by appealing to the nation as one and indivisible: *La France une et indivisible!* Only in the course of time can the heat of such words cool down and language become informal again. The new achievement of the nation-state, for example, becomes a common phenomenon—so much so that nationalism can be ridiculed. This is permitted because people know that too much nationalism can stand in the way of further progress. In such a case, a new crisis makes itself felt. The crisis of the twentieth century to a large extent can be considered the crisis of the nation-state—that is to say, the crisis of the concept of one state, one country, one language, and one capital as a model for political unity and sovereignty. This is a concept that is actually derived from the French Revolution.

Different Sorts of Crisis

There can be peace if different parties succeed in creating a common present. To maintain such a peace, it is necessary—however minimally—to agree upon a certain number of peace terms, even if this might occur as the result of quite different viewpoints. In the negotiations between unions and the employers, for instance, the atmosphere might become quite heated. But both parties know that they need to find a solution. The employers know it, because they need to prevent unrest and avoid damage to the companies. The unions know it, because they also want to secure the interests of their members on a longer term. Acting from different viewpoints, they might just find a solution that both of them can accept. It becomes an urgent matter if

8. Rosenstock-Huessy, *Origin of Speech*.

they do not succeed, because the crisis might become unmanageable. Without this sense of urgency, such negotiations might not even succeed. Every now and then, they do not succeed. Disaster might be unavoidable.

There are four reasons under which such a crisis can emerge. They hang together with the four aggregate states of language we mentioned earlier. A crisis takes the shape of a revolution if a group is inspired by new ideas and loses its patience with old power relationships. People are fed up and start a struggle for change, often with slogans of which they themselves have only a faint notion of what those slogans might concretely mean. The revolutionary speaks an unarticulated language, one in which he cannot express clearly what he wants. In any case, this language makes it clear that he does not accept the dominant consensus any longer. The subsequent governments of the first phase of the French Revolution, until 1794, tried to bridge the gap between the new civil liberties of liberalism and human rights on one side, and the old regime of king and nobility and church on the other. Every compromise was refused and cut off, however, by the radical wing of the revolutionary forces. They claimed over and over again that the "Revolution was in danger." The unarticulated language of the revolutionaries, however, has its counterpart in the over-articulated language of the conservative party, which is caught up in an outdated view to such an extent that it cannot find the way forward. A decadent language articulates a new situation in outdated terms.

Take the example of somebody defending the free market and free enterprise, even though at the same time there are some big players who control the market and their protectionism prevents new players from coming in. If the group that cooperated all along with the market suddenly falls apart because the different parties cannot find each other in the common view they agreed upon at first, anarchy steps in. If one nation imposes its views and values and norms, its "codes of speech," onto a different nation, there is war.

Revolution, decadence, anarchy, and war correspond with the time perspectives of future and past, and the two spaces, inside and outside. A crisis within the shared space of an inside group means anarchy. A crisis between two groups with external relationships means war. Revolution does not find the connection with the language of the past and decadence does not find the connection with the language of the future.

It is of great importance to distinguish among these four types of crisis in the interpretation of social conflict, because in the heat of political competition the opponents easily take over each other's terms. Even the Contras in their revolution in Nicaragua in the 1980s wanted to behave in an revolutionary fashion so that they could return under the cloak of revolutionary language to the old order. Should one, for example, look upon the terrorism of certain Muslim minorities as the harbinger of a new revolutionary language that anticipates great changes? Or do these people try to speak a language that is no longer adequate to the present situation? In the latter case, it is decadent, too much the language of the past. It can even be both at the same time. That would mean that people are in search of a new equilibrium between the western heritage and Islamic tradition, but can express this only if it is packed into old language. In the same vein, the Christian evangelical movement tries to anticipate a new future by making faith more personal. But it achieves this result in quite an ambivalent way by organizing big gatherings that have the character of mass meetings—even more so than traditional church gatherings. So, it too tries to innovate, but by old means. For that reason, one should not only listen to what the different parties say, but also to the key in which it is said. In other words, one should look not only at what the bird sings, but also at how it flies. Is it revolutionary or decadent? Is it an expression of anarchy or is it a war cry? Does the language announce a culture at the beginning of its development? Or is the group merely marking time, albeit with a lot of noise? These distinctions are not easy to make.

After the world wars, for instance, many people were convinced that the role of Europe on the stage of world power was over. Nothing new could come from Europe. However, the European Union learned to create new balances, up to a point, among many different interests. This happened only by a continuous process of difficult negotiations, in which many people started thinking that this attitude of taking other parties into account by creating always new balances, might as well be an example for the rest of the world. Europe might still have something to say, after all.

Table 5 shows the four types of communication failure.

Table 5. War, anarchy, decadence, and revolution

War The front, outside	Anarchy The front, inside	Decadence Too much past	Revolution Too much future
One group tries to impose its values and ways of speech onto another group by force.	Different groups within one and the same society do not speak and listen anymore, but shout and scream. Coordination is lost.	An old and obsolete "discourse" still functions and imposes itself on a new situation no longer covered by it. Too much articulation.	A new and unarticulated language tries to innovate, to deal with a new challenge and without being able to connect to past experiences.

The Combined Efforts of Three Generations

A revolution can have a lasting impact only if at least three successive generations are involved. The first generation in the midst of a historical crisis senses a new future, and listens to a new imperative. This first generation often proceeds without any external success. But even if there are no successes and everything fails, the new name and assignment are now on everybody's agenda. This first generation frequently has a vision, but lacks a plan. Lonely individuals break away from the traditional order of society and prepare for a new future in the margin of it. After a first trial, often everything seems lost. But a new generation takes up the thread in a new way. This new generation undertakes more realistic endeavors to turn the new approach into a reality. Rosenstock-Huessy calls this the *Law of the Twofold Beginning*. What first echoed as a loud clarion call could not be put into action because it had no support. Further, the innovators had an idea but no sense of reality. This new mountain of a vision must now be conquered, step by step, in a slow process by daily labor. Only after the third generation comes in can the new achievement become part of the normal bloodstream of society. Again, that means a test for the new truth, because if the new achievements cannot become part of the normal repertoire of action, but remains reserved for a special group, did this new truth really resolve the crisis? Was the new achievement really necessary and unavoidable? If the change is not critically important in the long term, it will not be taken on by subsequent generations. There are many such so-called revolutionary innovations with the ambition to change history, but they are in fact only one-generation phenomena, illusions of the day.

Of course, every generation feels the challenge to start something new, and does not like to take over the heritage of past generations automatically. That means that every new generation is put to the test, whether it has the power to convince the next generation of its truths. If not, such truths cannot be confirmed and cannot be turned into reality. They will not hold. The next generation will not believe them anymore, because life itself and the quality of life can just as well do without them. In that case, the so-called renewals are only temporary fashions and not really necessary phenomena. Like fashion itself, they are just transitory in character.

For all those reasons, there is a subtle intrigue going on between the generations. It is an intrigue of separating from, and inheriting, and convincing, and letting go of each other. The everlasting question is whether only one generation can be the owner of the truth and put its stamp on the next generation. Or can the truth take a different shape from generation to generation to such an extent that it is both inherited and renewed, because the next generation also has a say in it? Between the generations, there is always something like a dead moment. Nothing goes on automatically. From each new generation, a process of respectively inheriting, changing, and passing on is required. If the present generation puts the next generation into the straitjacket of its own truths, it cannot love the next generation. It might even make it into an object. The well-known Christian virtues of faith, hope, and love are the expression of this passing-on of truth through time.[9] It is essential that the heritage of the one generation is passed on to the next in a way that anticipates the future. Every new generation has to face the threefold task of faithfully inheriting (obviously, a matter of faith), modulating and rethinking the truth in light of the next generation (being changed by love), and passing it on in the expectation that a new generation will realize the truth of the past in a new way (hope). To be aware of this position between the two generations, to feel the necessity of translating the inherited truth and making it in a new way, a new version or twist available for the next generation, is what constitutes the Christian process of movement through life. The Christian virtues do not represent some entities in and of themselves. They are not static virtues, but related to time. Faith in the achievements of generations passed, being changed by love in the present, passing on this changed heritage hopefully to the future. These are the three human qualities that make it possible, that allow the spiritual outlook of one time to be translated into another time, so that it is allowed to go through different shapes and phases. The present generation is always inclined to deliver ready products to the next generation. All the insights that somebody has acquired in a difficult process of trial and error are put together conveniently and systematically in a book. And the present generation of students is expected to learn it. This is the way it works! Everybody involved in the passing-on of traditions should ask himself: What can we do without? What is the next generation allowed to forget from all the heritage that is so dear to me? And also: What should I pass on, whatever the costs might be, because it is essential to any society or form of life in the future? In the same vein, the next generation should ask the reverse question: What should I, despite all my thirst for change and renewal, absolutely take on and inherit from the former generation, because it is indispensable, because it is essential to the quality of life?

These are more than only intellectual questions. Our complete existence, our "soul" is involved in them. The transfer of traditions between different generations is always precarious. It frequently takes the pressure of an impending crisis for the current generation to start to recapture its

---

9. Rosenstock-Huessy, *Atem des Geistes,* 101.

older heritage. A terrifying crisis makes people seek orientation. At such moments, old memories emerge. In times of crisis, whatever made an earlier impression is what they will think of, first. Parents often start asking themselves what they really accept as orienting truths for their lives, when they themselves have to raise children. What they discover at that moment as truths, under the pressure of being responsible for the next generation, is what they pass on. They might even go one step further and ask themselves what might be orienting truths for their children at a time that will go beyond their own lifetimes.

Table 6 shows faith, love, and hope as time connectors.

Faith	Love	Hope
A new generation trusts in old tradition Going along with pre-formal traditional language Relying on codes of speech that have already been created	A new orientation makes itself felt A new imperative, opening new roads in the midst of crises, inviting formal language A revelatory new experience	The new orientation longs for realization and institutionalization In the course of its realization, the new language becomes more informal The re-creation of society, a redemptive solution

Intercultural Dialogue

What I have presented here is actually a theory of cultural development and of the transfer of culture. In the next chapter, we will look at the content of such historical achievements and at the qualities and institutions of different cultures. But first, I will pay attention to the meaning of all this for the intercultural dialogue within a globalizing society.

In the first place, it is important to be aware of the fact that no culture is static. This also counts for the achievements and qualities and so-called *values* of different cultures. Such qualities, institutions, or values always constitute the answer of this particular society to a particular crisis. It seems to be a plain fact that only in the face of death and destruction can human inspiration and responsibility really take off. Groundbreaking ways of dealing with things always take their starting point from a dead stop. When a culture becomes static, this means nothing other than the fact that this culture has arrived in phase four, the phase in which the achievements of a culture become institutionalized and materialized in the world outside. This is always a phase of fossilization. For that reason, it is also a phase of decadence: People try to get away with old societal codes in a situation that urges something new upon them.

In the second place, however self-evident it might sound, it is still important to realize that in questions of cultural development and renewal, time has priority over space. This means, among other things, that a new solution of the question of peace or a new social contract is not bound to a particular place. Spengler wanted to see it this way, and many history books still follow that method. Historians, for instance, still give a description of the landscape, first. They describe the soil on which it all takes place and then mention the tribes and peoples that have lived there in times long gone by. But this way of actually dealing with history causes to be brushed away the new insight or imperative that called this society into being. All nations originated only in a conflict with opposing forces, in conflict with old and obsolete forms of life. Further, a new invention is frequently successful only in a region in which it did not originate. This counts for both Christianity and Buddhism, just to name two examples.

Actually, the cultural and religious heritage that was created in a particular place always and soon travels around the world. Christianity actually is an Eastern religion, from Palestine. Islam even obtained a foothold in Indonesia. In imperial China, the heritage from Mesopotamia and Egypt lived even further. Western culture to a large extent has been transferred around the globe throughout the last hundred years. Let us assume that it is true that culture and religion can be defined as the totality of codes, values, achievements, and ways of behavior that made peace and justice possible. That is to say, it is true in an encompassing sense that culture and religion can be understood as "the ways of speech of the human race" (Rosenstock-Huessy). Then it is not surprising that people around the world have always been in search of and will always be in search of a better solution for the issues of peace and justice. That is not to say that there is only one good solution for this question. If that were the case, then this would turn all of humanity into grey mice that adapt themselves to the treadmill of repetition. That would be suffocating. It is quite an evident insight that peace and justice cannot be a static result, and that people lose their inspiration if they do not live into the conviction that they are on their way to a still more encompassing order of peace and justice.

Peace and justice only exist and can only be realized in the ongoing process toward peace and justice. And always people, in light of the establishment of a new order of peace and justice, have drawn from many different sources and examples, jumping to whatever is helpful. One could argue that whatever inspired people in the past to create some form of peace and justice can serve as an example and a source of inspiration for a new and higher form of peace and justice. That is also the reason that history so often proceeds by reformations, renaissances, and restorations. This leads to a plurality of values that always requires the establishment of a new equilibrium and a fine tuning between the different and often contradicting contributions. Just when a group of people has discovered something new, it tends to be deaf and dumb to everything the others have to say. Many wars have been waged with a feeling of mission, because people wanted to bring to all the others, too, the solution or salvation they discovered. China tried to bring the blessings of the empire to all of Southeast Asia. Great Britain founded the Commonwealth with a feeling of mission, as if the kingdom of God had come down to earth. Napoleon marched on Moscow, with his army, to bring freedom and civil rights to all of Europe. For Lenin, the Russian Revolution was only the first step toward the world revolution.

This drive for fulfilling a mission raises the question of whether only war or economic power can decide the different priorities in values and achievements of different cultures. Can there also be a peaceful dialogue between such values and achievements? This question has become more urgent since every war on this planet drifts into civil war within the one emerging world society. The consequences in terms of refugees, damage, and costs are on the account of all world society. Throughout history, the waging of war was always about power, but not about naked power. On the contrary, it has always been power with some sort of investiture, promoting a particular set of values to deal with reality. Power is not just a materialistic concept. It is more or less itself an idea.

Power means that one can impose a lifestyle and value priorities and achievements on others. In other words, even power is not the final aim. The values that one tries to impose are the final aim. What happens if the violence of military technology of today makes it impossible to really wage war, and yet people cannot accept each other's lifestyles? What to do, then? Is the term *dialogue between values and priorities* not too sweet a concept in a situation in which such priorities and values severely collide with each other?

Rosenstock-Huessy considered this to be the real question urged upon us by the two world wars. The struggle about how values were to be prioritized had to be conducted in peace, but not without conflict, and not really nice and harmonious, either. It looks as if today a significant shift is taking place between war and dialogue. All around the world, the military gets more and more involved in "peacekeeping" assignments. These are aimed at keeping the colliding parties calm, interfering with restrained violence, and also using conflict management and persuasion as methods for restoring order. In turn, should not dialogue between different cultures then receive the character of confrontation? It is a fact that the representatives of different cultures do not consider each other's values only as interesting, but also as quite inconvenient. *Confrontation* might be the name for dialogue that struggles over value priorities. Such confrontations already take place in negotiations between employers and employees, in debates between the representatives of different cultural neighborhood organizations. Even marriages are frequently the place of permanent confrontations, something for which the Americans have found the beautiful term *argue*. The partners do seek peace, do love each other, and at least take responsibility for each other. But this involves a permanent struggle about the terms of the next peace treaty, the terms of the next labor contract, and the division of labor between husband and wife.

In such confrontations, the power of speech receives a new quality. And that is the reason Rosenstock-Huessy's teaching on language is so eminently important. To speak does not mean primarily to transfer information. It is not even primarily an intellectual exercise. To really speak is to give articulation to what moves us in our emotional lives, in our hearts, in the existential layer of fears and wishes and longing and love. The one who really speaks gives expression to this emotional life, and is frequently surprised about what she or he has said, while being perfectly sure that he or she is fully standing behind the words spoken. Such words can come from the depth of the soul. To speak is to appeal. To speak is to experience an appeal by the word that goes between two people, and if the other too expresses his or her emotional life, both are changed. To speak, to use an expression from Levinas, is a manifestation of "the other in me." The voice of the other echoes in me, and a word really listened to influences a person's emotional life—that is, the place where our value orientations live. People who are indifferent to each other cannot listen to each other. Not to be indifferent means to be open to change.

Speech that goes from heart to heart makes people turn toward one another, even (or especially) people who were on the verge of entering into a conflict. Only on the brink of a crisis and disaster do people speak with full power. Or they fail to speak, and disaster follows. It is actually impossible to mechanically extort such a form of speech. The Spirit blows where it wants. One can create opportunities for such forms of speech and occasions, situations of trial and error; but nobody is in control of the situation if speech sets people on fire. And nobody is in control of the situation if a spark of understanding jumps from the one person to the other. At such moments, not only do people turn themselves toward one another and co-exist, value priorities open themselves up to each other, can look each other in the face, and get along. This power of speech frequently creates a new peace, on new terms, however temporary it might be.

Intercultural dialogue cannot operate without change. It also cannot do without love, a hospitality that is open to change. Four rules are indispensable for intercultural dialogue:

1. The end of the communication actually is the beginning of communication. If people and representatives of different cultures do not understand each other anymore in their usual forms and self-evident codes of communication, then that does not mean the end. It is instead the starting point of more serious communication. They have to talk to each other more intensely than ever before.

2. If intercultural communication is to succeed, every participant in this communication should be loosened somewhat from his or her background. The form that my life has taken until now might not be the final and definitive one. The repertoire of human behavior and interaction that I know and am used to is not necessarily the end of all truth.

3. If representatives from different cultures try to establish cooperation, the codes of communication between them should become an object of communication. These codes of behavior need to be established and agreed upon over and over again. What are our ways of dealing with each other? How do we handle particular situations leading to particular misunderstandings?

4. Intercultural communication takes a special effort. It is not automatic. It always takes us beyond ourselves and it costs something.

Only in this way can different cultures open themselves up to each other's heritage. In addition, the word *heritage* in this context might remind us that cultures are not bound to a specific locality. People have changed constantly all over the world and acquired from other peoples whatever they could use for constituting peace, righteousness, and survival. That makes all talk about the supposed superiority of western culture obsolete. It also makes obsolete the emphasis on indigenous development. Even if western culture represents the latest development in the emergence of new values (see chapter 7), this is not a spatial phenomenon, as if western culture has a patent on particular human qualities. Intercultural communication in a way is also communication among different layers of culture and human qualities, derived from the different geological layers of human history. Different times have to open up to each other. For that reason, this chapter has been about time.

The French social theorist Jean-François Lyotard gave us the expression of the *Great Story*, now long gone, in which people participated in their traditional communities. Nowadays, however, everyone lives on his own with fragments of this *Great Story*, via disconnected "discourses," contradictory in themselves, confused. We no longer fully stand behind our convictions, and we have detached ourselves from our backgrounds. In part, such a process is a condition for intercultural dialogue. People who are convinced too much of their own partial truths cannot listen. But it might turn out that this situation does not constitute the end of the *Great Story*, but only the beginning. For the first time in history, all of humanity lives together within one horizon. Until now, only small stories were told further—that is, the stories about the different cultures and traditions that inhabit the world. The *Great Story* begins only now and consists of what these partial traditions have to say to each other. They have to say something to each other, just as men and women have to say something to each other—not because they are the same, but because they are different. They complement each other; they correct each other. And *peace* means the state of having found the exact rhythm and alternation for their divergent contributions, a matter of time and circumstances. *To speak* also means this: To express oneself in different keys, depending on time and circumstances. The same person who needs to take the lead in an authoritarian way at one moment, and has to summon the courage to say what is necessary to say, in the next moment must be open to criticism. The person must be able to listen, and be vulnerable to change. In this way the separate cultures can also handle the plurality of values and codes of conduct within their spheres. Sometimes one must be loyal; at other times, one must be able to criticize, and so on. Timing is everything.

6

Fundamental Experiences, Human Qualities, and Cultures

Introduction

The repetitive fourfold rhythm of time, the fourfold rhythm of communication, and the fourfold rhythm of the different types of responsibility all originate from four fundamental human experiences. The forms of grammar are the expression of those four fundamental experiences.

These four fundamental experiences explain the development of the diversity of cultures and civilizations, just as these fundamental experiences in turn are developed further by those different cultures and civilizations. These four fundamental experiences are the innate possibilities of every human being. At the same time, however, they are unimaginable without the cultures that adopted them and articulated them more precisely by cultivating them. For that reason, it is impossible to discover these human capabilities without following the concrete development of the different cultures in which they are articulated.[1] Therefore, it is impossible to derive these fundamental human possibilities in the abstract from logical and universal principles, and to consider the historical developments as accidental articulations. The historical articulation of a human quality also constitutes the creation or development of such a human quality.

---

1. The concrete expression under which a particular human capacity develops constitutes and defines that capacity. This means it is unthinkable for the special human capacity to develop without the concrete events or narratives in which it is produced. Further, that capacity cannot be accessed by anyone without those events and narratives. See Levinas, *Totalité et Infini*, 148.

This fact has far-reaching implications for all attempts to provide a theoretical foundation for ethics and religion, and for the discoveries of the so-called sciences. I will come back to these implications.

After describing those four fundamental possibilities, I will also pay attention to the cultural traditions in which they are unfolded. And then it will appear that I have already extracted or abstracted the fundamental possibilities from the cultural developments that articulated them. Although these fundamental possibilities are open to every culture and every human being, different cultures have specialized in particular, fundamental possibilities to such an extent that it takes a special effort to recognize our own (form of these) fundamental possibilities from the way other cultures have articulated them. In this respect, we can compare the relationship between cultures to the relationship between an amateur and a specialist. One culture attends to a particular, fundamental possibility in an amateurish way, whereas another culture might fully specialize in it. Of course, there is no room to go into detail with respect to all those different cultures. To understand them fully, we would need to speak more languages. The language in which a culture expresses itself is a world of its own. It is difficult to find the entrance to a culture if one does not speak the language.

If we follow this trail, we find a sort of genealogy of human qualities linked to a genealogy of human cultures, a human pedigree. This is not a pedigree of the biological sort, but a pedigree of the learning process and of the spiritual growth of the human race. At the end of the chapter, I will relate this historical and longitudinal narrative to current sociological research in cultural differences, especially that of the Dutch social psychologist Geert Hofstede (at the end of this chapter) and the organizational theorist Fons Trompenaars (at the end of the next chapter). Using sociological reviews and statistics, they have conducted research into cultural differences all over the world, and developed universal (at least, as they pretend) "cultural dimensions." This research has made it possible to find out how different cultures score on particular qualities, lending themselves then to comparison. The result of such research is a cross-section of present-day cultures, which I would like to complement here with a longitudinal historical perspective. And of course, both in respect to this longitudinal historical perspective and the sociological cross-section, a lot of research still needs to be done.

Four Fundamental Experiences and Aggregate States

The imperative, the subjunctive, the pluperfect tense, and the indicative mood are more than accidental forms of grammar. They also constitute the declension or modulation of our existence. They put us in a different aggregate state, as I argued before. They put us respectively in the mode of *you!, I, we,* and *it*.[2] These four types of experience constitute the basic material from which the whole complex reality of sense and meaning is built up. Just as the partitions in 12 different pitches lies at the base of all variation in Western musical possibilities, these four fundamental keys of our existence combine in every possible way. They unfold the richness of our lives. They constitute the four voices or four angles in which our experience is pronounced. The specter of these four colors anchors us in reality. Anything that cannot appear in these four light refractions of language cannot yet be articulated. It is still unreal, not fully known.

The "it" experience: Anybody, any human being, is also a body among bodies, a thing among things. A bullet that enters our body, or a sword, causes damage. The body is at the mercy of the elements. In this sense the "it" is a form of our existence in the third person. In the third person, we speak about human beings and things, as if they cannot speak to us. They are not present as interlocutors. Sentenced in absentia, they passively undergo what happens to them like objects in the world outside. In the same way I can consider myself as an object. But in this consideration, something has already entered from a different key, since by considering myself, I am acting as a subject that looks upon an object. The mechanical existence, however, of movement and labor—that is, the effort to escape the grip of the elements and find food and shelter, is a type of existence that first grapples with things, before thinking about them.[3] This is very similar to a football player who, in the heat of a football game, reacts in a flash to keep the ball away from the goal. He doesn't reflect about it. In itself, labor and movement have this pre-reflexive character. We can get caught. Or we can pick things, ourselves. That is going quite fast. No reflection can come in between. In my primary vital force, I am in search of protection against the wildness of nature or against the grip of the enemy. In this feeling of taking or getting caught, with a primitive fear and vital force, the most elementary "it" experience can be expressed. In any form of organized labor—in shift labor, for example—more reflection has already come in between. In that case, labor has become conceptualized. For example, workers must work for eight hours with a given number of people in order to achieve a specific level of production. Agreements have been made about that (a matter

---

2. Martin Buber became famous with his book, *Ich und Du* [I and Thou], but he gives us access to only two of the four possibilities mentioned here. He distinguished the relationship toward things from the relationships toward human beings, approached as "Thou."

3. Levinas, *Totalité et Infini,* 142.

of the subjunctive), and such agreements have a tradition (a matter of the pluperfect tense). And that means that the other poles of the cross of reality already have made their impact felt on the "it" pole. Yet, even on this level something of this pre-reflexive "it" experience is kept alive, the experience of laborious struggle for existence, labor grappling with things, body against the body. A stucco worker, for example, uses knowledge and experience to smoothly spread plaster on the wall with mortar that is prepared according to exact rules. But let us say that an unexpected situation arises; the plaster does not stick to the wall, or it glides off the trowel too quickly. Suddenly, this pre-reflexive grappling with things emerges once again. All handling of matter, even the writing of a text, contains the mark of such laborious plodding. A word pops up—you write it down; you think it over; you might reject it. You grapple in search of a better word.

The "you" experience: Clearly the "you" experience is completely on the other side of the spectrum of fundamental experiences. Yet the "you" experience has in common with the "it" experience that it is a pre-reflexive event. Something happens to you of which you cannot have full consciousness. It is as if you are not completely present. *Poor me* is what the English say to point to an overwhelming experience they passively undergo, and *me voici* is what the French say in response to being called upon. This can be an unanswerable crisis or surprise, or a new challenge that asks the utmost and can cost everything. The *me* in both expressions shows the overwhelming character of the event—as if I have become an object of it. A person who loses a loved one feels both disoriented and challenged. This is the case too with a person who feels lost in a foreign country, or who has lost a job and is down in the dumps. It is a situation that asks for initiative, but at the same time the situation takes away any chances for initiative. In a disaster, but also in a declaration of love, it seems as if you were not fully present. The appeal that comes from it is bigger than our capacity to answer it. I feel mobilized and paralyzed at the same time. A person is conscious of more than consciousness is capable of. Difficult initiation rituals, in which the participants run the risk of death, also have this overwhelming character. By means of such rituals, one's identity was forever etched into the identity of the tribe. Tattoos can serve the same purpose. By such rituals, one's life receives a new destination, a new name, a new assignment. At first, people don't know what to do with it.

For many people, the outbreak of World War I—and later, World War II—meant that they found themselves in a profound crisis in which they knew only that nothing would be the same again. People could scarcely find the words for it. In such a situation, one feels appealed to and challenged to the innermost filaments of one's existence. But at the same time, the experience is unanswerable. A whole generation can be used up by such an event, and in that vein, many people after the Second World War were, for many years, silent about the atrocities. Many became speechless. A type of responsibility that is experienced as infinite is at the limit of terror.[4] A person can crumble under the weight of the new imperative. One is at the same time electrified and feels thrown off. One is inevitably called upon to do something, and at the same time one feels powerless relative to the weight of the imperative.

The "I" experience: In the "it" experience, we grapple with things so that we can grasp them and hold onto them. In the "you" experience, we are subjected to a power that electrifies us and which is beyond our grasp. Now, different from both of those experiences is the "I" experience, which denotes an exchange on the same level. The "I" actually should be thought of in the sense of the Latin *ego*. This long *o* in the Latin *ego* expresses the subjunctive, the feeling that we stretch ourselves beyond ourselves, as is beautifully expressed in the word *longing,* itself. As if we try to make ourselves longer. This long *o* finds expression in the search for agreement, for tuning in to my interlocutor. We seek each other, court each other, mutually influence each other, and propose.[5] In this mutual tuning, the language is sung and becomes lyrical, in the hope that the other will sing together with us. Every proposal we make to each other has something of a marriage proposal. A proposal, even if it is only a proposal to take on a particular viewpoint, is an invitation for approval, a begging for commitment, a question to stay tuned. In doing such proposals, a person is fully conscious of himself.

Saying *I* in a certain sense means saying, *But I*. That is to say, a person no longer merely participates in the group, but distinguishes himself from the others by saying *I*. Doing that requires a decision, a choice. The person takes the initiative: I! In this sense saying *I* is an act of becoming independent. I am on my own feet. As actor and taker of some initiative, sooner or later I will also become an actor in the world outside and manage things or people my way—as if such people can be handled as things, too. But if that happens the "it" experience is already making itself felt in

---

4. *Il y a* [there is] is the expression by which Levinas names the situation in which existence is experienced as a series of anonymous events. These can be events without a face and a name, raining down upon you, depressing you, and even being terrifying. But at the same time, Levinas says: "The *there is*—that is the weight by which the otherness presses on my subjectivity, which cannot support it." *Autrement quêtre*, 209.

5. In Anglo-Saxon philosophy, much emphasis is put on clear propositions. But at the same time, propositions are not only reasons. The very infinitive, *to propose*, also means to ask for marriage. In any proposal, I also propose—that is, I invite the other person to marry our insights to each other. We "suggest" proposals to each other, which literally means *bear together*, as if we are expecting a child.

the "I" experience. From the moment the "it" experience makes its influence felt in the "I" experience, we begin to objectify something. The actor indicates and states matters of fact much more than expressing a longing, proposing and asking for an answer. It is much safer to exchange thoughts about the world outside than to exchange feelings inside. In the original *ego*, however, we are not in search of a world outside, but of a partner with whom we share the room inside, share the same longing and desire, with whom we create community, find an open ear, tune in to each other in this exchange of expression and answer. Such openness inevitably also implies an exposure to the other. Saying *I* in that sense means giving of oneself. I bend toward the other, just the way love makes me. Love, if it is not a static concept, is this original event of openness and exposure to the other. We become "conversed," turned around, turned toward the other by love. We become declined. The *o* of *ego* expresses this mood—that is, this declension. In such exposure, we can easily receive "no" for an answer. Our inclination can be declined. That is part of the exposure. The mode of such exposure and determination and inclination and longing is the "I" experience.

The "we" experience: Whereas the "I" is conscious and alert, the "we" experience sinks away in routine, habituation, and comfort. What "we" do is a matter of course, something in which the individual does not have the initiative anymore, does not need to be fully conscious, but keeps the course, in agreement with the prevailing group codes. The "we" experience is one of belonging to the group and having reached agreement to such an extent that the "I" gets absorbed by the group. Unconsciously, or perhaps only half-consciously, one participates in whatever the group does. Not fully unconscious, not totally pre-reflexive, such as in labor or in grappling with things. This is the case because one is conscious of the jargon or the prevailing discourse that goes around in the group. By speaking the current language, one pays in the currency of the group. We adapt. Actually, we are members of a whole lot of groups. Apparently without any effort, we adapt to quite different discourses of all those different groups. This adaptation to the "we" of the group is the currency by which we pay our membership. We pay the price for our belonging—that is, to adapt to and adopt the prevailing symbols and ideas. What is not proper cannot become property of the group. It is not suitable and should remain outside. We leave part of us behind in each membership. That is the price we pay. To pose questions to somebody with whom we speak is implicitly already asking for belonging. If the current language as a shared identity also echoes in me, I inform others after the prevailing discourse, and I can join the conversation. That then is the language I listen to and am obedient to. By this shared horizon, I enter a shared membership. If the "I" experience is still an experience of exposure, the "we" experience is primarily an experience of going and letting go, of joyful participating in the group, of hiding behind something and feeling secure, thanks to a shared identity and investiture. I am part of something bigger. I go with the flow of the self-evident stream of language, safe and satisfied. I am not in search of mutual tuning, but I am already tuned. We can enjoy the ideas to which we are attached, just as well and just as materialistically as we can enjoy our meals. In the native soil where we come from, even the world outside bears the mark of this common group atmosphere of belonging. We feel at home over there, and remember the atmosphere of the group merely by returning to our roots. Participating in such a "we" experience implies a shared tradition and history. The grammatical form of the pluperfect expresses this by repetition (in many languages) or by extension: *had walked, had lived*, and so on. The language itself expresses this flow, this being in one's element. This is no surprise since language is nothing else but the conscious articulation of experience and makes the experience explicit and accessible by naming it.

The Magic of Language

Many historians try to treat history as a (positive) science. Adverse to speculation, they want to know the facts that can underpin bigger statements. But as a matter of fact, the question: *Which facts are the important ones?* is difficult to decide. Which facts are decisive? The storming of the Bastille—an example I mentioned earlier—is regularly taken as the starting point of the French Revolution. The people of that time experienced it like that. But after the storming of the Bastille, it remained quiet during an entire summer—a summer that is called the *grande peur* [the great fear], because people anxiously sensed the impending future. Can people feel that? In any case, the storming of the Bastille was decisive, not because it was in itself a big thing, but because it was a big statement. It caused inevitable, further steps to be taken, and that made it a turning point. That tells us something about the definition of what might count as a real event. An event has taken place if a lasting change in experience and perception of reality has occurred. In other words, where a different language starts being spoken—a different "discourse" as it is called today—there something has happened. For Goethe, the cannonade of the Battle of Valmy was such a turning point. At Valmy, the French army consisted primarily of volunteers and defended itself against the Prussian artillery. Although on the Prussian side 400 victims fell, compared to 600 on the French side, nevertheless the moral victory was to the French, because the Prussians were actually supposed to win. The

French, however, had re-grouped several times over. They kept firing while passionately singing the *Marseillaise*. In other words, here Goethe became conscious of the revolutionary élan of the French. Again, the event was a statement. The mere facts of such an event can be summed up by the historian in endless detail, while simultaneously missing the meaning of it. The meaning of the event consists of the new perception, the new language, the new imperative that causes a lasting change.

Even if we cannot trace the exact historical backgrounds of the creation of language, it still bears the lasting marks of such changes. For example, let us consider the terms or names *father, mother, son,* and *daughter*. Even now, such names still have a kind of magic power that unconsciously affects everybody who speaks these words—or better, names. Thanks to such names, an ordered family life becomes possible in which the family members are safe for each other. Such family names are mostly words in the comparative, like *bigger* and *deeper*, and so on. They express respect for the other (*other* is also a word in the comparative). They express distance. For that reason, they are not self-evident, since we can assume that an ordered family life would not be possible if the men especially were not to maintain a strict discipline among themselves. A man needs to say *no* to his direct desires, so as not to violate his beautiful daughters. It is not by accident that the incest taboo in the original tribes is maintained by means of the most severe sanctions. This "no" against erotic desire is wrapped up in the name *daughter*. You don't do that to your "daughter." In a sense, a father is a converted man, just as love and responsibility are converted desire. Halfway in the embrace toward the other, in which lust has already announced itself, desire turns around and changes into responsibility and love.

This original event, as it is wrapped up in the names *father, mother, son,* and *daughter,* is not merely an event that took place at one special moment in time. It is something that happens over and over again. As soon as these names are spoken, these relationships are re-established. Love is not a static concept, a feeling, or a value that has an "ontological" character of its own (of which one could try to establish the static "essence"). But it is the unfolding of love; or in other words, it is a process: (1) desire for the full embrace; (2) being frightened of one's own possible violence, or being frightened of possible long-term change; (3) stepping back, letting go—respect expressed by touch. Language is not only the articulation of this original event, but also the magical formula through which the event re-installs itself. Now that we have given it a name, we can more easily call upon it.

From this background, it becomes possible to understand the structure of the sociological work of Rosenstock-Huessy, his three-part *Soziologie*.[6] In this work he does not give more empirical underpinnings or historical data than are absolutely necessary to understand the new language, the new way of speech that enters history in a particular phase. For that reason, he first pays attention to the original historical event. When did the change in speech occur for the first time? Second, he pays attention to the lasting change of perception, thinking, and feeling, which is brought about by one's own experience of a culture. We already experience reality and our social relationships within it in a particular way, thanks to the language we use. Finally, he pays attention to the institutions—that is to say, the objective structures and arrangements of society that underpin and support this way of life. *Soziologie* has this threefold structure: event—self-experience—institution.

The self-experience is nothing other than the replication and repetition of the original event. The institutions are the ultimate structures and forms that support this experience. Here we have an example of the methodical reversal to which I pointed earlier. The relationship between father and daughter, and between mother and son has been changed by the original event. Somebody must have taken the creative step toward this new level of peace within the social group, and must have experienced it as an important, new imperative. Such an event does not constitute an accidental historic and empirical step toward an already existing general concept of fatherhood and motherhood, which would then constitute a type of ontological values independent of this event. In the original event, the original discovery of being a father or mother is not only discovered, but also *created*. And storing this experience in language by using those names makes it transferable through the generations.[7] The "abstract values" of fatherhood and motherhood are nothing other than the repetition of this concrete original event in the experience of the current generation. The concept of fatherhood or motherhood is not something abstract, stored up somewhere in the essence

---

6. Rosenstock-Huessy, *Soziologie I und II*. This two-volume work contains three parts, and is the source of the descriptions of the primary forms of language in this book and of the social forms corresponding to them, which are the articulations and concretizations of them. It is also the source for the subsequent examinations of language, here.

7. In the Book of Deuteronomy (literally meaning *the second version of the law*), the Ten Commandments are introduced by a long, fictitious speech of Moses to a later generation. In this speech, it is stated expressly that the Commandments from Mount Sinai are not so much meant for the generations before us, but made as a covenant "with us, with all of us who are alive here today" (Deuteronomy 5:3). The later generation is spoken to as if they were part of the event. The original *event* is repeated in their *living experience*.

of things so that the really living historical fathers and mothers become species of the general concept. It is completely the other way around.

The concrete experiences in which the names *Father* and *Mother* appear are constitutive for the general concept of this fundamental, creative possibility, and the general concept never becomes more than an abstraction from the concrete experience that tells its story. The general concept is an abbreviation of this story. And the story does not exemplify the general concept. Names acquire their impact when the history of those names is told. Their essence lies in that history.

This methodical principle is of eminent importance for a correct understanding of the language philosophy of Rosenstock-Huessy. In philosophy, it is still the case that moral values and norms are founded either in an ontology or in metaphysics in which these norms and values are supposed to be given within the universal horizon of being human. Or they can be traced back to an existential phenomenology, which does not take into consideration the concrete historical background of such phenomenological experiences. Actually, the historical background—just like the concrete events and narrations that are the starting point for the development of human capacity—is the starting point from which philosophical values and norms are founded.

Events in which new names and imperatives have been articulated are transferred via language as concrete names to the next generation, and such names provide us with a normative orientation. The history that tells the story of the contexts, in which these values come into existence—these names!—must be told in its concrete ramifications so that we can fully understand their values and realize them, and can renew them in our own existence. The concept of freedom, for instance, is incomprehensible without telling the story of the moral and material struggle for freedom. The value of critical observation and analysis (and expression), critically asking questions beyond what is apparent, cannot be fully understood without telling the story of Socrates. He, after all, had to drink the poison hemlock for insisting on posing the "questions beyond."

What Christianity means by *love* is incomprehensible without the concrete history of the Sermon on the Mount and the crucifixion of Jesus. The current attention to narration in theology and philosophy confirms this view. Rosenstock-Huessy's language philosophy had introduced this necessity before World War I.

Four Streams of Culture

Tribes

The history of religion and culture has developed the innate capacities of human beings to such an extent that it is difficult to distinguish what is still innate—and therefore "natural"—and what is developed by "nurture." "Being human" is actually what this history of religion and culture made of us all, until now. Individual people have "shares" in being full human beings. From the totality of human possibilities, different cultures adopted a particular specialization. In our time of globalization, the different ramifications of this history converge and the heritage of "being human" becomes our common stock. Although in all human cultures, all fundamental human possibilities are present, certain specific cultures or layers of culture developed specific human qualities more so than others. In a small, schematic way, I will put forward four streams of culture, each of which emphatically specialized in specific human possibilities. For convenience, I will discuss them in chronological order.

The tribes explored and developed the "we" experience. Nowhere is the order of society, of belonging and social control, as strict as in the tribe. The tribe obeys the commandments of the ancestors, the voice of tradition, and the fixed codes of behavior and customs of the group. The "we" feeling of the tribes has been so strong that no single tribe could consider another one as human—or, as we might express it today in humanistic terms, as members of the "moral community." The respect for tradition within this form of life was so strong that the new generation was incorporated into the tribe by harsh initiation rites. The sacrifice of the firstborn child, an old custom within many tribes, makes it unambiguously clear to the next generation who is in charge, and whom they are expected to obey. In nineteenth century Africa, one ritual was observed in which two tribes that had members related by marriage exchanges would enter into combat with each other at such an initiation rite. The young men of each tribe were sent into the jungle to fight the young men of the other tribe. The struggle went on until one of the young men died. At that moment, the struggle stopped immediately and the initiation rite was over. The boys were now considered to be mature men. Every one of them had faced death, because nobody could know in advance who would be the first victim. In this way the traditions of the tribe were confirmed once more.

The same thing happens in the fearful masks by which deceased ancestors were represented and by means of which the medicine man or shaman spoke in their names. The names of the ancestors probably are the oldest layer of language. They have sounded as imperatives for those currently alive, and have represented—literally, *made present*—the spirits of the ancestors. The eye of the ancestors and the social control of the other families have strictly kept the incest taboo, for example. The broader societal order was necessary to maintain this taboo so that probably the larger tribal order, the living together in families, and the incest taboo originated at the same time. In this way, they can speak a new language by which every individual is incorporated into the group, and by which the group can take guard over ordered family life. This shared language was essentially written on the bodies of the members by the tattoos, which were different from tribe to tribe. What you belonged to was written on your body.

Each new achievement also implies a one-sidedness. The language of belonging and shared obedience was so powerful that both contact with other tribes and with the open future could be avoided. There was one thing the tribe did not want: to change. If change was necessary, then the ancestors needed to be appeased by sacrifices. Despite, or exactly because of, the changes, the living needed to show their lasting loyalty to the ancestors by such sacrifices. Change was inevitable, because the future imposes itself, whether you like it or not. And because the tribes were not sedentary, they often encountered unexpected situations.

Even tribal life should not be thought of as static. We have a better picture of tribal history if we assume that conflicts were so omnipresent that tribes fell apart, or that anarchy broke out. The members who were ostracized from the tribe were considered as man-wolves, and many of them started a new tribe, with new rules that, from that moment on, were kept as strictly as the former ones. Tribes also formed coalitions among themselves. Time and again, new group codes were tried out. Need bends law. However, despite the fact that tribal history was full of crisis, the ideal still was continuity and tradition. After a crisis, the rules of the ancestors were maintained once more, and even if these rules might have changed, the memory of such change would have been obliterated. They were considered to have existed forever. After all, memory of actual experience did not typically go back further than three generations. To the tribe, we still owe our names and family life; and everything that turns into a lasting tradition sooner or later revives the old heritage of the tribes.

Empires

Empires developed the "it" experience. For the most part, imperial cultures are not sharply distinguished by historians and anthropologists or sociologists from tribal cultures, and indeed there are all kinds of intermediate stages and compromises. But the oldest empires, when the need for explicit opposition against tribal life was probably the strongest, emphatically distinguished themselves from the tribe. Unlike tribes, empires are anchored in a particular territory or domain. The word *domain* etymologically is derived from *to dominate*. An empire like Egypt or Babylon was hierarchically organized with a son of the gods, the emperor, at the top. The most well-articulated example of such an imperial culture is probably ancient Egypt. It was not the common past that served as the primary orientation point, but space, the cosmos, the domain with the stars above it. Consider, for example, the discovery that the Nile started to rise in July when only the star Sirius in the Orion constellation remained above the horizon, while the rest of Orion disappeared beneath the horizon. With this observation and the knowledge of its consequences, Egyptians could introduce an agricultural calendar based on what was "to be read in the stars." This made it possible to control such a territory from one center, and turn it into a "domain." Pharaoh, as the son of the gods, was simultaneously the head of this central hierarchy and considered one of the divine powers among the stars.

He and his followers would go down the Nile—at first, annually, and later, biennially—to demonstrate this apparatus of central power with new authority and legitimacy. A separation between Church and State, as we know it, had not yet been invented, of course. Pharaoh was the boss. Our word *boss* still has this connotation of a strong power that is simultaneously sanction power and legitimate power, and for which one needs to bow—as a self-evident matter of fact. It is a religious word in the sense in which the Egyptian hierarchy was religious in character. *Hierarchy* literally means "holy order." That is exactly what it was. For three months, the population worked on the Pharaoah's construction projects, as long as the flood lasted. After that, the population would work for nine months on the land, which was divided into small parts with the help of an early form of the Pythagorean formula. Big construction projects like temples and pyramids represented the overwhelming cosmic order in which the people worked and functioned like labor forces. Processions symbolized the slow but steady rhythm of the stars, which people tried to become part of. In the pyramids, the zodiacal light visible at night in a triangle in the Southern Hemisphere was brought down to Earth—first in the form of a stair-stepped pyramid, and later perfected with smooth sides, once they technically understood how to do that.

In this way, Pharaoh appeared as the one who controlled the cosmos: He made the zodiacal triangle that was visible only at night appear also in daylight on the horizon. In stylized form—in function—the bodies of the people were depicted on the temples. The higher up in the hierarchy they were, the bigger their representations in stone or drawings. This hierarchy made a stratified civil service and division of labor not only necessary, but also possible. As in a big factory, everybody was required to fulfill his labor in rank and file, and work and behave as a function of the cosmos. The advantageous result of this mega-machine was enormous agricultural production. The lasting disadvantage was what we would now call the *proletarization of labor*. Proletarization not only in the sense of poverty and exploitation, but also in the sense of loss of tradition and shortsightedness in time. People who move and function only according to the rhythm of their daily labor are robbed of the other qualities of their humanity.

The influence of the Egyptian Empire stretched into Babylon and Mesopotamia, and even to India and China. Pyramids and hieroglyphs have been found even in South America. India and China developed the heritage of Egypt and Babylon in two different directions. What they had in common is the centralization of power in kings and emperors, in a hierarchical form of government. This too was religious in character in the sense in which Egypt was religious. They also had in common a government structure that followed the rhythm of the seasons, with the help of an agricultural calendar, and attention to the movement of the cosmos. In China the emperor would live each season in a different part of his palace to make it clear who actually governed the cosmos. The different developments in China and India are nicely illustrated in the architecture of the Chinese and Indian temples. An Indian temple grows up in stages from the soil, with a new bulge above the former one. The movement is from the bottom, upward. A Chinese temple, on the contrary, descends from heaven; for each stage, there is a new roof beneath the former one. The movement is from the top, downward.

The Indian society consisted of many castes that competed with one another, and kingdoms in competition with each other; and there was struggle and competition between the different gods, as well. The three main gods of the Indian pantheon—Brahma (the creator), Vishnu (the maintainer), and Shiva (the destroyer)—indicate the rhythm of rising, shining, and sinking of all the life powers of nature. In this direct naturalism there is collegiality with Greece and even with Greek art. The different castes constitute a compromise between living in tribes and the ranks and stratifications of the empire. Families and clans are also castes—that is, each a professional group. They live in their own world. Bigger units of empires in India were always threatened with falling apart for that reason. Buddhism is a corrective reaction to this continuous struggle, in which only objective force is what counts. Buddhism strives toward emptiness from this vital urge. It looks upon this struggle and mutual competition as a world of illusion that we need to get rid of in order to reach the nirvana state of complete peace. As such, it is an antidote for too much competition and struggle. Nirvana made it possible to create occasional stronger forms of solidarity by teaching people to rise above their direct self-interests.

In China, the opposite road was taken. The Zhang dynasty (from 1200 BC (?) onward—the dates are not very accurate in Chinese history) appealed to a heavenly justice (Tian) that was meant to overcome earthly chaos. Through it, a balance could be achieved and maintained by mutual adaptation and tuning of the central power and the nobility. The centralization of power from the Han era and beyond (± 400 BC) substituted the power of the nobility by a civil service to which clan loyalties, in principle, did not provide the entrance, but a system of education and examinations did. The emperor needed this civil service to keep hierarchical control over the whole empire; the teachings of Confucius were one of the main ingredients in the education of that civil service. According to Confucius, the rhythm of movement of the cosmos and a virtuous life—honoring the ancestors, showing respect for authorities, and being tactical in one's work—come down to the same thing. The harmony of the social cosmos is both reflected and part of the physical cosmos. Therefore, there is essentially no confrontation. Instead of engaging in a confrontation, one prefers to give a hint. One does not openly criticize, but prefers correction through silence. The lower authorities were not allowed to speak up against the emperor. But often when the answer was "yes," their action was a "no." Of course, if they could, they created their own version of the truth or of the order they received from the emperor. And then it was up to the emperor to adapt to this new version of his orders, or to correct his subordinates more violently. Of course, the former action was often preferred, but new orders could try to re-acquire the initiative and prevent some negative effects. A continuous play of cat-and-mouse could be the result, constantly framing the adaptation in such a way as to take over the initiative by this adaptation itself. Yin and Yang, the alternation between initiative and its petrification, and taking over the initiative, beautifully symbolizes this peculiarity of Chinese (and not only Chinese) management strategies. On the surface, there is harmony and nothing changes. Beneath the surface, constant change is taking place. The person who became the object of the action of the other uses this state as a starting point for taking initiative and turn the scales. A nice example of this, and still in place today, is the practice of Chinese companies to wait on paying the bill from another company until a new order has come in. Being the object of someone's action—that is, the company waiting for the bill to be paid, is silently turned into a way to take over the initiative; in this case, soliciting new orders.

Taoism can be understood as a reaction to this continuous adaptation, fine-tuning, and smiling, and adapting, and maintaining this artful equilibrium. It continuously anticipates the actions of others and goes along with them, and in the process, tries to steer them to one's own advantage. In all adaptation and movement, which can be required by external forces, an inner openness and rest are necessary. It is a state in which there is no stress and in which we keep ourselves out of this game, according to Taoism. If Confucianism already constitutes a kind of moderation and ramping-down of the self, because it is constantly seeking mutual adaptation, the lucid openness of Taoism introduces a moderation to the second degree: ramping down the stress of mutual adaptation itself, even smiling at the habit of constantly smiling. *Wu wei,* the principle of doing nothing (even while being in action), precisely indicates this inner freedom from keeping up the appearance of harmony and adapting to stressful situations. Or in different terms: Moderation of the stubborn and proud self in the Confucian style actually creates a detour by giving in to others in order to reach one's own goals. In the process, the person doing that anticipates that the others will adopt the same strategy. The result is harmony on the surface, but continuous stress and unrest and anxiety underneath. This happens because behind every action there might be a dual intention. The moderation of the self, introduced by Confucianism, functions at the price of stress. To ramp down such moderation to a second degree, making oneself unimportant and not caring about respect, means a liberation from the continuous process of anticipation and giving in to others. In one's inner center, one remains free from giving in, free from stress, free from the cycle of the initiative turning into petrification, and petrification turning into initiative. Not needing to do something and to be quiet in one's inner center—despite all outward movement—gives one the freedom to look beyond the need for direct recognition and mutual adaptation, which in China threatens to suffocate social life.

Israel

Nowhere is there a tradition that has articulated the "you!" experience to such a degree as has that of Israel. From the time of the Exodus onward, this people has given the priority to an unknown future above a known and reliable past, the "fleshpots" of Egypt. Of course, as long as there have been empires, there have been rebellions against unbearable injustice and poverty. But always in the end, it meant the installation of yet another dynasty. People have always tried to reform the political cosmic system of the empire, and put it in place again, installing a better version than what just had occurred. It has never happened that people broke away from this political cosmic system, as such. Without the figure of Moses and the law-giving event at Mount Sinai, the founding of the people of Israel would not have been anything more than a rebellion as well. But the law at Mount Sinai gave Israel a special and articulated constitution. The firmament is not the fundament of Israel, but the future is—that is to say, the commandment and the promise of a justice that is bigger and more encompassing than the cosmos is capable of providing. For that reason, the God of Israel could not be expressed in a visible form. For the same reason, he is also exclusive.

In antiquity, people knew that the different gods were actually aspects of one and the same cosmic reality in different manifestations. In that sense, the monotheism of Israel was not something new. But to allow only one exclusive manifestation of God—that is, the command for a future justice that tuned down all other authorities—was unheard of. The God of Israel cannot be honored in addition to, or in identification with, or as an aspect of the universe. He is as invisible as the future of the justice to which he appeals. The prophetic faith of Israel gives to the uncertain and unknown future the moral priority above the safety of an oppressive cosmic imperial order. Instead, Israel ventured into the unknown and unsure future, rather than bear the safe and reliable hard work in the cyclical present of the fleshpots of Egypt. That is why Israel broke away from both the faith in ancestors and the reliance on the imperial calendar of the stars. For 200 years, it succeeded in surviving as a loose association of tribes and by the charismatic leadership of "judges." After this revolutionary period, Israel too had to compromise with the institution of centralized kingship, and allow the building of a temple. But even when this happened, King Solomon, simultaneously at the inauguration of the temple, proclaims that God is too big to live in a temple. In addition, there was the institution of the prophets, who raised their voices generation after generation. The prophet, acting against the king from the beginning, repeatedly remembered the king of the promised future. The critical form of history writing in the Hebrew Bible is not so much *critical* in the sense of detailed research after the facts. Instead, the holiness of God criticizes human actions. This holiness—or in other words, the promised future of justice and peace—as a holy moral command, served as a critical gauge for denouncing the exploitative practices of the kings and their elites. The Hebrew Bible, the book that writes the "national" history of Israel, exposes it as a history of injustice, pride, and exploitation. Which people knows of such a national history, contained in a "holy" book? Even after the arrival of Christianity, the Jews once more took their position in the margin of history, pointing beyond the status quo toward a peace and justice that went beyond the Church and its mission among the heathen peoples.

Nobody can completely break away from the existing order and be completely exposed to the imperative of peace and justice. The imperative stands in critical opposition to the status quo, in which widow and orphan, the stranger, and the poor are oppressed. The concession of Israel toward the status quo consisted of the fact that, at least on the surface, it had to fall back on a tribal constitution. Only in this way could Israel successfully live as a "future-oriented *we*." Only in this way could the orientation around a future of justice become a tradition itself. Now at least there was one people that cultivated the vision of the future of justice. By keeping the Torah in the margin of history, and disciplining itself in its inner life according to this imperative, a group of people could exist—for the first time—who could bear the exposure to the unknown future, and had the courage to do that. A future-directed *we*: a people. A people who are no longer dependent on priests, who do not relate the future to the spirits of the ancestors, who are not dependent on a pharaoh, and who do not relate the future to the cosmic order of the starry universe. They are a collection and a gathering of ordinary people, who together are oriented around the promise of justice. Private citizens without public office were the voices of this life experience; they were ordinary people. But still a people, organized in families and tribes. Only in this way, could faith in the future become a tradition itself.

The West

The West,[8] from the earliest church history until present day, articulated and developed the "I" experience through civil society. The Church—and later, the society of free citizens—made possible the free association of individuals. In this important value of the West, individual freedom is not the freedom of choice, but the freedom to associate always in new ways, without loyalties being dictated by the tribe, and without subjection to some hierarchy. In Western history, the free association of individuals has pushed back the power of the tribes and clans and the power of the state to such an extent that civil society has become an institution of its own, besides family ties,

---

8. To complete this thought, I should indicate how China and Greece articulated the "I" experience in a different way, as the inner pole of human existence. In mutual adaptation you and I both lose our contours. In this way China created an inner space of cooperation. The Greeks tried to create this inner space by a sympathetic contemplative attitude (*theoria*) of getting to know each other through theater and theory. In the Church, and later in parliaments, and later in society as such, this inner room is created by ongoing dialogue.

Church, and State. None of these old institutions can keep it under control anymore. But the modern society of free citizens could develop itself only in this direction as the successor to the Church, which blazed the trail toward it. There is one stream of tradition in institutions and the law. It comprises the earliest church congregations consisting of Jews and heathens; the monasterial orders, and later the papal party against the emperor in the Middle Ages; the cities, which often came into being as sworn communes of former serfs; the big church councils and synods; later, the parliaments, associations, and unions; and corporations and foundations. The revolutionary process, in which these freedoms have been conquered, step by step, is discussed in the next chapter. So I can be short at this point. The individualism of the West developed the "I" experience as a relation among equals who need mutual attuning to each other so that they can become partners over and over again. They also need to find a new form of agreement in competition, through opposition and cooperation. The consumer's freedom to choose whatever one likes, and the freedom to be left alone and seek one's own advantage, undoubtedly have been made possible by these achievements. But still they must be considered as secondary phenomena, as decadent appearances of the one important achievement: the free association of individuals in an orderly constitution. At the high points of history in creating all these liberties, the important thing was that every individual has a say in the public cause, and not that an individual can choose from twenty identical articles on the supermarket shelves.[9]

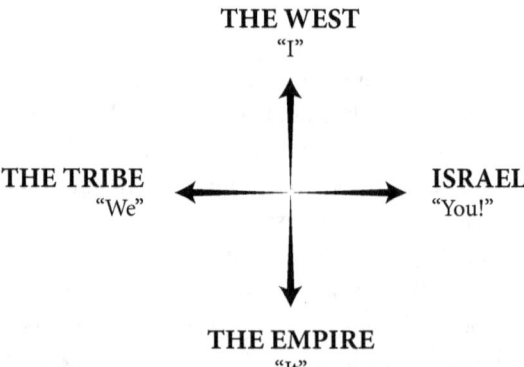

---

9. The one important correction to the one-sidedness of the Western development would be the Jewish tradition. It actually functioned like this, despite all the prosecutions. The achievements and steps forward of the West are inspired by the vision of the future and the prophetic criticism of Judaism. Against the secularization and decadence of the Western achievements, the prophetic criticism of Judaism is frequently the antidote. I return to that in the final chapter.

Relationship with Hofstede's Cultural Dimensions

Two Dutch sociologists have become famous for their research into the different dimensions and values of cultures. By analyzing statistics, based on information from questionnaires, they map out different cultures on many dimensions. They differ on the dimensions. Geert Hofstede has discovered four cultural dimensions, and Chinese scientists have added a fifth one to his work.[10] Fons Trompenaars distinguishes seven different cultural dimensions.[11] Because Trompenaars pays attention to several typically European cultural characteristics, we will comment on his work across these seven dimensions in the next chapter.

In this chapter, the work of Hofstede requires our attention, also because his four cultural dimensions show a relatedness and affinity with the four distinctions among cultures I have made here. And the extra cultural dimension the Chinese added also fits into the picture. We should be aware in advance that Hofstede's type of statistical research shows an appearance of objectivity, but that appearance does not match reality. The reasons are relatively simple. First, people who fill out questionnaires frequently do it in a hurry, and they know they do not have to provide accurate answers. Second and more important, many questions allow different interpretations, so that the aggregation of the results in general concepts and conclusions cannot avoid some subjectivity in interpretation. Further, the social value system of the researcher and his or her subjectivity can result in a certain degree of ambiguity in interpretation. As is so often the case, what one puts into the system is also what comes out of it. Inevitably the intuitions and spiritual baggage of the sociological researcher have a say in it. It never is quite clear whether their concepts and the distinctions are completely reflecting the statistical information. This is ideally, of course, their ambition, although I have said before that I do not go along with that type of presumably scientific objectivity. It is always an open question whether the statistical information and the categorization of the answers are actually adapted to the concepts and distinctions that the researcher already has in mind. Nevertheless, coincidence or not, the cultural distinctions made by Hofstede are very suitable for comparison to the four distinctions made here, in terms of primary human orientations to the past, the future, inside, and outside poles of reality.

Therefore, we can use the different dimensions on which Hofstede analyzes cultures as a first rough approximation of what is going on all over

---

10. Hofstede *Cultures and Organizations.*
11. Trompenaars and Hampden-Turner, *Riding the Waves.*

the world. Where I have until now presented a longitudinal analysis from the perspective of history, Hofstede and Trompenaars give a cross-section of the present. Here our focus is on Hofstede.

In the first place, there is the dimension of *power distance*. In one culture, it is easier for a subordinate to talk to the boss on an equal level than it is in another culture for a subordinate to talk to the boss as an equal. In one culture, the people dare to criticize their superiors more so than in another culture. All of this has to do with authority and the respect for authority, with status, and above all, with power. In short, a culture can be either more hierarchical, or more attuned to social equality.

Then second, there is the difference between *collectivism* and *individualism*. In a collectivist culture, people adapt to the group and the group has priority above the individual. Often—but not always—a collectivist culture is also a culture of shame. An individualistic culture is more inclined to be a culture of guilt. Shame and loss of face have to do with the relationship to the group in which people take part. A person can be ashamed if the group disapproves of his or her behavior. If someone feels guilty, an internal norm might be involved—for example, conscience, or something else like that. In an individualistic culture, people speak out more easily and more directly, and more often take responsibility for making their own choices.

Third, according to Hofstede, there is the difference between *feminine* and *masculine* cultures. The use of this terminology has been often criticized, but I am using it here only to try to bring some understanding to what he means. A feminine culture is a culture in which care is more important than competition, and in which the differences between masculine and feminine roles are less well defined. A culture is masculine in character if competition is important and if men prefer not to take part in roles and tasks typically carried out by women. A culture can be collectivist and still be either feminine or masculine. Japan is an example of a collectivist culture that is also strongly masculine. Achievement and competition are important. By comparison, China is more feminine, although China too is very collectivist. America, for example, is very individualistic, but also very competitive—and for that reason, masculine. A country like Sweden, by comparison, is at least as individualistic, but still more feminine.

In the fourth instance, Hofstede advances the dimension of *avoiding uncertainty*: the degree to which a society avoids uncertain situations and falls back on fixed procedures and rules and traditions. It also involves the degree to which a society is willing to take risks and to take itself out of its own comfort zone. In this respect, many misunderstandings can arise, because people in poor countries are forced to take risks that can be insured against in the rich countries. Therefore, one might conclude that rich countries are more likely to avoid uncertainty, but that is not what Hofstede means. China, for example, in Hofstede's research, stands out as an example of a country with high uncertainty avoidance. But that has much more to do with the question of the degree to which people dare to face unknown situations and to welcome change.

Chinese researchers added a fifth dimension to Hofstede's work. This is called the dimension of *long-term thinking,* or in other terms, *Eastern Confucianism,* a philosophy that emphasizes respect for tradition and authority, and at the same time respects a feeling for the contingencies of fate. While accepting such contingencies and going along with them as far as necessary, the Chinese still have an eye for the long-term goal. In that respect, tradition works as the orientation point in the midst of daily chaos. The way in which Hofstede introduces this fifth dimension in his book creates the impression that the Chinese researchers wanted not just to add this dimension to the other ones, but also to re-interpret the dimension of uncertainty avoidance in a more positive way. That counts all the more, because Hofstede mentions another Chinese piece of research from the same time in which the dimension of uncertainty avoidance is also left out. For the Chinese researchers, it does not seem to be an interesting dimension.[12]

Hofstede bases his research on statistical material and questionnaires that IBM used in the 1980s on a worldwide scale. His four or five dimensions can be taken as a rough conceptual framework that makes cultures all over the world quantitatively comparable, thanks to this statistical material. That leaves ample room for critical questions and misunderstandings. What looks the same in some cultures, according to this conceptual framework, might differ quite a lot on a closer look. For instance, both Japan and Germany have a high score on uncertainty avoidance. But in this case, quite different phenomena are put within the same category. Japanese uncertainty avoidance is a mixture of obedience to authority, to tradition, and to the collective—a mixture that cannot be seen without the Japanese high drive for achievement. German uncertainty avoidance is related to the German conscience of responsibility and the need for principled and fundamental oversight of the situation before making a really responsible decision. Obedience to hierarchy is an element in it, but not because the individual is not allowed to have his or her own opinion, but in spite of it. It is a typically German thing to do, to stand critically aside and obey authorities, without making an inner commitment to the authorities. The collectivism in China or India is something totally different from the collectivism in Arab countries or in some countries in Africa. In China and India, collectivism

---

12. Hofstede, *Cultures and Organizations,* 213.

is much more related to obedience to central authorities and to rules of politeness and social intercourse, whereas in Arab countries, family loyalty and responsibility for the clan play a much bigger role and the central state receives much less respect. To understand such phenomena, cross-sectional statistical research does not suffice. It is necessary to take into account the longitudinal development of these phenomena and to tell the story of a specific culture. This is also necessary to applying a more subtle eye to the differences. The same flag on a ship does not always mean that its cargo is the same.

Despite such comments and criticism, it is still interesting and illuminating to relate the dimensions of Hofstede to the cultural developments presented above as structured by Rosenstock-Huessy's cross of reality.

Let us first take the dimension of *power distance*. A culture can either be more hierarchical or allow for people from different layers within the hierarchy to still treat each other as equals. In the figure on page 151, this dimension covers more or less the tension between an "I" culture and an "it" culture. The last one always is hierarchical in character, in line with the chain of command within a labor organization I treated in chapter 3. If it is possible for people to treat each other more as equals, then there is more room for everybody to behave like an "I" and seek cooperation and agreement from different starting points. On the basis of such an agreement, once it has been found, once again the functional division of labor can take off to effectively—and hierarchically—implement the agreed-upon decisions. In a well-functioning parliamentary democracy, the policy is decided democratically. This means that reaching consensus involves taking into consideration different points of view, even though the implementation of such decisions takes place hierarchically and with functional division of labor of the state apparatus.

Next is the opposition between *collectivism* and *individualism*. In this dimension of Hofstede's, the tradition of the "we" group is pitted against the individualism of the "I" experience and maybe also against the experience of uniqueness, created by the imperative mood, which opens new ways and singles out unique individuals. A "we" is always more or less collectivist in character. A "we" is marked by a common history that binds this group together. And in as far as people share collective symbols and ideals, some form of collectivism is also involved.

Next is the opposition between *masculine* and *feminine*. A feminine society is one in which care plays a bigger role; competition plays a lesser role. Further, role differences between men and women are less strong than in other societies. Translated into the poles of Rosenstock-Huessy's cross of reality, in this dimension the "we" experience of tradition and belonging is pitted against the "it" experience of the struggle with nature and the drive for survival.

Finally, the degree of *uncertainty avoidance* is related to the question of the extent to which people allow a rupture in their lives, and dare to face an unknown future, and even strive for fundamental innovations. For that reason, it is related to the "You!" experience in the cross of reality.

In the fifth dimension, the Chinese researchers who came up with it reinterpreted this fourth dimension of uncertainty avoidance positively. What Hofstede would call *uncertainty avoidance* is something in which they see respect for tradition and thinking on a longer term. In all the contingencies of fate and the uncertainties that are inevitably involved in it, they still seek opportunities to return to old values, even if this might involve many detours. These old values are, foremost, related to respect for the family and respect for authority, as well as to thrift and economy. It might be unavoidable for the time being to go with the flow and adapt to the trends; in that respect, the Chinese culture is flexible and maneuverable, because it can adapt. But in this mutual adaptation from me toward the other, inevitably the moment will come in which the other cannot do anything other than to adapt to me in turn, so that the equilibrium can be reinstated. From that moment on, it is no longer clear whether I am used by the other to reach his goals, or the other way around. The Chinese researchers seem to seek, amid the ambivalence of mutual adaptation, the constancy of long-term orientation, and thus tradition.

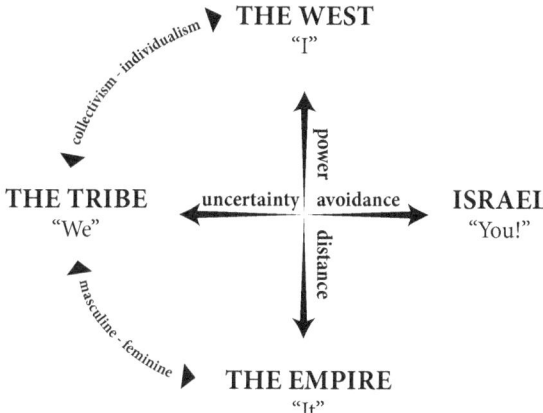

Having made these distinctions, we can now move toward recognizing the importance of timing and the dimension of time more clearly. The either-or distinctions are not absolutes, as though Western and non-Western cultures can simply be labeled along those lines. In the West, there is hierarchy, too, just as there is egalitarianism in the South, and individualism in the East. Even within one and the same culture, according to different settings and contexts, we can prioritize and accept different values and codes of communication. This is also a matter of timing. Of particular importance is the fact that cultural distinctions such as individualism versus collectivism, and hierarchy versus egalitarianism, are not just mutually exclusive. They can also be integrated into each other. They even should be! Timing again is everything: when to start and when to stop.

As a matter of fact, hierarchical control does not exclude an egalitarian dialogue. It does not even exclude criticism from the bottom to the top. It will probably function better if those in control can also accept criticism from below. In the course of Western history, hierarchies could become bigger and more efficient just because of that![13] This illustrates that the cross of reality indeed is a cross. Continuously we stand at the crucible, and we have to choose which direction we follow. Or which mixture of directions.

---

13. Gauchet, *Désenchantement du Monde*.

7

Western Qualities

Are Europe and the West an Exception?

In the course of the nineteenth century in China, Western law was introduced. In the beginning, it was only for the elite. Before that, it was considered a disturbance of harmony to start a lawsuit. Attorneys were forbidden. It was unimaginable to pay for the promotion of disharmony and opposition! Whoever secretly charged a client for advice to come up with a good defense in a lawsuit case, could be prosecuted or banned to a remote province as soon as it became known.[1]

Usually the magistrate would pass judgment, advised by a scribe, who in turn would base that advice not so much on legal tradition as on the basis of the philosophical tradition of Confucianism. The education of civil servants was primarily aimed at the reproduction of knowledge. The ruling dynasty was not interested in having intellectuals think independently.

This type of administration of justice in China did not differ essentially from India's or from those of the Arab countries or Africa. Why did an independent judiciary originate in the West and not somewhere else? For that matter, one can ask the same question about opposition in politics, the expression of public opinion, and the striving for fundamental change in society by careful planning and disciplined labor. The English invaders in India easily overthrew central authority with the help of a coalition of former vassals, and took over.[2] The Spanish did the same in Latin America, albeit more cruelly. The Aztecs and Incans could keep control over the many tribes they tried to integrate into their empires only by resorting to violence.

---

1. Chang, "Legal Education," 300–301.
2. Landes, *Wealth and Poverty of Nations*, 153.

Even more so in Africa, large empires have always had difficulty in surviving in the face of tribal life.

Two changes are of fundamental importance in Europe after the emergence of the Frankish empire in the sixth century. These changes started slowly, but accelerated exponentially in the last few centuries. In the first place, individuals were increasingly freed from their fixed bonds of loyalty, both in relation to their families and as subjects of kings and other authorities. This began in the way the manor or the farm during the Middle Ages was organized. This was not merely a family enterprise. People from different families could become members of the manor, and each member had rights, at least on paper.[3]

In the beginning, this legal status was merely a formality. But as time passed and these manors became more successful, the serfs working the land could increasingly exercise their rights. This disintegration of the clan did not occur only through the manor. People who became members of a monastery consciously broke with their families and for that reason they were no longer interesting to them. They had lost their meaning for the procreation of the next generation. Cities liberated themselves from the authority of princes and of the nobility by legal agreements, written by monks. So they acquired city rights. Puritan congregations treated everyone within their community as brothers and sisters and as "friends." In the Middle Ages the term *friends* was used to designate not direct family but laws.[4] This course of events continued until the time of the French Revolution, which claimed innate human rights for each individual, independent of rank or status. For the first time, each individual had the right to have a say, merely on the basis of the person he or she was, and not on the basis of family or clan loyalties or as a subject of authorities and kings, or as bearers of offices. Gradually, an open civil society came into being, step by step. This meant open cooperation and re-grouping of individuals, apart from family loyalties and state authority.[5]

Second, the unknown future received more and more priority, compared to the well-known past. Tribes and empires are organized as a continuation of what is. The best they can do is reach perfection by returning to the "original intention." For instance, they might start a new tribe or—as happened frequently in great empires—they chased away the ruling dynasty in a time of crisis and installed a new one.

---

3. Berman, *Law and Revolution*, Vol. 1, 328–29.
4. Rosenstock-Huessy, *American Social History*, 12.
5. Stackhouse, *Creeds, Society, and Human Rights*.

In Europe too, social and political renewals were legitimized by an appeal to the past. But increasingly fundamental innovations were always introduced despite, or under the cloak of, such an appeal to the past. The English gentry actually took over parliamentary power by an appeal to old rights, acquiring a power that they had never had before. The French Revolution wanted to renew history much more consciously and explicitly, but they still wanted to appeal to the "natural" order of things, just like the Greeks and Romans in antiquity. Only since the time of the French Revolution did the word *new* become legitimate. And now, something new is always considered something better. Advertisements gain from that perception.

With an Eye on the Future: Secularization

It is quite remarkable and characteristic of European history that every time a drive for change manifests itself, it functions like a "holy imperative" for realizing a promised future. The result of this driving force was always some form of secularization.[6] Secularization can be conceived as a form of saying "no" against authorities past and present. Secularization hauls down things that were once respected and met with awe. Whoever starts dealing with powerful authorities disrespectfully, because they are considered not good enough anymore, tears them down and robs them of their presumably divine character. The imperative to realize something new turns the status quo into "mere" material in the hands of human beings. Each new revolution proclaims such a "no" against outdated power, and in doing so creates room for something new. I mention several examples:

- The Christianization under Charlemagne, already begun before his time, implies a secularization of the belief in heroes and ancestors by tearing them down in the name of the Savior, the crucified Christ. Those who had been neglected before, victims and people of lower rank, now appear in high esteem. The victim of violence receives higher authority than do the heroes of the tribes. The future receives more weight than the past. When Boniface cut an oak among the Frisians, he did not do so to turn them into Christians in a narrowly understood religious sense. He is combatting a life form based on the solidarity within the tribe. He is trying to replace it with the inclusive spirit of a

6. History proceeds from pressure (from an old-fashioned order) toward freedom. That is to say, it proceeds toward the right ordering of the world. By this process, Europeans across their entire history have broken away from old orders. Freedom from and freedom toward something different indicate the rhythm of this process. Rosenstock-Huessy *Europäischen Revolutionen*, 92–93. I follow his interpretation of the European revolutions here.

Christian community. He is fighting for a higher level of morals, so to speak. He replaced the reverence for ancestors with what we might call a *victim ethics*. According to our experience, the victims are always to be respected. They are never "mere" victims! They challenge the right of those in power. That is actually caused by the fact that we already perceive them from the perspective of the victim of all times (Christ), who for the first time made them appear in a different light and who gave them a voice. According to the experience of the Church and the monastic orders, this higher level of morals and this more inclusive community was already a reality, but only inside their communities. From Charlemagne onward, this higher level of morals has also had an impact on the political power game. Charlemagne acquires legitimacy by proposing himself as a Christian emperor, not only on the basis of his personal conviction, but also as a political goal. That is, to gain authority over all the other tribes. He couldn't do that merely on the basis of loyalty to his own tribe. It took the supra-tribal orientation of the Christian faith to legitimize his authority over the other tribes, as well.

- A monastery in Burgundian Cluny during the tenth century was at the forefront of a reform movement. This monastery actually secularized the other monasteries by organizing them into a supra-local corporation and then also even counting them. This organizing and counting was not done until that time, and it certainly was not allowed because it was considered disrespectful. But now it is, because chaos, the last judgment, is pending, and it is no longer forbidden to count the sinners, if you can lead them on the right path and if you can organize them and teach them higher moral standards.

- By the struggle of investiture from 1075 onward, the pope tried to subordinate the emperor and the bishops to his authority. He alone represented the coming Christ. The emperor was no longer considered in charge of a holy office, but he was considered "merely" a political entity. In theology, the Church fathers were secularized by treating them (*erörtern*) in a systematic treatise (the *Summa* of Thomas Aquinas), which implied that they were compared to each other and that the pros and cons of different positions could be summarized. The writings of the Church fathers were no longer considered immediately holy, as they were before. They are allowed to be critically examined. Only Christ is considered to be holy, as the British scholastic Anselm of Canterbury says.

- The pope and the Franciscans from the twelfth century onward secularized the politics of the Italian city-states by opposing *temporalia* and *spiritualia*. *Temporalia* meant the worldly powers, the state of affairs that could not be changed for the moment—or simply, the state. The *spiritualia* meant the coming Kingdom of God and the earthly representations of it, like the sacraments, canon law, and the work of the church in changing the world.

- In turn, Luther secularized the pope and the institutions of the Church itself by appealing to his personal conscience and by resisting the all-too-visible church. He turned the princes into executors of a holy imperative, the next step into the future, because they were responsible for exercising political power over the church too, from now on. He depicted the pope as the Antichrist. The monks left the church, and by doing so, the worldly calling or profession became sacral. In their professions, people began to fulfill their calling to improve the world. The world became the place where the invisible church could live its life, by personal conscientious decisions in one's professional life. In Lutheran Germany, professional life was kept free from state interference.

- The English Glorious Revolution of 1688 secularizes the power of the princes by declaring them to be tyrants despite their sacral powers, just as the Dutch national anthem does: "Drive out tyranny . . . " The community of the Commons, the lower nobility, now becomes the bearer of a sacred imperative; the Commonwealth of Great Britain and its colonies is eventually founded.

- The French Revolution secularizes both the church and the nobility and puts the sacred imperative of changing the world into the hands of man by means of reason, virtue, and natural benevolence.

- The Russian Revolution even secularizes man himself by robbing him of all human dignity and reducing him to a bundle of nerves and needs, to be organized by science. But this analytic perspective, which subjects the totality of social reality to scientific planning, and this calculating approach are sacred imperatives from the perspective of the revolutionaries, because these are necessary entries into the future.

Revolutions and Human Qualities

Until now, we have looked at the traditional powers that a revolution denounced. Time and again, part of our traditional humanity, traditional patterns of life, and forms of governance were treated with disrespect and pulled down. But in the same moment and at the same time, a "yes" is said to the future, not only in terms of the larger political and economic organization of a territory, but also in relation to values and human qualities that are necessary and even indispensable to organizing these larger territories. This is never a matter only of law and regulations, but also a question of human attitudes and social intercourse. From what perspective do human beings look upon each other, and how do they encode their behavior toward each other? Or as Rosenstock-Huessy put it: How do people speak?[7] And in addition, by speaking, how do people arrange their social relationships? This question puts the understanding of language in the center of attention.

Such human qualities and new ways of speaking are necessary because people are less calculable, to the extent that they live and work together in larger systems. Historians, sociologists, and philosophers have often pointed out that larger organizational systems require more discipline. Civilization would have brought about, and been itself in turn brought about by, a disciplined type of human being. These people keep themselves in check and adapt to the larger framework of society. Living together would cause more uniformity, just as it would require more uniformity. But this is only part of the story. An organization or a company or a country will not flourish if its people behave only like cogs in a machine. That is not even desirable. Larger organizations that are under hierarchical control might even rely too much on the command structure and be inclined to standardize human behavior as much as they can. In the short term, this might seem to be more effective, but in the long term it is the cause of stagnation. That is because it can be realized only at the expense of what is priceless in humans: their commitment and effort, their creativity, and their professionalism (chapter 1).

It is difficult for larger economies to be sustainable without a more pronounced articulation of all sorts of human qualities. It really takes something to create cooperation. This is all the more so if people are less familiar with each other. In larger economies, where the powers of family loyalty and state authority are pushed into the background, these traditional forces of social cohesion—the family and the state—need to be replaced or compensated for. This cannot be done by only a more disciplined type of behavior. It also takes more developed human qualities like loyalty, openness, and a willingness to put in some extra effort if that is necessary for success. It also requires consideration for others, in case something does not work out. And it requires respect and responsibility, even for people whom you do not know at all. In effect, it requires an enlargement of the moral community, more inclusive thinking, and acting. A combination of criticism and respect, and the ability to start over after a disappointment are all necessary. To maintain peace in a large organization, a continuous

---

7. Rosenstock-Huessy, *Sprache des Menschengeschlechts*, 269–73.

investment in such qualities is indispensable, much more so than in smaller organizations, where people more easily adapt to each other. For the sake of social cohesion in large social systems, social relations need to be invested with new qualities. Social intercourse is a form of spiritual life. What the Middle Ages used the word *spiritual* for is more or less the same as what we refer to today with the word *social*.

In the next sections, I will indicate the main steps that are taken in Western history and which constitute the focal points of the European repertoire of values and of more pronounced, outspoken, and acquired qualities. Again, these human qualities, virtues, or values allow for self-regulation of a civil society apart from family loyalty and state authority. They make it possible to overcome the compartmentalization of society. Compartmentalization is the consequence of the collectivism of closed in-groups. Even now, in Africa, this is the case. These qualities, virtues, and values also make it possible to overcome the lack of voluntariness in large state bureaucracies. They make it possible on all levels for people from different social ranks and affiliations to respond to historical imperatives and necessities by the voluntary action they initiate. This volunteerism and responsibility are the mark of a living civil society. Let us give a small historical inventory of such acquired values and virtues.

Authority and righteousness: From the time of the struggle for investiture, the pope claimed authority above the emperor. He demanded the right to appoint bishops. He also called for the Crusades, which in all their ambivalence contributed to the unity of Europe and to the emancipation of the knights. After they returned, they became more independent of their superiors, thanks to the authority that they too had acquired by their sacrifices and the cause they had struggled for. The pope granted every believer the right to appeal to him as final judge. Despite all ambivalence, the struggle was about a more articulated type of authority—namely, authority without political power. In the end, the pope did not have armies to command. By mere authority and diplomacy, the pope tried to motivate political leaders to advance his goals, and several times he failed. He even went into Babylonian captivity, because he had to flee Rome. This had been an exercise in creating a civil society, because people learned to respond not to mere power, but also to authority without power. Even up to now, if a need is felt—for instance, to eradicate poverty or to work on environmental sustainability—civilians at all levels of society start responding to such a necessity of their own initiative. Such a need can be articulated by representatives of nongovernmental organizations or individuals, by well-known people, or by people without power. These might be people who have acquired more authority because they were victims of established power. One might think of a statesman like Nelson Mandela.

Exactly because the the pope was in a position of authority, but without power, this authority became more outspoken and articulated. This type of authority also became an inherent quality of bishops, monks, and priests everywhere in Europe. By force of this authority, everywhere in Europe the law was codified and developed. The papal party struggled hard to put an end to the arbitrary rule of emperors and kings, systematically applying and further developing the law. General concepts of law and theology were developed and refined in interaction with concrete cases brought before court. Generations of theologians and jurists succeeded each other in working on the development of a body of law with the tangible result that gradually "rule by law" and "rule of law" could be enforced throughout Europe.[8]

This last expression, *rule of law,* meant that political authorities were no longer above the law. They themselves were now subject to the law as long as they did not change it. The first expression of *rule by law* adds an equitable rule to that: avoiding arbitrary decisions. It was the competition and struggle between pope and emperor that greatly stimulated this development of law. Right should of necessity be spoken between two parties, who each in their own ways are right. Confirmation and opposition came to be expressed from within the framework of this development of pros and cons. This included the independent defense for the defendants.

At the origin therefore of Western culture, there is already a certain plurality of voices that cannot be reduced to one denominator. Very early, the ability to deal with differences had been cultivated. These differences were both allowed and tolerated exactly by the fact that they were all subject to the same treatment, the same rule of law. Justice and playing by the rules created equal treatment of different parties, even if such rules were often only respected in the breach. Huge mechanical clocks that were exhibited in churches and which also showed the movements of the planets, symbolized this longing for justice. The message was that the universe itself was subject to universal rules. So in analogy with it, canon law, universal theological concepts, and church institutions (the seven sacraments, which pertained to everyone, everywhere) should determine the life rhythm. Through church bells, the life rhythm of the monasteries also spread beyond them. Arbitrary rule, granting privileges on the basis of particular relationships, should be avoided. Instead, universal rule was gradually put in place, something that could not have been achieved without the interventions of the Church,

---

8. Berman, *Law and Revolution,* Vol. 1, 292.

being the one institution that was dependent neither on family loyalties nor on state authority.[9]

Civility and compassion: Instead of civility, we could also speak of courtly culture, which was promoted by chivalry and Madonna devotion.[10] By the end of the twelfth century, the emperor was by treaty no longer allowed to enter the northern part of Italy with his armies. The nobility and patrician families took over the administration of the cities, legitimized by and under the spiritual guidance of the pope in Rome. Everywhere, temporary political offices were introduced to prevent any lasting concentration of power. The Franciscan and other mendicant orders tried to soften the competition between the different cities as social workers with compassion and education and care for the poor and the sick.

Madonna devotion plays an important role in this civilizing movement. Typical for Italian painting is the picture of the holy Virgin in the landscape. If such a Madonna painting was finished by a great artist, the painting would be carried in a procession through the landscape. This was a demonstration and an appeal to civil and courtly behavior. It was also an appeal to civility and compassion with human beings, who in all their quarrels were considered nothing else but sinners under the custody of the Holy Mother Church, and should for that reason overcome their rivalries.

Under guidance of the Holy Mother Church, the sphere in which family members deal with each other becomes the model for social order. Even now, we have an image of Italians who deal with each other as quarrelling children within a big family, and even now the relationship between mother and son is very special in Italy. The Italian cities came into existence as part of this civilizing movement; as a result, the people outside the city walls received city rights, too. As a consequence, the difference disappeared between city and countryside. The new reservoir of labor and creativity that had been tapped laid the basis for the later prosperity of the Renaissance. Everywhere in Europe where "Our Lovely Lady" churches were built, this civilizing movement of the Holy Mother Church in Europe had its way. During this time, many cities were founded and they acquired city rights. From city to city, such bills of rights were copied and acquired by each other throughout Europe. The city movement was a great event in terms of creating solidarity beyond and apart from family clans and tribes. Supported by the city laws, an attitude of civil cooperation was cultivated, a cooperation that was no longer confined to family lines. The church was the mother of

---

9. Fukuyama, *Origins of Political Order.*

10. Charles Taylor ascribes the origin of civility mainly to the seventeenth century, having in mind England in particular, although he knows about the origin of the term in Italy. Here his Anglo-Saxon background probably plays out. Taylor, *Secular Age*, 99.

all of us . . . and we are part of one big family, one social body. That was the idea. Needless to say, it was not always the reality.

Conscientious inwardness: The human type of the German Reformation. Ever since Luther broke with the authority of Rome, every Christian became directly—that is, without mediation by the Church—responsible to God. This inner responsibility produced an attitude of accuracy, strong discipline, and thorough scientific research. The central focus of this attitude was not so much empiricism, but rather judgment by principles. The church hierarchy of Rome had become all too visible and had made the people spellbound to that which was visible before their eyes—that is, statues, pictures, and relics. In reaction, the Reformation searched for the invisible perspective point from which everything fitted together in one system, and visible things were approached and conceptualized only within this framework.

For this reason, the German spirit is always inclined not to take things as they present themselves, but searches for the principle behind it, the general concept in which it fits and from which it can be explained. By such a conceptual and systematic approach, the risk of being overwhelmed by the impressive appearances of authorities could be avoided. Instead, the Germans sought counsel from their inner consciences, standing before the face of God in a personal relationship. But the intensity of this responsibility implied that people felt urged to show that they indeed could take responsibility for the totality of things. They should prove that they could put their views in a systematic framework that legitimized such personal conscientious decisions in the face of external authorities like the state or the hierarchy of the Catholic Church. This helps explain the German attitude of thorough and systematic thinking. You really had to be sure of the rightness of your decision, and this implied the necessity of giving a systematic account of it. The key point is judgment by one's own consciousness, independent of the social surroundings and independent of external authorities. This meant a tremendous freedom for the individual, which also could be expressed in the conduct of business. It was expressed in making high-quality products with a high level of reliability.

This attitude of conscientious responsibility induced German philosophers and theologians to construct encompassing conceptual systems. At the same time, the German princes took over ruling the Church from Rome, legitimized in that respect by Luther and other theologians. But in turn, they constantly had to be reminded of their responsibility, as well. This responsibility served as the authorization and legitimization of their resistance toward the emperor and the Roman Catholic Church. It also legitimized their authority inside their territories and their rule over the church institutions.

After the Peace of Westphalia in 1648, they were sovereign within their own territories,[11] but for that same reason, their power had to be kept in check by their conscientious responsibility before God. This explains the special relationship and balance in Germany among universities, scientists, and civil servants on the one hand, and princes and political leaders on the other. The learned scientists were free to enter upon a scientific debate on whatever political matters they wanted. Theologians, jurists, and philosophers in this way exercised their academic freedom in which the princes were not allowed to intervene.

This, on the other hand, proves that academic freedom was not just a matter of individual willfulness to do whatever one pleased. It was the freedom to open a debate to find the best option for a particular problem independent of the authority of princes. This inner freedom of consciousness, combined with a certain attitude of protesting Protestantism, made many Germans opt for loneliness and total criticism. *Ohne mich* [without me] is a very German attitude. Nevertheless, by thorough and conscientious research, the German scientist could have a lasting but indirect influence on politics. He gave advice in freedom and independence. It was up to the prince to decide and take on whatever he could use.

It is the achievement of the German principalities to respect this mutual independence of princes and universities. Only in the long term could the solid advice of civil servants and learned professors have an impact. Learned professors could not count on immediate success. But by their conscientious attitude, the German civil servants set a new standard of incorruptibility. That people had to pay extra to civil servants for their services had been common practice all over the world. The extent to which that practice is no longer considered acceptable now is due to the example of the German civil servant.

The use of a long-term perspective is one of the qualities still to be added to the list of historical achievements brought about through this German responsible and systematic approach. The delusions of the day were overcome by the responsibility for having an inclusive perspective also in matters of time. This long-term thinking was expressed, for instance, in forestry, which for the first time was implemented in a sustainable way in Germany. That is, forestry was developed with a view of lasting availability of these resources. This was also important because the combination of

11. The very concept of *sovereignty* has its origin in this. It meant that the emperor could not intervene in the civil rule of the princes. Therefore, the concept of sovereignty didn't have its origin in the authority of the French kings, as Saskia Sassen proposes. The German sovereign princes served as the model, when the French withdrew civil law from the authority of the church. See Sassen, *Territory, Authority, Right*s, 44–45.

water power and wood constituted the technological regime of the time. It was important to have these resources available in the future, too.

Because of this long-term perspective, with an eye on the next generation and different from the "motherly" attitude of Italy, the German spirit can be called "fatherly." In the professions, this was expressed by preparing the next generation for taking over the task of the previous generation. Schooling was important because every Christian should participate in the responsibility of one's individual conscience before God. Free choice of professions was also stimulated by the fact that so many monks and nuns left the monasteries. Education and independent professions in small workshops were the concrete result of these new courses of events. Even now Germany is well recognized for the strong role of its civil authority, for professional education, for thorough learning, and for solid long-lasting products.

Team spirit and loyalty: The type of the English Revolution. In England it is the lower nobility, the Commons, who made revolution. It was not the high nobility or the princes. This revolution was a reaction to the absolutist rule of the kings, which developed everywhere in Europe in the wake of the Reformation. In Germany, the princes had become independent of the emperor by claiming sovereignty in all civil affairs of their territories. But this actually meant that everywhere the administration of law and justice—which until then were for the greater part church affairs—now went into secular hands. Kings and princes everywhere in Europe followed this example of withdrawing the rule of law and jurisdiction from the hands of the Church by an appeal to their royal office, using the expression, *by the grace of God*.

Especially in England, which after all was an island with only one king, this removal of authority from the Church by local royalty strongly reinforced top-down relationships and threatened the old and traditional rights of the lower nobility. In the Netherlands, the same problem caused the Eighty Years' War. In Great Britain, it resulted in the Great Rebellion of Cromwell and later in the Glorious Revolution of 1688, when the Dutch stadtholder William III became King of England. By the exercise of close solidarity and team spirit, and by calling upon old traditions, the lower nobility, the Commons, defeated the King and the higher nobility, and overtook Parliament. In order to protect the Members of Parliament (MPs) against the arbitrary power of the king, neither the MPs nor their opinions were allowed to be mentioned in public. Only the Speaker of the House could speak on behalf of Parliament, and pass on the decisions of Parliament to the king.

Where in Germany principles and systems were decisive, in England particulars and empirical circumstances, local privileges, and customs settled the matter. Tradition and a feeling of togetherness were strongly cultivated in Puritan church congregations both in England and in the Netherlands. In the troublesome days of the Eighty Years' War, this same feeling of solidarity and togetherness tipped the scales. The Presbyterian congregations were organized from the bottom up, under the leadership of patrician families and lower nobility. They were not organized by princes and principles from above, but by cooperation from below.

Scientific research too was cast in the same mold of community life and cooperation. The scientific community of professional researchers, assembled in associations, decided on the scientific quality of theoretical treatises and practical experiments of individual members. Nature was not the only thing explored with the help of practical experiments on the basis of group cooperation; the same team spirit enabled the oceans to be fared. Likewise, in the economy, shared ownership in the enterprise was introduced first in the Netherlands and then later in England. Loyalty, mutual trust, creditworthiness, team spirit, and public spirit are the achievements and characteristics that were articulated and pronounced during this period. This team spirit, which was introduced by the example of church congregations, dealt the final blow to clannish and family systems of solidarity. Congregational life and later civil life replaced belonging to the clan and securing an economic level of subsistence. Insurance and relief to the poor by the Church and the State deprived the clan system of its economic meaning. Creditworthiness, making one's promises true, was so much valued in eighteenth-century England that even poor people who evidently could not pay their debts, were put in prison. One should stick to one's promises also in public life. In social systems in which the family is still of major importance, the habit of keeping promises to people perceived as outsiders is traditionally held in less esteem.

Passion, naturalness, reasonableness, and individual genius: This is the human type of the French Revolution. At the time of the English Revolution, the French lower nobility was in turmoil because it felt attracted to Protestantism. Louis XIV had the grandiose idea of binding the nobility to him in Versailles and to entertain them with feasts and parties. His regime increasingly sought support from the Catholic Church, and especially from the Jesuits, all while relying too on this idle, but privileged nobility. In the long run, they stood in the way of the modernization and the centralization of France. Voltaire once said that one changes in France as much from law as from horses. For instance, up until the French Revolution, it was usual to raise taxes at the borders of the counties; the taxes were to be paid even in kind, the *taille*.

The gap between hard-working civilians, primarily concentrated in Paris, and a feasting nobility in Versailles, was increasing. The resistance of the ordinary population began to rise against the *ancien regime,* and it became increasingly expressed in public. The theater and the salons were especially the places in which public opinion was formed, in an atmosphere that was outside the control of both the State and the Church.

The philosopher Jean-Jacques Rousseau spoke about the *volonté generale,* by which he meant *public opinion,* the melting pot of opinions of ordinary civilians who, on the basis of their natural feeling or common sense, publicly expressed their opinions. This public opinion and general will can be considered the decisive factors in the success of the French Revolution.

In France the word *tradition* still smells of antiquated privileges. As a civilian, you do not need any status, you should not even have one, other than by what you are and what you do and say. Therefore, one does not call upon tradition, but on what each reasonable and logical thinking human can clearly see. Passion is what from now on takes the lead, and in combination with that, emerging new opportunities gained priority over old-time traditions. The most ordinary man still has a say in things if he has only the creativity and genius of a passionate speaker who cleverly puts into words what the spirit of the moment makes felt to everyone. His words are therefore logical and reasonable.

In a certain sense, it has become possible for everyone to say "I," after the French Revolution, which means it has become possible to give one's opinion without speaking in the name of somebody else or of something beyond oneself, and still demand that other people listen. Every person has a say in things without representing higher authorities. Every human being is to be valued according to his own power, ability, and faculties. This power can be understood in a material and financial way, just as it can be understood in a cultural, spiritual way. Rationality and virtue replace obedience and tradition. With a "messianic" drive, virtuous citizens from now on try to realize today what the church tradition promised for the end of history: freedom, equality, and brotherhood.

After 1801, the Jews were granted civil rights, a fact that makes it clear that the French were serious about this. The appeal to original human nature that does not discriminate was at the same time the source of inspiration for the realization of a "messianic" future in which all humans would be equal. The same attitude appeared in the economy. Here too, everything could be dealt with rationally, and this meant that science should take the lead in factory production, and that people should have equal opportunities in competition with each other. Improving production under the lead of rationality and individual genius was central. The French Revolution did not pay attention to the material human needs, the equal distribution of products, or the reproduction of the labor force. This was reserved for the next revolution. For the French, the human being as subject, not as object, was the focal point of attention.

Cool calculation is a characteristic of the human type emerging from the Russian Revolution. The negative sides of being human—selfishness, wanting to satisfy material needs, and egoism—from then on could be used to reach positive and concrete goals, and in turn great and beautiful ideas were met with cynicism or skepticism. The language of numbers, tables, and models, in which even human beings appear only as production forces or consumption units to be dealt with in a calculative approach, is characteristic of the specific Russian contribution to the revolutionary repertoire of Europe.

Fulfillment of material needs and organization, or in the language of Lenin's "electrification and *soviets*," are the terms of living and living together. The new social order of the Russian Revolution most emphatically is expressed in the five-year plan, which serves to organize not only the production, but also the reproduction of the labor force. Scientific socialism was labeled with the name *materialism,* but at the same time it was emphatically scientific in the sense that it subjected humans and means unscrupulously to an encompassing rational calculation. Social reality was treated as a part of nature.

The fate of the rising, small middle class, the *kulaks,* who were destroyed in the course of the Russian Revolution, is typical for this approach. Their annihilation was looked upon as possibly economically disadvantageous, but desirable in ideological terms. In this group of middle-class people, the individualism of the Western civilian attained a foothold. This did not fit into the ideology of total calculation, which was meant to satisfy the needs of real proletarians.

During the Great Depression of the twentieth century, the West became much impressed by the Soviet Union, because the Russian economy did not suffer from this crisis, thanks to the central planning policy of the state. The Russian example was followed. Even America allowed state control over the economy via the New Deal. The Second World War and the total mobilization in its consequence meant another strong impetus for the development of the state apparatus. After the fall of the Berlin Wall in 1989, the language of the Russian Revolution was even more outspokenly copied by the West. Admittedly, government authorities retreated in many domains so that they could leave the organization of society to the social actors themselves. Nevertheless, thinking in calculating terms was copied almost everywhere. Paradoxically, cloaked in the victory of neo-liberalism, this calculative language has been established in economies and societies all over the world. Only in the communist counterpart was the starting point different for this calculative rationality: there it was the state, in neoliberalism it is the individual. All societal factors and actors are dealt with in one encompassing calculation, as much indifferent to values and as standardized as possible. Even health systems and educational institutions have become subject to this calculative rationality to the extent that a patient's care is expressed in standardized procedures and minutes spent on health care tasks, whereas educational institutions calculate time spent on student supervision. In this management approach, there is little regard for the professionalism and dedication required. Such dedication and professionalism are taken for granted and do not need to be specially maintained. Only at the beginning of the twenty-first century did companies and institutions increasingly feel how one-sided such a policy and management mechanism are. People started asking for more ethical concern, personal conviction, and values, instead of mere management.

In all these revolutionary transitions, new human qualities emerged in the tension between a promised future and an antiquated past. This occurred in steps, to begin a different kind of political and social articulation. In this way, the revolutionaries contributed to the re-creation of man. Man was invested with new achievements, or at least a sharper articulation of existing human qualities, and in that sense our humanity was re-created once more. These human qualities, achievements and values in turn have opposed each other in order to correct each other's deficiencies and they continuously compete for priority.

Conscientious deliberation, for instance, is something inward for the individual standing before God, whereas team spirit and loyalty take place in a group. The group feeling that results from this team spirit or public spirit is quite different from the French individuality and passionate genius. This passionate individuality is, in turn, in sharp contrast to the Russian cynicism and cool calculation.

These human qualities came into being as a reaction to one another's one-sidedness. The process of the European revolutions is like a discussion between opponents. A continuing line in this European spiritual development is pluralism, the combination of criticism and opposition, and continuous mutual correction. There are continuous political and social struggles and competitions going on between opponents, but it has become impossible to turn the opponent into a monster. However vigorous the struggle with the opponents might be, the other party might also have something valuable to say. In this vein, Europe has continuously exercised its ability to disagree—and nevertheless give in, if the other clearly has a point (even if you do not like it or do not like the other party). In this way, opposing forces could mutually penetrate each other. Different times and the spirit of different times could be put together.

The World Wars: First Step toward the Planet

The Soviet Union began with the intention of initiating a world revolution. However, in the end, the Bolsheviks could establish socialism only in Russia and in a few more satellite states. In the course of history, the Russian Revolution became more and more Russian and less and less revolutionary. The language of the Russian Revolution—that is, the language of planning, total calculation of needs and interests, and numbers and figures—has amply been copied by other nations. Nevertheless, it still makes sense to question whether the Russian Revolution indeed was the "real" revolution of the twentieth century. The Russian Communists anticipated the world revolution. They tried to plan the revolution and push it forward. Had it not been for the unplanned and unexpected mobilization of the Russian army during the First World War, the Russian proletarians would probably never have allowed themselves to be subjects of propaganda and agitation as a revolutionary mass. What then is the meaning of these two World Wars?

Historians such as Rosenstock-Huessy and Eric Hobsbawn look at the World Wars as one period of time, one experience.[12] They consider World War II, which Winston Churchill called "the superfluous war," a repetition of or a part of World War I. It was a war that broke out because the nation-states refused to learn the lesson from World War I. But what was this lesson of the World Wars?

There is a striking difference between both World Wars, a difference that can give us a clue as to what was at stake. On the battlefields of World War I, technology proved unexpectedly to be a decisive force, unlike anything else seen before. Even though courage was in abundance, it was the firepower that was decisive, and it turned humans into mere resource and matter. Cannon fodder feeding the war machinery. Nation-states, which took their own existence as an absolute, tried to turn each other into objects. They were frequently shocked themselves by the effectiveness of their own machine guns, cannons, and poison gas. The Battle of Verdun was fought in the stench of decomposing bodies, because there was no time and no truce that allowed them to be buried. People were treated as parts of nature.

A characteristic of the nation-states at the time of World War I was that they felt *superior* to each other. In distinction, the characteristic for World War II was the *hatred* toward the other human being, expressed in

---

12. Hobsbawn, *Age of Extremes*.

the Holocaust and in all the concentration camps throughout the world. Now people were not only treated as matter and resource, or as nature. In addition, they were meant to witness this treatment and suffer it consciously. It is the paradox of cruelty and torture that human beings are reduced to material and to mere nature, but that at the same time, they are meant to suffer this reduction consciously. Torture and hatred are directed to the otherness of the other human being, while at the same time this otherness and the moral responsibility it requires are denied.[13]

Fascism can be looked upon as a reaction to Bolshevism, a counter-revolution. People were shocked by the fact that in the ideology of Communism, they could be treated as mere material, bundles of nerves and functions within the machinery of modern industry. Uprooted by that shock, in response, they clung to race, national identity, and hatred toward foreigners—especially the Jews—in order to maintain their self-esteem and honor, and their feeling of human identity. In reaction to the experience of being treated as an "it," they chose the attitude of a "we." This attitude of a "we," in combination with the hatred toward the other, makes the difference between the First World War and the Second. The treatment of human beings as mere material in World War I, compared to World War II, was still a regrettable consequence of the power of modern technology. But in World War II, it was deliberately exercised on human beings who were intended to consciously suffer the denial of their humanity.

If World War I already implies a refusal to speak to the other human being, then World War II is the same refusal, squared. Hatred, cruelty, and torture are more than only the denial of somebody's humanity, and more than a refusal to speak. It is anti-language. The refusal to speak is paradoxically *expressed* to the other at the very moment someone treats him or her as an object. In this treatment, his personal presence is still appealed to. The intention is that he should be nothing more than mere matter, but still should suffer this treatment consciously.

The treatment of human beings as objects, but at the same time as human beings who witness their own suffering—concurrently being human and non-human matter—is expressed in many monuments, books, movies, and even music about the Holocaust and World War II. This indicates the lack or refusal of language, and at the same time the necessity of it, and the appeal to it. Human beings are turned into matter, but you can still see that they are human and hear the call to respond.

After World War I, Rosenstock-Huessy and a group of his friends—among whom were the Jewish philosopher Franz Rosenzweig, the Protestant

---

13. Levinas, *Totalité et Infini*, 216.

theologian Hans Ehrenberg, and the scientist Rudolf Ehrenberg—rediscovered the meaning of language and the living word. It would not suffice anymore if the world were merely to exist of thinking subjects and objects to be dealt with; a third force was needed that could make people turn toward one another. After World War II, the meaning of language and of "re-sponsibility" was rediscovered by Emmanuel Levinas under the explicit influence of Rosenzweig. Levinas introduced the experience of responsibility as a possibility to put an end to the totality of war, which consists of people colliding with each other as forces in space, or reducing each other to economic competitors.[14]

If the answer of the Russian Revolution to the problem of the exploitation of the labor force consists of the total calculation and regulation of society, then what is the next step in the history of revolutions? We need to look for the answer in the appeal coming from the all-encompassing violence of the World Wars: the necessity *to speak*. Rosenstock-Huessy—and later, Levinas—discovered that language starts as a command, an imperative that reaches the heart and soul of the hearer. A real imperative causes a rupture and a change in the course of events. A certain amount of violence is implied in such an imperative. That is, it is an overwhelming power if a command makes me suffer, and burdens me with the need to say something I had not planned on saying. This burden of responsibility is an obsession, and a burden bigger than humans can bear. The World Wars have caused such a rupture and overwhelmed us with shock and indignation about so much suffering, violence, and terror. In this sense, refusing to speak, to use language, once again calls for bringing language back—that is, taking responsibility.

The rediscovery of speech as the power that makes people change, and the explicit and articulated exercise of such speech, constitute the lesson learned, the "imperative," from the two World Wars. Rosenstock-Huessy's grammatical method was indirectly picked up by Levinas in his expression that an imperative puts us in the "accusative." By this, Levinas means the burden of responsibility and the necessity to give an answer in front of the naked face of the other human being—these transform me into an object of the action by their overwhelming power. This intensity of speaking and responding is the "human quality" that is currently in the process of creation, in response to the suffering of two World Wars. Levinas uses the metaphor for responsibility as an investiture. We are essentially putting on new clothes. We still live under the impact of this imperative, and are frequently confused by it. All around us, we still see the inclination to

---

14. Levinas, *Totalité et Infini*, IXff.

deal with each other in instrumental ways by means of a total calculation of forces. But at the same time, we feel this does not really work, because we cannot see how it solves the problems of our time. We are urged to speak to each other, confront each other, and talk. That means that communication, the power to speak and to listen, is a crucial human quality now, to be developed to respond to the predicament we are in. Rosenstock-Huessy's theory and interpretation of language provide the theoretical means to deal with this challenge. He is the first to offer an interpretation of language as a process of change. In our daily dealings with each other—in marriages, as much as in world politics—this has become the most crucial issue of our times. This also is the case in relation to communication across cultures and intercultural management.

Europe and Trompenaars' Cultural Dimensions

At the end of the previous chapter, I compared my historical overview of social history to the sociological analysis of cross-cultural characteristics from Geert Hofstede. Fons Trompenaars originally collaborated with Hofstede, but later he chose a different course. Instead of five different dimensions of cultural characteristics, Trompenaars distinguishes eight. Their content can be related very well to the European heritage of human qualities, because he frequently mentions characteristics of specific European cultures, especially their Protestant variants, in the context of his eight dimensions. By the end of this chapter, I shall relate his sociological cross-section to my historical time perspective, just as I did in the previous chapter with Hofstede's cultural dimensions.

Trompenaars distinguishes the following dimensions on which cultures differentiate:

1. *Universalistic versus particularistic:* Is a decision made according to general rules and regulations, or is it induced by particularistic relationships and privileges?
2. *Individualistic versus communitarian:* This distinction more or less covers one addressed by Hofstede, relating to individualistic or collectivist cultures.
3. *Egalitarian versus hierarchical:* This one essentially covers the dimension of power distance, introduced by Hofstede.
4. *Neutral versus affective:* Do we place emotional neutrality and analytical rationality in high esteem when we make decisions, or do contingent situations and affective preferences tip the scales in one direction

or the other? Is, for instance, an affective relationship important in the business trade, and do people show their feelings in negotiations? Or is an object-oriented, "professional" attitude more suitable?

5. *Specific versus diffuse:* Do people differentiate among roles and persons, or do they mix them up together? Do people want to know more of each other's context or do they meet each other only in terms of their professional roles?

6. *Achievement or status:* Are people valued for what they have achieved as individuals, or are they valued according to their position in a particular family, tribe or clan, education, or profession?

7. *Sequential or synchronic:* Are people doing things in parallel and are they easily distracted, or do they work in a sequential order according to plan? And do they plan ahead?

8. *Voluntaristic or fatalistic:* Are people in control of their environments because of their own initiative (from an inner center, so to speak)? Or are they uncontrollably exposed to the influences of their environments and to the course of events, and do they take things as they come?

The *universalism* (1) of European culture has its origin in the eleventh century, when canon law was introduced to regulate all of Europe, and when the seven sacraments were the rule everywhere in Europe. Through scholasticism, the teachings of the Church fathers and of the law (common law, Roman law) were homogenized and systematized. This universalization of law and of Church regulations brought about the unity of Europe as one common, inner world. The rule of law (instead of arbitrary rule) actually was the result of the competition between pope and emperor, who kept each other in check. Neither of them was legitimized and able to exercise absolute power.

Later revolutions like the Reformation, and the French and Russian revolutions, abolished papal supremacy, but kept the same universalism in new versions. This universalism is also related to what Spengler calls the *faustic* character of Europe, the habit of always looking beyond the moment in space and in time. Everything should be covered and nothing left out. Instead of contingent circumstances, general rules and concepts should tip the scales and separate cases should be dealt with from one and the same perspective.

Rosenstock-Huessy traces this habit back to the Christian character of Europe: The remotest future and the least-recognized interest have an impact on us today. In chapter 5, we explain why Christianity can be thought of as a connector and translator of different periods of time, one to another. The Christian spirit of this habit consists of the fact that the powers governing us in the moment are deprived of their crude legitimacy, but at the same time, they are not completely abolished. People live in two realms at the same time—that is, in the field of tension as well as in the mutual penetration of both. For that reason, their lives are subject to constant change. The greater justice promised for the future has an impact on the existing, often unjust, order. The rights of the weak and of the victims confronts the right of the strongest, and tempers it. We need to perceive the current moment as part of something bigger, and need to justify it within this framework. We compare and connect different times and different spaces to each other. The homogenization of time and space serves that purpose exactly.

This concept of the homogeneity of time and space was not brought about for the first time by the philosophy of Kant. He gives only the Protestant and Enlightenment versions of it, derived from the authority of reason and the categories of the human mind. This means only that Kant perceived an established practice as inherently derived from the functioning of the human mind. But the disenchantment of time and space,[15] of the here and now, so that they can be related to other times and spaces—all this had already taken place and had become an established fact.

Even more so, we tend to see the relationship between things in space and events in time before we see the different things and events separately. In painting, this is readily apparent with the use of perspective. The same thing happens in mathematics: The individual number is seen as a function of a whole series of numbers. If time and space are the same everywhere, we can't treat specific times and spaces in any special way.

Thus the secularization and homogenization of time and space in turn reinforces the universalistic approach. Not even the king is above the law. Even a friend is to be handled by the same rule. At best, there is some room for flexibility, just as there is in general in the application of law. But each special case should be accounted for within the framework of the general rules. It is important to notice that a person's complete way of perception and experience is framed by such habits. It makes it understandable why in different cultures—especially among the uneducated populations, where

---

15. *Disenchantment:* To look beyond what is right in front of you and connect it to something else is a way of treating it with disrespect. Living under the full impression of the moment—for instance, the person who is suddenly right in front of you—forbids you to look beyond. In part, this explains why people in many cultures let themselves be interrupted by the events of the moment, and don't mind the bigger perspective. I do not want to judge which attitude is better. The important question is, as I already pointed out: *When* is which one better!?

Western values are not very evident—such different codes of behavior are the rule.

Considering the universalistic application of the rules in Europe, there are major differences. In the Catholic South, the visible institution of the Catholic Church traditionally represents the universal rule. As a consequence, the individual believers might more easily deviate from the rule, because it is already firmly anchored in the external authority of the Church. If people respect only the rule, thanks to the external authority of the visible Church, then it is not that bad if individual mortals juggle a bit with the norms. Or to put it more positively, it is not that bad if they apply the norm creatively.[16] If instead the rule is not in much evidence and has no external authority or guarantee apart from conscientious human subjectivity, it might easily evaporate and cease to exist altogether, if people no longer apply it. The Protestant emphasis on inwardness and conscientiousness makes them more serious about the accurate application of the rules. It is as if a Protestant might say: Don't think that the larger order of things repairs your deviations from the rule. There is no larger order of things apart from your conscientious derivation and application of the rules."

In the previous chapter, I paid enough attention to *hierarchical* (2) and *collectivist* (3) cultures, so that I need not belabor those points here. But I would like to make a point that Western culture too knows of hierarchy and collectivism. In the previous chapter, I explained that empires live by hierarchy and tribes by collectivism. They discovered and installed these human qualities and institutions. That egalitarianism and individualism also became respected values within the framework of a self-regulating and well-functioning civil society is due to the forward thrust of the Judeo-Christian tradition. Egalitarianism and individualism were mostly considered, from the perspective of hierarchical empires or collectivist tribes, to be dangerous human qualities to be avoided. But in Western society too these new achievements can function well, only if they know when to start and to stop. It is the mutual interpenetration and alternation between egalitarianism and hierarchy, and collectivism and individualism that makes civil society work. Even in the most democratic associations, the chairperson at the end of the deliberations will try to draw a conclusion and base a decision on sometimes contradictory and confusing pros and cons. At such a moment, a hierarchical element comes in: The chair brings the decision to a vote. The members of the association might easily approve it, because they know that

---

16. This explains the indignation in Italy about the Dutch laws on euthanasia, despite the fact that morphine is used on a much larger scale in terminal cases in Italy.

some decision needs to be made. This insight provides an opportunity to make an important point in relation to individualism.

The West is often considered individualistic, and this assumption is interpreted as if everybody does what he likes, the way egoistic and arbitrary consumers act. More often than not, such behavior is there, but it is not the origin of Western individualism. That feature goes back far more to the freedom of conscience and the right to express one's individual opinion in public. This approach to individualism leads to a less stubborn and autocratic understanding of individualism than is typically assumed. Yes, in the West the average person does have an individual opinion and likes to express it, but it is a type of individualism in which differences of opinion are already anticipated. You know in advance that others will disagree with you, and that the expression of your own opinion is only the starting point of the negotiation and discussion. It is not the conclusion. In that sense, individualism and egalitarianism complement each other to the extent that people converse as participants in the process, and on the same level. This in itself has been exercised so much more after World War II, when differences grew exponentially, and conflicts could no longer be decided by mere violence. Thus, we have seen an emerging process of participatory discussion becoming a human quality, the quality to deal dialogically with a plurality of opinions.

The differences between *neutral* and *affective* cultures (4), as well as between *specific* and *diffuse* cultures (5), has played an important role within Europe. These are typical differences distinguishing the Protestant North from the Catholic South. The Protestant North is more neutral, shows feelings less, and is more role-specific. This results in a stronger differentiation and separation between private and public. The application of a universalistic rule in public life is actually supported by neutral, role-specific behavior. People are treated more as replaceable components of a smoothly functioning civil society.

In Italy and Spain, the relationship needs to be established first before doing business, which is a sign of an affective culture. The apparently less emotional attitude of the Protestant North to human relationships is still the result of a more clearly articulated form of social discipline and solidarity. Everybody was supposed to be included in the responsible social body, but on condition that they would also behave as disciplined members of this social body. They are not allowed to discriminate—but then again, people should also stick to the rule and behave equally and according to the same discipline. The North installed relief for the poor, for instance, but part of it was to put disciplinary measures in place so that the poor could be turned into hard workers. The role or office became more important than affective relationships, which could easily lead to particularistic treatment. The driving force behind this neutral and role-specific attitude in a sense was not indifference, but responsibility.[17] A conscientious role-specific attitude requires a more strict discipline of the civilians involved. This is expected from everybody. Begging was forbidden in the Protestant countries and everybody was put to work. And inasmuch as equal rules and neutral roles are concerned, even now, foreigners might be surprised to discover that they are treated on an equal basis like everybody else, even by totally unknown civil servants. The formation of Protestant congregations played an important role in bringing about this change. These communities created an inner space of civil mutual responsibility, which in earlier times was possible only in the monasteries. The well-known, direct communicative attitude of the Dutch can be understood in this light. Many foreigners consider the Dutch as very direct, and sometimes even crude. The Dutch could afford this attitude, because their solidarity was already an established fact. This counts not only for the Dutch; the Germans, although they might be more polite, make a direct and crude impression on many affective people from southern Europe. They say what they think. However, within the framework of an already established community, the fact that things can be said without much fuss or criticism does not lead to loss of face. Clashes in communication belonged to a process of seeking agreement not only in family life, but also in public life. To relate this to a more direct example: Because people were already brothers and sisters in Christ, as members of church congregations, they could afford to be more crude. Even in casual conversation, they did not need to fear that things would run amok, or that a breakdown of the relationship would result. Of course, the difference between the North and South in these respects is gradual and generalized, and it does not take into account that the attitude produced by the Reformation in the long run also had its impact in the southern countries of Europe.

Affective cultures are frequently diffuse cultures. Within the context of affective and diffuse cultures, "corruption" is often not perceived as such. It is almost logical that a person has to pay extra for State services. I have already pointed to the incorruptibility of the type of the German civil servant. This is something new in history. In this sense, public relationships become impersonal and neutral, and are no longer diffuse and affective. Above all, they are no longer particular; there is no special treatment for friends. Whoever passes by the ticket office, known or unknown, gets the same treatment.

17. Charles Taylor calls this a next step in the development of the "buffered self," and connects it to the utopian ideal of a mechanistic society of well-adapted and disciplined individuals. Taylor, *A Secular Age*, 290.

The difference between *sequential* and *synchronic* cultures (7) is related to the earlier discussion about homogenization of space and time. Time is used as an instrument in our hands, and is dealt with through planning and discipline. The story is well known of an African pointing out to a secularized Westerner that the Westerner is still serving a god: the watch on his wrist. Africans in many contexts frequently stop what they are doing when a visitor shows up. If, in the middle of a conversation the mobile phone rings, an African will bring the conversation to a halt, sometimes even in front of a large audience. Whoever deals with time in an instrumented way can do so only by an act of abstraction. This reduces the different times and the different intensities of these times to one denominator: neutral time, instrumented time. Time that serves a future purpose. This means that separate events, and the privileged "now" are treated with disrespect and that they are secularized. The momentary presence of events and of other human beings are, by this process of abstraction, not fully lived through, and they are not sensed with their full impact and respect. Instead, they are robbed of their uniqueness and perceived within a larger perspective. One does not allow oneself to be interrupted so easily, with all the accompanying advantages and disadvantages. But this unwillingness to be interrupted takes a special attitude of the mind. In this attitude, one relates the *here* to the *there* and the *present* to the *future*. The individual moment evaporates in a process of abstraction and generalization, because it is "used" only to achieve a specific purpose. We can derive from this criticism that Western human beings are never completely and fully present in the moment. In Buddhist meditations, people today exercise mindfulness and they want to live in the moment itself in order to be fully present to it. Once more, the question is not whether something is better or worse, but *when* one or the other attitude is appropriate. In many cases, abstraction is also necessary, because without it, planning and discipline are not possible. Here, my aim is to point out only that this process of abstraction and generalization is typically Western, and even more so, typically Protestant, at least in its origin.

This act of abstraction might more easily be understood with the help of a similar abstraction, which also took place in the Middle Ages. It relates to the practice of "IOUs" [I owe you . . .] or promissory notes. The abstraction begins with the possibility of turning these IOUs on debentures from a specific debtor to a specific lender via an interchangeable transaction at the bank. According to specific agreements (phrased in the debentures), the bank could handle these debts as tradable. Therefore, debentures lost their specific character of being agreements or promises between two specific persons. They actually became securities. The category of securities too has been brought about by an act of abstraction. The individual promissory note could suddenly be considered only a special case of the general concept of an IOU, for which there are certain universal rules. Owing money would no longer be something specific and particular between you and me. Suddenly, a third person can buy my obligation so that I now have to pay that person. Moreover, I pay that person via the bank. This can be done even by several third parties. The individual IOU can now be seen within a broader perspective. But this is possible only if all banks are committed to the rule. This again is not only a matter of abstraction, but of discipline and—not to forget—an act of increased solidarity. Without generally valid laws in place and practiced consistently, it would not be possible.

By this example, we can observe that an instrumental way of dealing with time can be understood as a concurrent act of abstraction and discipline. Fixed meals and fixed times of prayer during the day, as well as the clocks in the Middle Ages, served that purpose in the monasteries and later in the cities. Using discipline and instrumentation to deal with time is again a form of secularization as well, because in a certain sense, the passage of time is treated without respect now. Instead of ruling over us, it is now under our command—confirmed by the presence of an instrument in our hands. The individual moment and the individual encounter are no longer treated as something unique and overwhelming. It is we who are in charge. This, by and large, is also what Charles Taylor means by the *buffered self*, the self that is no longer caught off balance by the outside world, and no longer impressed by it. There is no longer any influence on us from the things around us, and we approach things from a distance. We are neither carried along nor taken away, but we find in ourselves the center point from which to act.

What Trompenaars calls *voluntarism* or *internalism* (8) has its origin in this training of the will. It was already in place at the time of the obligatory penances after confession in the Middle Ages. Even more so, in the Protestant tradition, the group confession of sins was the first step of a more intense discipline. After a general confession in which we are heard as much as we hear others intoning the liturgy of confession, we are more resolved to be hard on ourselves, and not to let ourselves be carried along by the influence of others. We strive to keep our impulses in check. This reinforces inner self-control. A life of gratefulness, the Calvinist formula for life after the confession of guilt, was typically a life of hard labor, the subjection of impulses to the will, and to self-discipline. If a person confessed his sins because he had given in to his impulses and was sorry about it—or caught in a crime—then gratefulness after forgiveness demanded from then on that he improve his behavior. The ego as the center of inner control is in this way reinforced. Things and experiences no longer affect us and we do not need to use our circumstances as a foundation for an unavoidable fate. You can do something about them, if only you confront them! Only if you want change, will you consider yourself a pivot point and put your will and initiative between the past and the future. Only if you want to reach a particular goal in the future will you start using time in an instrumented way, dicing it up and planning a process of steps to get there. Kant considered this attitude as characteristic for the Enlightenment. But I propose that the Enlightenment offered only a secular version of the same process. We leave our self-chosen dependence and childhood behind us and are no longer influenced and overwhelmed. Instead, we position ourselves as competent judges against the rest of the world and assume responsibility for our own lives, governed by reason.

Another issue can also be clarified in this context: the difference between a culture of guilt and the culture of shame. Shame means falling out of a group. Whoever feels shame feels that he or she no longer belongs to the group. To confess guilt is easy, if it is already an established fact that although everybody has weak moments we can all still be part of a community of sinners like anybody else. This—to be a community of sinners—was the self-understanding of the Church. Of course, the difference between a culture of shame and a culture of guilt is gradual, because in Western culture, shame and guilt frequently overlap. But with respect to guilt, the inner conscience—or in Catholicism, the authority of the Church—plays a bigger role. *Shame* refers to the group to which one belongs. One does not feel ashamed when one is judged by an inner authority, but only when one falls out of the group.

A reference to the Russian Orthodox tradition shows how specifically Western and unusual this approach is to reality, this collection of universalism, disciplined labor, planning, initiative, and regulation. Or at least it was, compared to the rest of the world. In the Russian Orthodox tradition, two things are important: the heavenly light that befalls us via the icons from an inaccessible reality—and adjacent to that, a holy life of compassion and love. The more miserable the realities of this earth are, the more room there is for real acts of compassion.[18]

A Russian friend wrote the following lines to me in an email correspondence:

---

18. From an edition of Rosenstock-Huessy's *Jenseits all unsres Wissen wohnt Gott* [Beyond All of Our Knowledge Lives God]: "The *agape* / love is a keyword of Christianity. Eastern Christianity for this reason remained 'strong and hard,' because it had to live in a 'barbarian atmosphere.'"

You in the West substituted love with organization. There is no compassion. You pay taxes and you have a social security system, and that is it.

The disorder of the world makes it possible to love your neighbor in such a way that it really affects your inner self.

In Russia, nothing is well organized, but neighbors help neighbors get through the winter with a sack of potatoes if they can and if they are good people.

8

The Christian Way of Dealing with Time

Living in Time Periods

Throughout history, people and societies have changed course. People have always been confronted with upheavals, and yet they have started anew. Both in their personal biographies and as societies, people have liberated themselves over and over again from the pressure of stalemates. Tribes fell apart and different subgroups developed in different directions. Sometimes those who were banned formed a new tribe. In empires, new dynasties avenged the injustices of the previous ones—or at least they destroyed each other and replaced each other.

Never has there been a static society or a harmonious golden age of which romanticists dream. At best, those have existed only occasionally! After such lucky times, these societies cannot avoid the necessity of fundamentally rearranging the whole spiritual framework and orientation of their members. This willingness to rearrange, this plasticity of human beings, the ability to move from one way of life into another—that is the human soul. It is that part of us that suffers from decadent or hypocritical or petrified states of affairs. It is also that which energizes people and makes people breathe whenever changed circumstances allow new opportunities for peace and justice to emerge.

Most ruptures and changes have just taken place without planning or foresight, when people were fed up with oppressive regimes. It was a long time before humanity learned to deal with such ruptures and changes more consciously. If one societal form replaced another, the past was frequently and totally denied. A new tribe did not keep alive the memory of the previous tribal form. A new dynasty did not look at its achievements from the perspective of its predecessor dynasty. Each time period regarded itself in absolute terms. The Christian era is the first to break with the closed universe of this self-absoluteness. The fact that the Church maintained the Old Testament beside the New Testament made it possible to look at sequential periods of time from one perspective. And the Church looked at her own era, the New Testament, from the perspective of a previous period of time. According to its own self-consciousness, the specific achievements of the Church could be understood only from the perspective of the prior phase that began with the people of Israel and the Jewish tradition, amending it, drawing from it.

Throughout this book, I have frequently spoken about the historical achievements and human qualities that constitute the core and growth of history. Likewise, the ability to break from and still reconnect to a previous period of time is a characteristic achievement of the West and of Christianity. From now on, an upheaval does not mean an absolutely new beginning, but a passing point from a time before the upheaval to the time thereafter; it is a link in a chain. From now on, a rupture can take place in one era, even though the indispensable achievements of that previous period of time can also be inherited and maintained. The urge to think in periods of time and to write a history that consciously relates a previous phase to the present is characteristic for this Western and Christian approach.

My point here is not to defend a specific set of beliefs as "Christian." My point is to arrive at an understanding of the achievements and qualities of the Christian tradition, in dialogue with the contributions of other religions and older cultural traditions. These together constitute the common stock and repertoire of our humanity.

All such new human qualities first entered history with religious pathos. After they became more common and people got used to them, they could dress themselves in more secular garments. Religion and societal order, and cult and culture have always been connected, and they have never been without the other. According to popular understanding, faith and religion deal with the afterlife. However, if you look at both more closely, it appears that faith and religion are all about life before death. Impending death for the social body frequently requires new religious inspiration. The core question of each religion and each culture is how to create peace amid anarchy, amid the threat of the struggle of all against all. What can bind people together? Which power can prevent the disintegration and petrification of society, and can prevent the terrors of war and revolution? That is the primary question of religion. The binding power of religion rests on the assumption that there are things for which people are ready to die, in any single moment, and that they are attached to values and convictions that are more important than anything else, including their own lives. Therefore, the central question of faith and religion is not whether there is life after death, but instead: What is it that is worth dying for? Or also: What is worth killing? The warriors of the tribe died for the spirits of their ancestors, because the authority of the ancestors constituted the backbone of their society. They were also prepared to use violence to defend the specific form of peace that they had experienced within their tribe. For whatever people are willing to sacrifice either their own lives or others' lives, that is the higher power, the religious core of each society. That is sacred. That is binding (again, the literal meaning of the word *religion*). That still pertains in the most secular society, even if it seems as if all of that plays no role—something that is likely to be concluded during quiet times.

My point is not to sell a specific truth as the exclusive property of the Christian tradition. The truth that I want to "sell" is Christian, but it is not exclusive. What is Christian in it lies in an acquired quality that in the learning process of human history becomes conscious, or comes to be revealed by the cross of Christ. That is, it is the ability to break occasionally from old states of affairs and yet to connect to them spiritually. Thanks to a process of translation of the achievements of one time into a subsequent time, a reconnection between such times becomes possible, despite the rupture or upheaval.[1] One period is translated in the other period, despite—or thanks to—a fundamental rupture. Now human beings can switch between each of those periods. They can consciously say "good-bye" to days past, and still inherit the achievements of those times in a new era. A particle of death can in full conscience be admitted into life. The original plasticity of being human, the ability to change, can now be exercised and used more consciously. A more articulated and developed form of love might live together with the fruits of former forms of (societally institutionalized) love. In that sense, all of the human qualities and cultural values mentioned here are the fruits of growing love, the fruits of a growing tree of humankind.

According to St. Augustine, human beings are Christian by nature. To do the right thing is actually the most logical and natural thing to do. That a human being can be evil is what requires explanation. It is only natural to do good. In this vein, the plasticity or the ability to change is also the most natural human characteristic. It is something in which all humans already partake in, a little bit; it became more articulated and pronounced

---

1. An extensive explication of this human quality as specifically introduced by the Christian tradition is presented by Wayne Cristaudo in *Religion, Redemption, and Revolution*. Love is impossible to be constrained by the straitjackets of any social formation; love is central to that formation. Such love can grow. Revolutionary upheavals, if societies have become stalemated, liberate society from this stalemate by sacrifice, and take love to a next level, more encompassing and intense than the previous level.

after Christ. Each new imperative that makes itself felt in the course of time requires such plasticity. A new appeal asks for a new response—and a breaking-off from older times. People can collide with each other only if they stay the course like automatons. This actually makes them soulless.

The human soul responds. The soul gives us the ability to take a risky step, to be open and vulnerable in giving a new answer. Between each previous and each next answer, there is a "moment of death." The human soul refers to the human experience of being thrown into a new time, and it is related to the experience that the petrification before the previous upheaval was painful and suffocating. The person involved needs to be born again. The person who emigrates to a new country has to ask him- or herself which features from the former existence can be kept alive. One way or the other, it is always the case that whatever a human being stood for, heart and soul, somehow needs to be rescued in this new context. But not without change. In a new period, the achievements of the past can receive a new emphasis and a new place within the whole picture. Past achievements can be rejuvenated because (and when) newly achieved qualities compensate for their shortcomings. Everything that really brought peace in a specific time must find a translation into another time, because living and loving people are too much attached to it to let it go. It has become part of their souls.

Inside, Outside, and Periods

It is important to note that change is not something that people do, but something people undergo. It requires a certain passivity. I have called that moment of passivity the *human soul*. The passivity and passion of the soul form the turning point for change. Levinas speaks about the "passivity of responsibility," referring to the experience of being urged to respond, even before taking any initiative. It is this passivity of responsibility that takes the lead over our thoughts and over our will, time and again. In the language of Rosenstock-Huessy, a new imperative makes itself felt. A new marching order announces itself. A new language is spoken.

This has enormous consequences both for our *economic life* and for the *scientific method*. The Christian symbol of the cross, which creates periods of time, has not yet penetrated the fields of economics and science. The ability of consciously entering upon new periods of time and accepting change might therefore be most difficult to integrate into science and into economic policy. In a sense, science and economics are still pre-Christian. Neither in science nor in economics is there an awareness of the occasional necessity for change, under the weight of a new imperative that redirects the scientific research and reorganizes it. A new moral imperative and a new appeal actually drive the research. Science becomes dead and boring if it only adds data to its mountains of knowledge without any kind of lively appeal. To the extent that some effort to articulate meaningful periods of change takes place in science and economics, it happens more or less by accident. It is not part of the method as such. For the most part, such changes are considered merely the product of a chain of cause and effect, represented in a mechanical way.

Of course, new periods of time do occur both in the economy and in science. But there is no awareness of the fact that such periods are founded by the passivity of responsibility, for which I have used the word *soul*. Science is always inventing new concepts and ideas. But according to its own self-understanding, such concepts and ideas are derived from reasonable thought and reflection only. They can also be derived from the power of criticism and growing insight, but not by a new existential experience that makes us look upon the old facts from a new perspective. And even if that is admitted, it is assumed that paradigm shifts occur from time to time without any possible explanation.

This is the opinion, for example, of the science philosopher Thomas Kuhn, who does identify them, but can give no reason for their emergence.

The human soul and responsibility are not considered to be in the lead in this process. Consequently, science and economics are actually driven forward by a power that does not play any role in their self-understanding. Because of that, this power can do its work only under the surface. In reality, it is the soul, passion, and the passivity of responsibility that give new names. The names derived from such new experiences lead to new concepts.

In the 1950s, for example, environmentalism could not and did not mean what it means now. An environmentalist at that time would probably, if the word were used at all, hold that the environment, as opposed to heredity, was the primary influence on the development of a person. From the 1960s onward, an environmentalist all of a sudden was somebody who was concerned about the harm done to the natural environment. Such a shift in meaning is not the product of reasonable thought, but an answer of a living soul, a human being with sensibility and love, to whom it occurs at one moment: This cannot be allowed to happen, just like that! At such a moment, people jump to a new word or add a new meaning to an old word.

In this sense too in the field of economics, the legislation on social security is not a product of reasonable thought. It came into existence because there was a moral problem—that is, felt injustice and human suffering. Living people could not allow the older generation to sink into poverty, and for that reason they started searching for another way to analyze economic processes and from there, they created an argument for social security. The origin of such new ideas lies in the moral layer of existence. The word *morality* today often replaces the old word *soul*. If something is not "morally sound," this layer of existence is actually appealed to, for which I have used the terms *soul* and *passion* and *passivity of responsibility*. Before something can be named "not morally sound," somebody must first have been frightened about the existing indifference in relation to a particular problem.

Until far into the twentieth century, the methods and the rationality of science were considered to be independent from our emotional lives and from our responsibilities. Actually, Friedrich Nietzsche had already made several breaches in this understanding of pure reason. Left to itself, our reason is flexible and adapts to each person's wishes. By wiping out God as the horizon of our experience, by wiping out a final authority that gives meaning to our experiences, so Nietzsche says in his aphorisms, meaninglessness and senselessness enter in. There is no longer any moral compass for our knowledge. People and their rationales tumble indeterminately around in space, without below and above, or left and right. They can construct "truth" in as many ways as their imagination allows.

Franz Rosenzweig has shown that science does not know where to begin and where to end. An arbitrariness of system building, and of change and construction, and an endless interlinking and differentiation of concepts occurs, if reason is left to itself without "revelation." That is to say, without a loving commitment, without moving in the orbit of a fixed point outside its own mere intellectual functioning that provides orientation.[2]

Levinas speaks of the "there is" to indicate this senselessness and meaninglessness: Events and experiences befall us without structure, a terrifying maze that in the end also appears to be similar to the chaos and horrors of war.[3] That so many people allowed themselves to be used as agents of a tyrannical system, without any protest from their souls, is the end point and result of a development in which the rationality of reason was considered to be independent from the soul and in which the soul was considered nonexistent. If people believe in such an image of soulless human existence, they indeed have lost their souls. To draw the consequences from such an insight, and consequently pull the power of thinking away from its own internal logic, is a scientific task that still lies ahead of us. This book tries to contribute to that task by thinking and answering in the context of periods of time and by considering living language to be the core of our human existence.

---

2. Rosenzweig, *Der Stern der Erlösung*, 91ff.
3. Levinas, *Autrement qu'être*, 207ff.

The same counts for the external space of our economic existence. Today, economics still predominantly views the core of our humanity as seeking pleasure, fulfilling needs and desires, and calculating the next steps according to each individual's interests. From this starting point, taking human beings as self-interested rational agents, economists can calculate production and consumption, and mathematically model them. It looks as if society consists of an accumulation of human needs that are met by organization—that is, by calculating management. And *"That's all there is."* That was more or less the vision of Lenin on socialism. He might even have been quite satisfied about the management ideology of the twenty-first century. People and processes are standardized and subject to an encompassing, calculating approach—both in the sphere of production and consumption. This approach is applied in social intercourse, in hospitals, education institutions, and so on. Such an approach supposedly is more effective, at least more cost-effective, although many times it turns out to be not even that.

Standardization and calculation of production also constitute the basic pattern of labor organization. Human resource management, career coaching, and all sorts of other training and learning trajectories are introduced only as corrective measures, positioned on top of this default procedure, to the extent that there is room for it in the budget. The market forces constantly urge change and a flexible dealing with human resources. Often that means that people have to exchange the "luxury" of meaningful work for short-term efficiency. Frequently overlooked is that the rhythm of change is—or should be—not only dictated by the forces of the market, but also subject to new moral imperatives that re-orient and reorganize the sphere of labor. For instance, people work differently at different ages, but this quite relevant issue is never sufficiently counted. This problem becomes more urgent if we all have to work longer in our lifetimes than did the previous generation. Such a new imperative, keeping the elderly longer at work in a suitable way, should have an impact on the science and reality of economics. The different periods of our biography cannot be subsumed in the abstract unity of "workforce."

The spilling of human capital in the sense of conviction and commitment, and orientation and perspective of the workers that are invested in the work, is even less accounted for in this abstract model of being human. In other words, the most priceless aspects of being human are those least accounted for and counted. The most priceless: the involvement and inspiration that empowers action at its most effective state.

What is also not accounted for is the fact that different moral imperatives can organize different parts of the world economy in different ways. The development of societies, cultures, and economies is path dependent.

There is an ongoing dialogue about different cultural values or path-dependent imperatives and different economic orders and strategic choices. Although these orders and choices are real, they are typically not consciously taken into account. From context to context, such emerging new moral imperatives might be different. We cannot expect Africa or Asia to copy the Western economic culture just like that. They will and will have to create their own versions, even if they cannot avoid taking Western heritage into account. The existential answer given by a living human soul to such imperatives can and should become the creative origin of different economic orderings and management methods.

It is striking that in science, an abstract human reason—and in the sphere of labor, a monotonously organized economy—still operate as inner (scientific theory) and outer (economic behavior) space of our existence. It is also striking that both have survived 2,000 years of the Christian-modulating treatment of time. It is just as striking that in India and China, with Buddhism and Taoism, the inner and outer spaces of our existence have already been freed and delivered from this *abstraction* and *monotony*. Can these achievements from the East become meaningful factors in the re-orientation of *science* and *economics*? If Judaism and Christianity have created a breakthrough of the cyclical conception of time for the East, we might want to consider whether Taoism and Buddhism can help break with the abstract and monotonous experience of time in the West in science and economics.

Taoism and Living Inside

At the inner pole of the subject, it is the truth that demands to be recognized. At the outside pole, only real force has lasting consequences. In these expressions, we can summarize the meaning of the inside and outside poles. Science validates itself in the quest for truth. Profit and fortune follow the power of economic production. This is the way in which the conceptual world of the subject, and the development of objective forces in the outside world, have their dynamic tension and follow their course. Can these dynamics be interrupted—that is, can they be re-oriented and changed?

The French philosopher René Girard discovered or re-discovered the mimesis as an organizing principle of society. People imitate each other and copy their opinions from each other. They vary, and they seek recognition by speaking a current type of language, a certain discourse. For the most part, this discourse usually constitutes the average around which public opinion circles. Girard points out that this process can easily lead to violent confrontations, because there is increasing competition for what many people identify as attractive. If everybody competes for recognition by participating in the current discourse and in trying to set the tone, then the space for expression automatically becomes scarce, and struggle might ensue. The result is a struggle of all against all, of which the energy in the end finds an outlet in targeting a common victim. Unless, of course, somebody at the top of the hierarchy clearly sets the tone to keep everybody tuned to this center of command!

That is the way in which imperial authority functioned in the hierarchical society of China. The imperial court set the tone and everybody had to follow. Whoever wanted to acquire a high position would have to acquire recognition from the higher authorities and flatter them. In a conversation, it was appropriate to say only what the other person liked to hear. If lower officials wanted to set a course that differed from that of their superiors, then a common strategy consisted of formally going along with them, and appearing always to do what their superiors wanted them to do. But in the end, they would have done it a different way. That is to say, they would give a different twist to the "shared opinion." In this way, they could create some room for making their own policies, pretending that everything was all right. They could even hint at differences in opinion, knowing that the best way to criticize their leaders was to wrap up the criticism in a compliment.

One poem, for example, hailed and glorified the emperor, but without at all mentioning the beautiful empress. The readers knew that she was very cruel, and they understood the criticism.[4] If the smartly wrapped criticism of the subordinates could be read between the lines, they risked banishment or worse.

Confucius aimed at maintaining respect for the tradition and the authorities, and wisely promoted a harmonious society. In the period of the quarrelling states (between 400 and 300 BC), when there was not yet a united empire, this sort of wisdom came at the right moment, because it tactfully corrected the competing princes and dukes, and reminded them of the larger perspective. His wisdom promoted unity and harmony.

After the Han emperors (approximately 206 BC until 220 AD) brought about this unity of imperial China, the Confucian striving for harmony and mutual adaptation became a conservative power. The Chinese emperors were always ambivalent toward Confucianism. On one hand, they needed this tradition of wisdom to build up a unified civil service. The Chinese civil service created unity in education and maintained strict objective criteria for the examinations that opened a career for civil servants. In this way,

---

4. Jullien, *Detour and Access*, 65.

it served but to push back the predominance of family loyalties and corruption. On the other hand, the emperors had no interest in an intelligent and well-educated and possibly critical civil service. The emperors were as much inhibited by the wisdom of Confucius as they promoted it. The neo-Confucianism after 1100 acquiesced in an apolitical role.[5]

The wisdom of Confucius did not allow for open opposition, but only for implicit criticism by hint or understatement. The finest art, as already stated, was to wrap criticism as a compliment. Open disagreement was not tolerated, and therefore difference in opinion was packed only as a variation of the unchangeable and shared truth. Even now, discussions in China proceed in such a way that the present speaker of the Party has an "addition" to the ideas of the previous Party speaker, when actually this addition implies a totally different point of view or a refutation of the previous speaker's ideas.

The analogy to science, to the extent that it is controlled by reason, is very close. Since everybody is in possession of the same reason, everybody should end up with the same insight. Differences of opinion are, in such a process of collective reasoning, reduced to a different aspect of or accent on the one shared truth. In unity, the group lays out the problem and everybody adds a piece to the puzzle. That is the self-understanding of scientists devoted to reason. It seems as if only an impersonal and subject-less reason is at work here. Although reason can accept only what is clear and distinct, as a matter of fact many "self-evident" viewpoints appear to slip in and out of the mazes of this critical look. Reason is not totally in control. The views that everybody repeats seem to have more clarity than those less frequently spoken of.

For instance, if the American political philosopher John Rawls gives his interpretation of rational and moral behavior in his account of ethics, he nevertheless takes as natural and universal the type of the individualistic American who optimizes his opportunities. What else could one think of, after all? It is so self-evident. Shared and traditional opinions and approaches make an all-too-easy appeal to "rational self-evidence." What is accepted as natural, however, is often nothing else but the current opinion or local habit. Whoever wants a scientific article accepted by peer reviewers does well not to offer up unheard-of things, but instead present a variant on a current discourse. The peer review system has come down to us through the Anglo-Saxon concept of science. That means that a particular analysis is accepted as scientific if the community of trained practitioners approves it as scientifically probable.[6] This approach differs from the French and Ger-

---

5. Zongsan, *Nineteen Lectures*.
6. Berman points out that the empirical method in the seventeenth century came to

man conception of science. The genius expression of passionate new ideas is the hallmark of the French scientific tradition and the thorough systematic scholarship that was handed down from one generation to the next is the German conception of science, from *Doktorvater* to *Doktorandus* [graduate advisor to graduate student]. The one-sided reliance on the peers of our present days leads to repetition and application of accepted views, just like in Mandarin China officially nothing changed or should change. In other words, reason today is on the side of current opinion. It has become a matter of convention. Keeping step with everybody else is the currency to be paid to belong to and be respected by the scientific community. Recognition from "accepted" authorities and a large number of footnotes serve the same purpose. If you want to be successful in our era, it is not advisable to bring forward new insights according to your own authority or genius. It is better instead not to be special or conspicuous, and just to go artfully with the flow and follow the fashion, and try to reach the top by some version of accepted and traditional views, presented under the cloak of innovation, backed by thorough (often quasi-) empirical evidence.

A reaction to such a too much of mutual adaptation was bound to emerge even in China. This reaction emerged at the same time as the teachings of Confucius in the person of Lao Tzu. According to his biographer Ssu Ma Chíen, even Confucius learned from him. Lao Tzu broke with this mutual imitation and adaptation, this following of the current discourse and trying to gain recognition by superiors with a friendly smile. He did so by making his own person even more inconspicuous than the ordinary grey mice that wanted to be counted and be seen. It is told of him that he withdrew from public life and disappeared behind a mountain. Only at the request of a border guard, as he was about to leave forever, did he decide to write down his famous work, the *Tao Te Ching*.[7] *Lao Tzu* is not even his real name. He effaced his own existence. That happened to be his recipe both against the stress, the artificiality of mutual adaptation, and toward the game of imitation, being fashionable, and of competing for recognition.

His recommendation for doing nothing (*wu wei*) can be understood as a recommendation not to keep up appearances and not to show off. It is

---

be understood in probabilistic terms, so that the degree was established of the probability of hypotheses "believed to be possibly but not necessarily true." The acceptance of such probability "depended on repetition and verification by the community of trained practitioners." *Law and Revolution II*, 267, 269. He points out that both natural sciences and law operated in this fashion. Indeed, "probability" in the natural sciences, like "probability" in law "had the qualitative meaning 'worthy of approbation,' and not today's quantitative meaning expressed by degrees of likelihood," (citing Rose-Mary Sargent, *Law and Revolution II*, 300).

7. Chen, *Tao Te Ching*, 10.

a recommendation to stop with unnatural artificiality, with the unreality of moving like satellites around the center of power. The one who does nothing—for example, by keeping silent in a discussion—automatically attracts the attention of all. People start asking themselves what it is that he has to say. The hub of the wheel stands still and does not move, and even so, everything gravitates around it. The one thing necessary is only to let go of all ambition and let go of all urges for recognition. It takes courage to face the emptiness of doing nothing, and to approach this Point Zero of activity. It takes quite something not to bother about recognition by any special effort, and to erase oneself in order to attain authenticity and regain the power of a truly and naturally spoken word.

Only the one who can also keep his truth for himself can at the right time be the one who really has something to say. That makes for power. Whoever has the power not to be ambitious can, at the right time and if it is really necessary, effectively make his true ambition be felt. In this way, Lao Tzu liberates the subject from too much stress and artificiality. He introduces a Point Zero in an environment in which everyone else searches for recognition. If this search for recognition can be looked upon as the usual form of mutual adaptation at the inner pole of existence, then this decline toward Point Zero represents an extra step inside, essentially a stepping inside oneself. Remember that it was at the inner pole of existence where people adapt to each other, and where they leave behind the part of themselves that does not fit into the current discourse. For the other part, they can in turn receive recognition.

But what if we no longer ask for any recognition? What if we let go and do not bother? What if we can remain invisible and leave ourselves out of the story? That would imply an enormous moderation and relaxation of all the reciprocal social tension. By suggesting this attitude, Lao Tzu acquired a new quality with a lasting impact on the inner space of inter-subjectivity.[8] Through him, it becomes possible to stop, and to alternate between activity and non-activity, between need for recognition and letting go. Whoever comes up with fundamental new insights in science should be able to bear this invisibility. Whoever searches for too much recognition for his or her new points of view will become disappointed and frustrated. A person can maintain creativity only if he or she does not need to be noticed. Whoever can do that succeeds in closing a specific period of the scientific enterprise, and by a paradigm shift enters the realm (actually, the time!) of new truths. In this way the Taoism of Lao Tzu makes it possible to live a periodic and changeable life at the inner pole of reality. And in this way too, scientific

---

8. For inter-subjectivity, see chapters 2 and 3.

discourses can be renewed. A thorough renewal of scientific discourse now requires that those who work on it remain invisible within their own epoch, in order to prepare for a time to come, and thereby they become the pivotal points of change.

Buddhism and Living Outside

Something comparable has been realized by Buddhism at the outside pole, the object pole of existence. At the inner pole, we tend to become unreal, artificial, and insincere by attuning ourselves too much to each other. But at the outside pole, we have to deal with struggle and competition, just as it is in the economy. Nature can be beautiful, but at the same time it is not a unity. It is an ongoing chaotic mix of competing forces. According to Bertrand Russell and his colleague, Alfred North Whitehead, the universe itself is nothing else but a new throw of the dice at any given moment, without continuity. Unconnected happenings and events follow each other up in nature, and even where it looks like a continuous process, reality "decides" only to leave it for the moment as it is.

It might not be a coincidence that in the time of Darwin, Buddhism made its inroads into the West.[9] Darwin discovered the extent to which the principle of continuous struggle is also viable in biology. But in this discovery, for himself unconsciously the emerging industrial society, with its competition and imperialism, could be concurrently reflected and make itself felt. The uprootedness of people's lives in the industrial society of the nineteenth century without the Western social security system of today, threw masses of individuals into poverty and misery. Struggle for life is everywhere, and to live without killing is not possible. The present age of globalization once more recalls that sort of imagery. In his time, Buddha discovered the same struggle in the cosmic lifestream of Hinduism, both among the gods and between human beings. He resisted this struggle. He neither wanted to take part in nor be a party to this cosmic struggle.

He achieved this by objectifying his own will to be, his passions, his emotions and impulses. He detached himself from them just by looking at them, as one looks upon to the struggle in the world outside. In this way, he saw through his passions and emotions: They are all merely appearance, unreal. The world is *maya*; it is covered by a veil of unreality and insincerity that one needs to get rid of. It is better not to be—at all—than to participate in this ruthless struggle. The only reason not yet to enter the *nirvana* (nothingness) is the urge to rescue the people who still have to live under this

---

9. Rosenstock-Huessy, "The Penetration of the Cross," *Complete Works*, 23.

veil of struggle and unreality. Buddha does not try to moderate the struggle by moral exhortations. That would not have made any impression. Instead, he applies the principle of struggle—that is, objectifying the opponent as a force outside, by looking at him with a detached eye from a distance—also to his own impulses. He also looks with detachment upon the passions behind the struggle itself. In this sense, the Buddha adds an extra step to the process of externalization. He not only externalizes the opponent, which happens by spying on him as prey, but also externalizes his own passions and will to power. And in this way, the passion for struggle, so to speak, dissolves into nothingness. If you take a close look at your anger and passions, they disappear into nothingness. You cannot remain angry and combine that with a detached look upon your own anger. The detachment makes your anger evaporate.

With Lao Tzu, the mutual adaptation in which part of oneself is repeatedly left out of the story and is therefore eliminated, ends up in complete self-elimination. With Buddha, the struggle and competition in which one repeatedly inserts oneself into the objective forces of nature, ends up in complete self-objectification, and as a result, in a complete annihilation of that will to be. As soon as one starts looking at the passions and impulses one feels, in a detached mood and at a distance, the feeling of anger and passion evaporates. It is not possible to be angry and look upon your own anger with detachment. Then the anger disappears. And just as Lao Tzu pushes the movement of self-elimination to the extreme—that is, not being in any need for recognition—Buddha in his way pushes the movement of objectification to the extreme, to the limits of self-objectification, and thus, to self-annihilation. The one who is all eye, and casts that eye upon his own will to be, his passions, and impulses, destroys them. This self-annihilation by the eye has a moderating and reconciling effect on the struggle of all against all, which is at work in the caste system. It also has a moderating and reconciling effect in the midst of ruthless competition in modern organizations.[10] Many modern managers can bring themselves back into balance after lunchtime, just by a moment of meditation.

In doing this, Buddha adds a new quality to the human repertoire of historically achieved character traits. His self-annihilation into *nirvana* is not just a negative movement. On the contrary, it leads to a positive result. He himself must still live a long life so that he can preach this self-annihilation, and to teach the eye that looks through the passions. Mahayana Buddhism especially is an exercise in continuously coming from non-being

---

10. In *The Christian Future*, Rosenstock-Huessy develops the parallel of Taoism and Buddhism with tendencies of the twentieth-century society.

into being, an exercise of giving up one's own way, and making one's force felt only at the right moment—that is, where it is really necessary. With such forbearance and self-restraint, it also is most effective. It helps to avoid interventions out of one's own impulses. Interventions by those who gave up on themselves and left their own desires behind have much more impact.

Later Hinduism, which integrated much of Buddhism into its own world view, can be understood as a compromise between being and non-being, between the unavoidable struggle and in a timely way giving up the struggle. It might not be a coincidence that the Hindu temples on Java, for instance, are all of a later date than the Mahayana Buddhist Borobudur Temple. It seems as if the high expectations of Buddhism later had to make concessions, ramping itself back in its rigor. In India, Buddhism was expelled and ended up leading a marginal existence. Strikingly, it could develop better in China. Hinduism integrated the contribution of Buddha in itself as one of its many life forms. In this way, at least, Hinduism could offer the possibility of a break in the continuous struggle for life. So the struggle for life in the space outside could occasionally be subjected to another life rhythm, interrupted by non-being. From time to time, and especially at the right moment, struggle can and should be stopped.

Judaism and Past beyond Past

The Jewish people through the ages have constituted only a small minority, wherever they have been. How is it possible that such a small number of people can have such an enormous impact on religious history, as well as on world history? The answer: Because they have had the courage repeatedly to challenge existing loyalties, and the courage to return to the origin before any other origin—that is, the unity of all people beyond their differences.

The people of Israel criticize the splitting-up of the human race into different partial truths and partial gods. Israel refers to a God who is representative of a justice not yet realized—that is, a God beyond all other powers. "Who is like the Lord our God / the One who sits enthroned on high, / who stoops down to look / on the heavens and the earth?" (Psalm 113). In this way, Israel evokes the thought of a justice and peace that especially considers the low state of miserable people, the widow, the orphan, the stranger (Psalm 113).

Whereas all people and tribes tend to be proud of their history, which of course is referred back to a faraway past, Israel goes back to the Year Zero, the creation of heaven and earth before anyone else's origin, and counts the years from that moment onward. The biblical expression itself, *Creator of heaven and earth*, is polemic in character. Where in Babel and Egypt the earth was considered temporary and created, and heaven considered eternal and unchangeable, the Bible instead speaks about the *Creator of heaven and earth*, and for that reason also about the *creation* of heaven. The throne of the God of justice is above the heavens. And heaven is only a stove for his feet. Note that the heaven is there, where the stars, the sun, and the moon prescribe how the people on earth should behave! The son of the gods—Pharaoh or the emperor of China as the ultimate authority in the heavenly empire—is in this way downgraded, diminished, and secularized.

In a similar manner, Israel has broken with tribal life. This is expressed in the story of Abraham, who is considered the tribal ancestor of Israel. He thinks that because he is now to be the first tribal ancestor, the gods want him to sacrifice his only son Isaac, but in the end, he is prevented by YHWH from completing the act. In this way, YHWH puts an end to the traditional powers of those tribal gods in order to replace them (or for that matter, re-orient them) by the claim of future justice. In this way, the story in which Abraham "sacrifices" his son actually becomes the story of the non-sacrifice of his son by "offering him up" to the God who releases him. That same God also claims his son Isaac as the next entry for a justice to come. Which means: His son Isaac has his own history with God, and is not a copy of his father, because this God is beyond all existing loyalties.

Israel, resisting the repetition and petrification of existing traditions, overcomes these traditions by taking an extra step backward. It proclaims an authority before any other authority and a beginning of time that is older than all the empires of these three thousands of years. In the same moment, Israel looks to a future that is still in coming. God is invisible, and does not appear in visible forms (as do idols). He is beyond the origin of these tangible and visible forms, and his authority derives from a time before the foundation of the earth. That is the reason these forms and idols do not suffice. True justice is still to come, and because of that, the true God is still invisible. Any visible forms of justice are idolatrous. They present a very poor version of the ultimate, final justice.

In this way, Israel exercised its capacity to stand alone, going against the group and enduring banishment and persecution. This happens to have been the case from the moment of the Exodus from Egypt under the leadership of Moses; the journey through the desert; the charismatic period, in which "judges" occasionally rescued Israel from foreign domination and internal injustices; the subsequent prophetic criticism of a small minority in the time of the Kings; and after that, exile and the diaspora. Israel has always been on its own, and every new enthusiasm of any new movement that wanted to realize justice in the present was met with skepticism and criticism.

This was the role of the Jews too against the Church and against Western society until the time of the French Revolution, which for the first time granted civil rights to Jews. Israel always pointed back toward a God that existed beyond any existing loyalties, and in this way also toward a future beyond present commitments. The extent to which a capacity of standing alone can become an acquired quality and culture for all should be considered the contribution and gift of the Jewish people. Such a quality never can become merely an inherited quality, because it never goes by itself. Everybody who needs to break away from an existing group suffers from this as a painful event. It costs a lot. But it does make a difference if there are already so many examples from a long chain of prior events in which people could not avoid doing the same, over and over again.

This ability to stand alone and lead a marginal existence has resulted in one of the most remarkable historical cultural documents: the Jewish Bible. Which people, describing their national history, have the nerve to interpret their national history from the perspective of a continuous, prophetic self-criticism? Which people describe their national history by tearing it down to the bottom?

In doing this, the Jewish people have erected a symbol that points forward and backward toward a higher level of peace and justice. In the feasts, the liturgy, and the observance of the law, in the family traditions inherited from father to son—in all of this, the identity and the tradition of the Jewish people consists of this pointing beyond the origin and beyond the present. This character of pointing beyond is the contribution of the Jewish people to the great dialogue, the great story and history of humanity. This attitude evoked anti-Semitism just as much as it has evoked respect. It evoked anti-Semitism because proud nations do not like to be criticized as only temporary phenomena. They tend to take themselves as absolutes and want to be eternal. It also evoked respect, because every nation in its revolutionary stage has used as its paradigm the historical example of Israel opposing the powers that be. The Jewish religion and culture are nothing but the cultivated ability to break with too-small loyalties and to wait for better times.

Christianity and Movement toward the Future

Is there a possibility to deal with the promise of future justice other than by pointing to it from a marginal position in the present? If the identity of the Jewish people rests in waiting and in pointing forward, then a question automatically pops up. Can prophetic self-criticism refrain from criticizing the possible self-justification and pride that can also hide in such an identity, too? Human existence is full of paradoxes and ambivalences. The tribe of Judah has led a very long existence as a small "island," constituting a tradition of pointing toward a future of justice and of being a memorial of a united origin of humankind beyond existing loyalties. Note the paradox in this expression: a tradition of pointing toward the future! At least, shouldn't an "island" like that, constituting the group loyalty of Israel, be allowed to maintain its existence and not give up or give in? Or is self-justification and petrification lingering around the corner once more, as soon as this is admitted?

Giving up this last stronghold of the self-justification silently implied in this role and identity, both pointing toward an unfulfilled future, is the meaning of the life and death of Jesus. He lived by moving into the future and died by drawing it into the present, and realizing it in his own way of life. The failure of his inspiration is built into his way of life. He does not merely point toward the future, but actually sacrifices his life to it. Everybody who takes it up where he had to drop it revives his name, revives the sacrifice. Thereby the openness for a future of justice is no longer limited to the people of Israel. The promise of the future is, from now on, thanks to the death of its bearer who died for it, without a harbor. It is an open position, a vacancy awaiting someone to take responsibility for it. It is an imperative in search of its subject. This longing for future justice now can enter into existence only once more if others stand up or wake up and follow this mode of existence, and take the next step in anticipating the promise of a future of justice and peace in an intractable presence. They live by longing for what is bigger than themselves, and in turn die of that same longing, devoting their lives and spending their lives on it. This indeed too is a form of dying. Others are called upon now to follow suit and once more take the next step. Those who do so are more alive, even if they lose their lives, than all of those who don't. Since the crucifixion of Jesus Christ, everybody's life is fractured and constituted by the rhythm of death and resurrection, times ending and times beginning, translated into each other.

This way of dealing with time is the specific achievement of the Christian tradition, and it has resulted in the ongoing change and revolutions of Western history. I have given many examples of this throughout this book. Although the specific danger of an existence in the margin of history—like that of the Jews—is sterility, this Christian way of dealing with time is accompanied also by a continuous danger—namely, that of illusion or deception.[11] The danger of the Christian life form consists of making a fool out of yourself, if only such small steps into the future are taken, so that nothing really changes anymore.

Falling back into old paganism, into self-justification, is therefore the specific risk of the Christian way. This always happens whenever the next step is no longer really taken. For that reason, it might not be a surprise that the last three great revolutions—the French Revolution, the Russian Revolution, and the revolution of the two World Wars (see chapter 6)—take the next step in history, without intervention from the institutions of the Church. This continues to be the case. As soon as churches cultivate their own identity by confirming their existence as a group, they should also be continuously left behind. The Christian way finds its justification only in repeatedly taking the next step. The Jewish identity, however much it might be petrified, even in this petrification still points to the beginning and to the end of history. In that sense, the self-justification of Jewish tradition is less severe. If the Christian identity, however, is petrified and turned into a merely Christian culture and into the self-confirmation of an in-group, it has become too much a part of the present, too much part of the partial loyalties making up the present state of affairs and no longer anticipating the future. Then it has once again turned into paganism.[12]

The Christian quality of continuously living in the tension between past and future has by its own inner dynamics transcended the framework of the Church and has become part of societal life. It requires the ability to unite one voice continually with its opposite voice in one's inner life, and it requires the ability to decide which of them is most urgent and of interest, now. In other words, a plurality of options and opinions and values and responsibilities, and a continuous search for improvement, go together and need each other. The one cannot do without the other, because real pluralism can be tolerated only within the framework of a search for improvement, the search for doing better.

Without the inspiration of a search for a higher form of justice, people lose their patience with each other. This is because *pluralism* also means having difficulty with each other. Each next step runs the risk of turning into

---

11. In their famous correspondence about the present meaning of the Jewish and Christian traditions, Rosenzweig as a Jew and Rosenstock-Huessy as a Christian used this kind of terminology for each other. Rosenstock-Huessy called the life of the Jewish synagogue sterile; Rosenzweig called the Christian belief in progress an illusion. Both agreed that these traditions liberate each other from their one-sidedness.

12. By the word *paganism*, we shouldn't think only of very special, old religions. Rosenstock-Huessy defines paganism pointedly as "repetition," continuing on the same treadmill.

an achievement to which one has become too much attached. Each group tends to close itself off from outside influences. If the cross of Christ is more than a church symbol—that is, a symbol of cultural history as such, then it points to this ability to give up one's attachments. This is what Rosenstock-Huessy means by introducing the "cross of reality."

Often the good is the enemy of the better. New achievements tend to turn into "sunk costs," ballast standing in the way of further improvement. "Christian" existence, without emphasizing the word *Christian* too much, is therefore primarily a human quality and achievement, as well. That is, it is not so much a belief in transcendental truths, but a life form. It is the "capacity" to break with oneself, with an old form of existence, and to take up a new form of existence. It is a process in service of the next step.

In this light, mentioning *the Spirit* in the Creed of the Church—"which proceeds (*procedit*, in Latin) from the Father and the Son"—acquires its special meaning. Whereas in the Trinity, the Father stands for the achieved goodness of the existing creation, and the Son for ultimate justice, love, and mercy, the Holy Spirit consist of the "proceeding" in this field of tension between both.[13] Between human beings, love can exist only as increasing love. Love is not a static quality, but is instead, always when it happens, a new act of turning toward each other and opening up, of change and re-creation of human existence, of living and of living together. Love can exist only as growing love.

Such a step forward requires giving up sunk costs and old attachments. The perspective of an unknown future, if the next step has been taken, gives us a new self-understanding, and puts us at another shore. Only from there can we once more connect to the treasures of the past. In that sense, the Christian way requires self-sacrifice. Together, therefore, Buddha, Lao Tzu, Abraham, and Christ represent the four "no" statements that are the condition for an inspired life and for living together. They break with the one-sidedness of the four poles of the cross of reality, and prevent us from having our lives absorbed by only one of these four poles and being deprived on unfolding ourselves to the full potential of reality. These four "nos" of *self-sacrifice* (Christianity), *self-criticism* (Judaism), *self-annihilation* (Buddhism), and *self-elimination* (Taoism) constitute the plasticity of a

---

13. In this respect I differ, and I think Rosenstock-Huessy would have differed, from the interpretation of the "cross of reality" given by Clinton Gardner in *Beyond Belief*, 107, 190, 209, where the Son is presented as the mediating process and the Spirit under the aspect of final redemption. This is not a trivial matter, as appears at p. 108, where Buddha, Mohammad, and Moses are identified and lose their contours, subsumed under this undifferentiated category of "Son."

full-grown biography, and are at the same time the condition for peacefully living together and living along the path of increasing love.

I know this chapter delivers too short a treatment to these different religious traditions, and that I am doing an injustice to them. All of these traditions are too rich and pluriform to be merely wrapped up in such ideal types, as I am doing right now. In each tradition, being human and living together always meant to be confronted with the four poles on which we as humans must stand guard, so that we can maintain our human faces. That I describe them here so briefly is justifiable only in the fact that I am not seeking to describe the world view or the representational system of these different traditions. I am looking instead at the kernel of acquired qualities that these traditions contribute to the human repertoire of living together. I am looking at the fundamental human qualities that these traditions pronounced and articulated. Without such qualities we, religious or not, and independent of any membership, would also lose our human faces and the ability to speak responsibly. Therefore, I will also risk making some comments on Islam.

Just like Judaism, Christianity, Hinduism, or Buddhism, Islam in its origin is not "just another religion." Like the others, it is a trial to create a new peace in a situation of crisis. For Islam, the crisis situation of its origin consisted of the lack of unity between the Arab tribes and the impossibility for those same tribes to integrate easily into the city life of those times or to go along with the forms of the Jewish and Christian traditions in those cities. Until that time, these tribes managed to live outside the uprootedness of the existing imperial cultures, maintaining strong cohesion and identities, yet facing disintegration. Islam, inspired by the Jewish and Christian contributions, meant taking the next step in this context, as far as it was possible for the Arab tribes.

Mohammed made it possible for the Arab tribes to gain a more comprehensive unity, the *ummah*, without undergoing the uprootedness of living in big cities. In this sense, the identification of the Quran, holding the tribes together, with the Paraclete in the Christian tradition—that is, the coming of the Holy Spirit after Christ—as it is claimed by the Muslim tradition, is an understandable self-image. It exactly was like that. In its monotheism, which reminds us of the unity of humanity before all periodical loyalties, Islam has also preserved the Jewish voice. In circumcision and in the food laws, Islam too has maintained an exercise in standing alone and going against the norm.

The Christian way (the "step forward," so to speak) is expressed in the creation of one big tribe, the *ummah*, and in the daily *salat*, by which all tribal elders, despite their pride, kneel before Allah in the dust, and bend before the five pillars of Islam. A more inclusive societal order is created for everybody. Both the Jewish and Christian voices, however, are adapted to what Mohammed and his followers couldn't give up. They couldn't give up communal life—that is, the belonging and obedience of an ordered (extended) family life, the clan, the tribe, the unity of the group.

In a certain sense, this is why Islam does not add much new to the history of acquired qualities. From the perspective of our time, Islam represents an earlier phase, as if there had been a standstill after the first historic step forward, which was thought to be a definite and final step, too.

Because of this, in the context of the present-day Western world, Islam is confronted with the question of how it can be renewed. Can Islam create a new self-understanding? Can Islam understand itself as representing *one* particular phase within the Christian history of continuous renewal and change, from one form of existence to the other? Or should the tradition of Islam indeed be understood as mechanical and static for all eternity? Can another change still come in after the Quran and the *hadith* (the tradition of words and habits of Mohammed), bringing about adaptation and translation to new times? Can Islam allow for new historical periods and translations of the original message? This might be the kernel questions in the search for a European and Western Islam. Islam might insert itself once more into the succession of bodies of time originating from Christianity, from which Islam too originates. It would then become an Arab answer to revelation in dialogue with the Russian Orthodox Church, a Catholic and Protestant answer, one denomination among others, observing one particular version of a more encompassing truth.

On the other hand, even if we admit that Islam did not create totally new qualities within the repertoire of the Jewish and Christian contributions, still it represents an older repertoire of human qualities—like the achievements of the tribe, community, belonging, obedience, and unity. One might say that Mohammed and his followers took over as much as they could from the Jewish and Christian traditions, while still maintaining these achievements. This might also mean that Muslims can start to accept and cultivate a translation of their original inspirations into modern times, only if those modern times in return can integrate new forms of community, belonging, obedience, and unity into their one-sided individualistic repertoire of behavior.

The Quran refuses to accept that the son of God died at the cross; this also means a refusal to accept the possibility of complete upheaval in one's own identity, the identity of the believer, who leaves everything behind and starts a new life. Pushed to the extreme, however, this (Christian) ability to break and to renew one's existence has led to the uprootedness of modern individuals, who seem to change their spiritual outlook almost every day. Of course, it is true that these ruptures and upheavals are also connection points, and that through those ruptures—as I have repeated many times—old heritage is translated into a new context. But modern society has difficulty in finding the right rhythm of continuity and change. Change is advocated so much that modern society has difficulty in creating opportunities for long-term commitments. The achievements of the tribes—community, belonging, obedience, and unity—are almost forgotten and completely lost in the individualistic network society of our days, so that everywhere people are in search of new connections.

Isn't the present conflict between the radical Islam (at least in part) and Western society, between "McWorld" and *Jihad*,[14] precisely about this issue? It looks as if just now the extremes of the Christian West and Islamic conservatism seek confrontation with each other, the too-much-closed tribe and the too-much-uprooted individual. Possibly Islam can renew itself and insert itself into the process of seeking the next step forward, only if the West, from its side, can reconnect to the traditional qualities of the tribes: community, unity, and identity. The search for a new equilibrium between what can be done quickly and what takes time and continuity also belongs in this sphere. The creation and maintenance of deep communities takes time. Individualistic networked societies want to be fast in everything. Western society could—although it might be burdensome—use some resistance from the side of Islam.

The Living God and a Flexible Ethics

Both in theology and philosophy, the scholastic habit of searching and constructing general concepts is still very strong. Summarizing truth in general systematic concepts is a characteristic feature of scholastic thinking, which originated in the eleventh century. By this procedure, the truth is conceptualized as generally valid, independent of time and place. This movement results in the homogenization of space and time. Thanks to this procedure, the clergy could, with or without inspiration, on the basis of mere theological reasoning and Church regulations, apply general rules to practical situations in pastoral counseling. They could also apply general rules to situations involving penance and in the application of Church law.

Another characteristic of scholasticism is the distinction it makes between human concepts in which the truth is conceptualized and reflected, and truth itself, which remains outside the grasp of human beings. This

---

14. Barber, *Jihad versus McWorld*.

is expressed in a famous formula of Anselm, namely *credo ut intelligam*, meaning, "I believe in order to understand." Belief and understanding in this procedure are no longer one and the same thing, and so a free space is created for the construction of human concepts. Now one is allowed to order and reorder those concepts by human construction, and to speculate on the truth. Only on condition that the general concepts do not themselves present the truth, but point toward the truth beyond concepts.

In the mirror—that is, in the reflection of such concepts, we make the truth understandable for human reason. But as concepts, they still merely refer to something outside the concept itself. It is, for instance, impossible to think God. God is beyond thinking. As general concepts, these speculations of course can be understood as generally valid, but at the price of giving only an indirect access to the truth. One can point to God (but not think God) by the interface of such self-constructed concepts and definitions. In former times, the Church fathers would operate differently. They would proclaim and state the truth only in relation to a specific time and situation, and these proclamations were for that moment inescapably and directly meant as the truth. So a sacrament—in the time before the seven sacraments that accompanied human life were even fixed throughout Europe—could refer to any situation that was experienced as holy. In other words, it was a situation in which God was experienced as directly present. A special event at a special time and place could become a sacrament. Scholasticism, on the contrary, made it possible to create an inner space within Europe and to subject this space to a common set of rules and truths. This was very helpful in the spatial organization of civil life. This is also the justification for this procedure. Scholasticism, however, made a special effort to create such general concepts in close correspondence with concrete experiences and practical situations. In this way, even Scholasticism did not fix the truth for all times into immobile general concepts, but left room for growth and further development of such concepts. In this way, even Scholasticism made concessions to the temporal meaning of general truths and values, which were nevertheless conceived as generally as possible.

Philosophy and philosophical ethics inherited this way of thinking in general, and also its emphasis on systematic concepts from Scholasticism. In doing this, philosophy also took over the basic assumption of the homogeneity of time and space. The truth is always and everywhere the same. It should be just like that. If that were not to be the case, it would lead to relativism or even skepticism, and so both philosophy and ethics would become essentially impossible. If everybody at will adopts his own values and truths, no agreement—and, as a consequence, no shared moral policy—will be possible. But ethics too pays a heavy price for the general validity of its truths and values. To reach general validity, the truths and values of ethical theory become static.

Philosophy and natural science, these two old companions, expressed this in the Cartesian formula, *Cogito ergo sum;* "I think, therefore I exist." This formula, just like the Scholastic formula, *Credo ut intelligam*, makes a difference between the general concepts that are constructed by our thought, and the reality corresponding to these concepts. Values and truths that are expressed in these general concepts should, according to this procedure, exist somewhere in reality, *in re*, as external reference points for our concepts. Thanks to this procedure, truths and values cannot be understood either as historical learning processes or as historical constructions, originating in the great and impressive human experiences of history. They are supposed to be part of the reality outside—that is, they should be somehow *out there*, just like the facts of natural science.[15] And in this way, the concepts referring to them are conceived as universally valid—but again, at the price of being turned into fixed absolutes.

Values and truths, however, are discovered and "revealed" by historical experience, pronounced and articulated in every era, as the Epiphany of the Other (Levinas) calls upon us to mend our ways. Only if articulated can they become valid. History proceeds from articulation to articulation, and indeed many of these epiphanies confirm each other and can be more or less generalized. They complement each other and correct each other. But there are always exceptions in which concrete situations require concrete and different solutions. For example, in a country like Bangladesh, where the drinking water is contaminated by unacceptably high levels of arsenic, it does not make much sense to impose the United Nations' minimally allowed universal norm for arsenic in drinking water. Even if the norm were to be set at a level 10 times higher than it is, which is the official norm of the Bangladeshi government, still the water supply for two-thirds of the population cannot meet this requirement. What does this mean for moral theory? Is a human life in Bangladesh less valuable than elsewhere? Nevertheless, this concrete situation, exceptional as it is, requires exceptional norms.

"Thou shalt not kill" is also a universal norm or value. But situations frequently occur in which it is not only unavoidable, but even imperative and justifiably so. Doing something or not doing it is not in itself good or bad. Time, occasion, and circumstances make an action good or bad. In our globalized world, many cultural traditions, values, and truths need to find ways of living together. It is impossible and even undesirable to reduce so

---

15. Jonathan Dancy, for example, in resisting a merely psychological conception of truth, tries to found value judgments in the end, exclusively in the world outside. See Dancy, *Practical Reality*.

many values and truths to one shared, uniform set of concepts. That is as undesirable as a world government.

Mutual understanding of these differing values and truths is a necessary, but not sufficient, condition for intercultural communication. Depending on time and circumstances, a new composition and order of priority and trade-off among differing sets of truths and values frequently need to be agreed upon. What is possible and desirable is not prescribed in all eternity, but is instead path-dependent and open for optimization.

The dialogical approach of this book pleads for listening and answering to historical urgency, to the concrete appeal that sounds different according to time and occasion. It is dependent on the interaction of different stakeholders. This approach leads to a dynamic ethics in which a once-proclaimed appeal might gain support in a time-consuming process of communication and dialogue, and in which it can eventually be realized by the contributions of many stakeholders. After each settlement, there is yet another next step, and an opportunity for a new appeal to be articulated.

Rosenstock-Huessy's formula for this process is expressed in the words: *Respondeo etsi mutabor,* "I respond, although I will be changed." I need to respond to an appeal, regardless of whether it is understood in religious or in secular terms. This new appeal is the inspiration of my life. When I respond to such a new appeal, I do not remain who I am. The appeal that I experience draws me away from the course I was following up to this point. This appeal, this inspiration, coordinates my efforts with those of others in a communicative process. Through this process, we might hope, we end up on common terms—at least in part and in as far as necessary. Only in such a communicative process can something like a shared ethics, a set of norms and values, a system of more or less general concepts be envisioned, no matter in how preliminary or temporary a manner.

This understanding of ethics within the framework of a dialogical approach to language leads to a flexible ethics, an ethics of time, and also a temporary ethics. It also leads especially to an ethics of the right moment, of timing. Those who are familiar with the language of the Bible might think in this context of the notion of the living God. The biblical name of God, YHWH, in many translations rendered by the word *Lord,* in its literal meaning refers to the future ("I will be"), and would be better translated as *the coming one* or *the living one.* The Bible too speaks and thinks always in concrete encounters in which God reveals or hides his face. In more pregnant terms, the name *God* could be expressed in the sentence: "Don't think that tomorrow I will be as you came to know me yesterday" (Rosenstock-Huessy). In a more secular way of saying it, in the language of ethics: The appeal of a concrete presence in front of me frequently tips the scales, despite all ongoing reasonable, utilitarian, political, and communicative deliberations.

In each response we give, we partake in the creation of the face of humanity and as a consequence also the face of the Living God.

Bibliography

Andriesse, C. D. *Titan kan niet slapen: een biografie van Christiaan Huygens* [Titan Cannot Sleep: A Biography of Christaan Huygens]. Amsterdam: Contact, 1994.
Barber, Benjamin. *Jihad versus McWorld: How Globalism and Tribalism Are Reshaping the World.* New York: Ballantine Books, 1995.
Bauman, Zygmunt. *Postmodern Ethics.* Oxford: Blackwell, 1993.
Beauchamp, Tom L. *Philosophical Ethics.* New York: McGraw-Hill, 1982.
Berman, Harold J. *Faith and Order: The Reconciliation of Law and Religion.* Grand Rapids, MI: Wm. B. Eerdmans, 1993.
Berman, Harold J. *Law and Revolution: The Formation of the Western Legal Tradition.* Vol I. Cambridge, MA: Harvard University Press, 1983.
———. *Law and Revolution: The Impact of the Protestant Reformations on the Western Legal Tradition.* Vol. II. Cambridge, MA: Harvard University Press, 2003.
Braudel, Fernand. *Civilization and Capitalism 15th-18th Century.* Vol. II, "The Wheels of Commerce," and Vol. III, "The Perspective of the World." Translated by Siân Reynolds. New York: Harper & Row, 1979.
Chang, Wejen. "Legal Education in Ch'ing China." In *Education and Society in Late Imperial China, 1600–1900.* Edited by Benjamin A. Elman and Alexander Woodside. London: University of California Press, 1994.
Chen, Ellen. M. *The Tao Te Ching: A New Translation with Commentary.* St. Paul, MN: Paragon House, 1989.
Cristaudo, Wayne. *Religion, Redemption, and Revolution: The New Speech-Thinking of Franz Rosenzweig and Eugen Rosenstock-Huessy.* Toronto: University of Toronto Press, 2012.
Dancy, Jonathan. *Practical Reality.* Oxford: Oxford University Press, 2003.
Daniels, Norman. *Justice and Justification: Reflective Equilibrium in Theory and Practice.* Cambridge: Cambridge University Press, 1996.
Davis Polk & Wardwell. "Executive Summary" in *Report of Davis Polk & Wardwell to the Shell Group Audit Committee,* March 31, 2004.
Davis, Michael. *Thinking Like an Engineer.* New York: Oxford University Press, 1998.
Fukuyama, Y. Francis. *The Origins of Political Order.* London: Exmouth House, 2011.
Gardner, Clinton C. *Beyond Belief: Discovering Christianity's New Paradigm.* White River Junction, VT: White River Press, 2008
Gauchet, Marcel. *Le Désenchantement du Monde: Une Histoire Politique de la Religion* [The Disenchantment of the World: A Political History of Religion]. Paris: Gallimard, 1985.

Bibliography

Girard, Rene, *Des Choses Cachées depuis la Fondation du Monde*. Paris: Grasset, 1978.

Habermas, Jürgen. *Between Facts and Norms: Contributions to a Discourse Theory of Law and Democracy*. Cambridge: Polity Press, 1996.

Hobsbawn, Eric. *The Age of Extremes: The Short Twentieth Century, 1914—1991*. London: Michael Joseph, 1994. Also published as *The Age of Extremes: A History of the World 1914—1991*. New York: Vintage Press, 1996.

Hofstede, Geert. *Cultures and Organizations: Software of the Mind*. New York: McGraw Hill, 1997.

Jaworski, Joseph. "Destiny and the Leader." In *Insights on Leadership: Service, Stewardship, Spirit, and Servant-Leadership*, edited by Larry C. Spears. New York: Wiley, 1997.

Julien, François. *Detour and Access: Strategies of Meaning in China and Greece*. New York: Zone Books, 2000.

Kant, Immanuel. *Kritik der Praktischen Vernunft—Grundlegung zur Metaphysik der Sitten* [Critique of Practical Reason—Groundwork of the Metaphysics of Morals]. Wiesbaden: Suhrkamp, Taschenbuch, 1977.

———. *Kritik der Urteilskraft* [Critique of the Power of Judgment]. Frankfurt, Germany: Suhrkamp, Taschenbuch, 1974.

Landes, David.S. *The Wealth and Poverty of Nations: Why Some Are so Rich and Others so Poor*. New York: WW Norton, 1988.

Levinas, Emmanuel. *Autrement qu'être où au delà de L'essence*. The Hague: Nijhoff, 1974.

———. *Difficile Liberté*. Paris: Albin Michel, 1963.

———. *Totalité et Infini*. The Hague: Nijhoff, 1963.

———. *Totality and Infinity*, trans. Alphonso Lingis. The Hague / Boston / London: Nijhoff, 1979.

MacIntyre, Alasdair. *After Virtue*. Notre Dame, IN: University of Notre Dame Press, 1984.

———. *Whose Justice? Which Rationality?* Notre Dame, IN: University of Notre Dame Press, 1988.

Martel, Leon. *High Performers: How the Best Companies Find and Keep Them*. San Francisco: Jossey Bass, 2002.

McNaughton, David. *Moral Vision*. Oxford / Cambridge: Blackwell, 1995.

Mintzberg, Henry. *Structures in Fives: Designing Effective Organizations*. Englewood Cliffs, NJ: Prentice Hall, 1983.

Mowshowitz, Abbe. *The Conquest of Will*. Delft: Eburon, 1989.

Plessner, Helmuth, *Die Stufen des Organischen und der Mensch*. Berlin: De Gruyter, 1975 (original edition 1929).

Roberts, Siobhan. *Wind Wizard: Alan G. Davenport and the Art of Wind Engineering*. Princeton, NJ: Princeton University Press, 2012.

Rosenstock-Huessy, Eugen. *American Social History*, Lecture 14. In: *Eugen Rosenstock-Huessy: The Collected Works on DVD*, Essex, VT: Argo Books, 12.

———. *Der Atem des Geistes*. Moers: Brendow Verlag; and Vienna: Amandus, 1990 [1950].

———. *Heilkraft und Wahrheit*, Moers: Brendow Verlag; and Vienna: Amandus, 1990 [1951].

———. *The Christian Future—or the Modern Mind Outrun*. London: SCM Press, Ltd., 1947 [1946].

———. *I Am an Impure Thinker*. Norwich, VT: Argo Books, 1970.

Rosenstock-Huessy, Eugen, *Die Europäischen Revolutionen und der Charakter der Nationen*. Moers: Brendow Verlag, 1989 [1931].

———. "Hans Ehrenberg under der Osten." In *Jenseits all unsres Wissen wohnt Gott— Hans Ehrenberg und Rudolf Ehrenberg* [Beyond All of Our Knowledge Lives God—Hans Ehrenberg and Rudolf Ehrenberg.] Edited by Rudolf Hermeier. Moers: Brendow Verlag, 1987.

———. "Im Jahre des Heils 1527" [In the Year of Salvation, 1527]. In *Heilkraft und Wahrheit* [Healing Power and Truth], 114–137. Moers, Germany: Brendow Verlag, 1990.

———. "Die Kopernikanische Wendung der Grammatik" [The Copernican Twist on Grammar]. In *Die Sprache des Menschengeschlechts* [The Speech of Mankind], Vol. I, 354–418. Heidelberg: Lambert Schneider, 1963.

———. *The Multiformity of Man*. Norwich, VT: Argo Books, 1973.

———. *The Origin of Speech*, Norwich, VT: Argo Books, 1981.

———. *Out of Revolution*. Norwich, VT: Argo Books 1993 [1938].

———. "The Penetration of the Cross." In: *Eugen Rosenstock-Huessy: The Collected Works on DVD*. Essex, VT: Argo Books. Rosenstock-Huessy, Eugen. "Der Selbstmord Europas" [The Suicide of Europe]. In *Die Sprache des Menschengeschlechts* [The Speech of Mankind], Vol. II, 45–84. Heidelberg: Lambert Schneider, 1963.

———. *Soziologie I und II* [Sociology I and II]. Stuttgart: Kohlhammer Verlag, 1956 and 1958.

———. *Speech and Reality*. Norwich, VT: Argo Books, 1970.

———. *Die Sprache des Menschengeschlechts*. Vol. I. Heidelberg: Lambert Schneider, 1963.

Rosenzweig, Franz. *Der Stern der Erlösung* [The Star of Redemption]. The Hague: Martinus Nijhoff, 1976 [1921].

Sassen, Saskia. *Territory, Authority, Rights: From Medieval to Global Assemblages*. Princeton, NJ, and Woodstock, England: Princeton University Press, 2006.

Spengler, Oswald. *Der Untergang des Abendlandes: Umrisse einer Morphologie der Weltgeschichte* [Decline of the West: Profiles of a Morphology of World History]. Munich: DTV, 2003 [1923].

Stackhouse, Max.L. *Creeds, Society and Human Rights, Study in Three Cultures*. Grand Rapids, MI: Eerdmans, 1984.

Taylor, Charles. *A Secular Age*. Cambridge, MA: Harvard University Press, 2007.

———. *Sources of the Self: The Making of the Modern Identity*. Cambridge, MA: Harvard University Press, 1992.

Taylor, Mark C. *After God*. Chicago: University of Chicago Press, 2007.

Toulmin, Stephen. *Return to Reason*. Cambridge, MA: Harvard University Press, 2001.

Trompenaars, Fons, and Charles Hampden-Turner. *Riding the Waves of Culture*. London: Nicholas Brealey, 1999.

Van de Bom, G. H. *Oneindige Verantwoordelijkheid: De cultuurfilosofie van Georg Picht en haar betekenis voor de theologie* [Infinite Responsibility: The Cultural Philosophy of Georg Picht and Its Significance for Theology]. Zoetermeer, Netherlands: Boekencentrum Zoetermeer, 1999.

Wennekes, Wim. *De Aartsvaders*. Amsterdam / Antwerp: Atlas, 1993.

Whitbeck, Caroline, *Ethics in Engineering Practice and Research*. Cambridge: Cambridge University Press, 1998.

Whitehead, Alfred N. *Process and Reality*. New York: Macmillan, 1929.

Williams, Bernard. *Ethics and the Limits of Philosophy.* London: Fontana Press, 1985.
Zongsan, Mou. *Nineteen Lectures on Chinese Philosophy.* www.nineteenlectures.org. 2007.

www.ingramcontent.com/pod-product-compliance
Lightning Source LLC
Chambersburg PA
CBHW070315230426
43663CB00011B/2135